Haunted Europe

I0593025

Haunted Europe offers a comprehensive account of the British and Irish fascination with a gothic vision of continental Europe, tracing its effect on British intellectual life from the birth of the gothic novel to the eve of Brexit and the symbolic recalibration of the UK's relationship to mainland Europe.

By focusing on the development of the relationship between Britain and Ireland, and continental Europe over more than two hundred years, this collection marks an important departure from standard literary critical narratives, which have tended to focus on a narrow time-period and have missed continuities and discontinuities in our ongoing relationship with the mainland.

Michael Newton (Leiden University, the Netherlands) is the author of the cultural histories, *Savage Girls and Wild Boys* and *Age of Assassins*, and two British Film Institute Film Classics books, on *Kind Hearts and Coronets* and *Rosemary's Baby*, as well as *Show People: A History of the Film Star*.

Evert Jan van Leeuwen (Leiden University, the Netherlands) is author of *House of Usher* (Auteur Press 2019); is co-editor of *The Literary Utopias of Cultural Communities* (Rodopi 2010); and has published articles in the *Journal for Eighteenth-Century Studies*, the *Nathaniel Hawthorne Review*, and *Studies in Gothic Fiction*, among others.

Routledge Interdisciplinary Perspectives on Literature

For more information about this series, please visit: https://www.routledge.com

Haunted Europe

Continental Connections in English-Language Gothic Writing, Film and New Media

Edited by
Michael Newton and
Evert Jan van Leeuwen

Routledge
Taylor & Francis Group

NEW YORK AND LONDON

First published 2020
by Routledge
605 Third Avenue, New York, NY 10017

and by Routledge
2 Park Square, Milton Park, Abingdon, Oxon, OX14 4RN

First issued in paperback 2021

Routledge is an imprint of the Taylor & Francis Group, an informa business

Publisher's Note
The publisher has gone to great lengths to ensure the quality of this reprint but points out that some imperfections in the original copies may be apparent.

Library of Congress Cataloging-in-Publication Data
A catalog record for this title has been requested

ISBN 13: 978-1-03-224086-2 (pbk)
ISBN 13: 978-0-367-27184-8 (hbk)

Typeset in Sabon
by codeMantra

For Lena, Alice, and Hannah, my favorite Europeans—
from Michael Newton

For Alexandra, my Dutch-English-Swiss sister—from Evert

Contents

Acknowledgments

We are deeply indebted to the team at Routledge—especially Jennifer Abbott and Veronica Haggar, Veronica Rodriguez and Polly Dodson. For their financial support regarding the conference that was the seed of this book, we offer our thanks to the Leiden University Centre for the Arts in Society (LUCAS), the Leiden University Fund (LUF), and the *Koninklijke Nederlandse Akademie van Wetenschappen* (KNAW). Many thanks also go to the highly resourceful and committed Lenneke Maan, Jan Siglé, and Myrte Wouterse, and to Robert Dines. We also thank Jen Baker, Ailise Bulfin, Daný van Dam, Lawrence Jackson, Melissa Kaufler, Paul Stock, and the many other excellent speakers at the "Haunted Europe" conference, including the very talented Lorna Gibb, and especially Leslie Megahey, for agreeing to be included in this book. Michael Newton offers his gratitude to Paul Laity and Nicholas Wroe at *The Guardian* for their generous support and for permission to use in a much-altered form some material from an article first commissioned by them on the BBC ghost films. We are grateful to the staff of Leiden University Library, and particularly to our colleagues Nadine Akkerman, Jan Frans van Dijkhuizen, Lotte Fikkers, Minke Jonk, Joke Kardux, Peter Liebregts, Tessa Obbens, Sara Polak, and Wim Tigges.

List of Contributors

Agnes Andeweg is Assistant Professor in Literature at University College Utrecht, where she teaches courses on literature and research methods in the humanities. She specializes in modern Dutch literature, gothic fiction, and cultural history and memory, with a focus on gender, sexuality, and nationality. She has published in journals such as *Early American Literature, Cultural History, Journal of Dutch Literature*, and *Sexuality and Culture*. With Sue Zlosnik, she edited *Gothic Kinship* (Manchester UP 2013) and wrote a monograph on the Flying Dutchman for the city of Terneuzen. Furthermore, she edited the volume *Seks in de nationale verbeelding: culturele dimensies van seksuele emancipatie* (Amsterdam UP, 2015) on the topic of the cultural dimensions of sexual liberation, and a special issue on this topic of *Sexuality and Culture*. In 2014, her essay on the Flying Dutchman won the Essay Prize of the International Society for Cultural History.

Scott Brewster is Reader in Modern English Literature at University of Lincoln. He is co-editor (with Luke Thurston) of *The Routledge Handbook to the Ghost Story* (2017) and is currently completing (co-authored with Lucie Armitt) *Climates of Fear: Gothic Travel through Haunted Landscapes* (Anthem Press, 2020). He has published widely on gothic literature, the ghost story, Irish writing, and psychoanalysis.

Nick Freeman is Reader in Late Victorian Literature at Loughborough University. Enthralled by the supernatural since his childhood discoveries of anthologies by Peter Haining and Michel Parry, he has embraced the darkness in essays on gothic and weird writers such as E. F. Benson, Arthur Machen, Edith Nesbit, and M. John Harrison. He has also contributed to *The Edinburgh Companion to Victorian Gothic* (2012), *The Routledge Handbook of the Ghost Story* (2018), and other reference works. In a parallel life, he publishes widely on the decadent literature and art of the 1890s and is the author of *Conceiving the City* (2007) and *1895* (2011).

Avril Horner is an Emeritus Professor of English at Kingston University, London. Her research interests include women's writing and gothic fiction. With Sue Zlosnik, she has co-authored many articles and several books, including *Daphne du Maurier: Writing, Identity and the Gothic Imagination* (1998) and *Gothic and the Comic Turn* (2005); their most recent publication is *Women and the Gothic* (2016). She has also written several articles with Janet Beer, with whom she co-authored *Edith Wharton: Sex, Satire and the Older Woman* (2011). Her edited books include *European Gothic: A Spirited Exchange* and (with Anne Rowe) *Living on Paper: Letters from Iris Murdoch, 1934–1995* (2015 and Vintage Press paperback 2016). She has an essay entitled "Gothic and Surrealism" forthcoming in David Punter's *Gothic and the Arts* and is currently writing a biography of the author Barbara Comyns.

Evert Jan van Leeuwen is a lecturer in English-language literature and culture at Leiden University. His field of interest is the history of Gothic, Horror, and Science Fiction. In this context, he has published essays on authors such as Poe, Godwin, and Hawthorne; themes such as haunted houses; and subgenres such as Spaghetti Westerns and Graveyard Poetry. He most recently completed a study on Roger Corman's *House of Usher* for Auteur Press and is presently researching a history of Dutch-language Science Fiction.

Roger Luckhurst teaches at Birkbeck College, University of London, and, among other works, is the author of the British Film Institute Classics on *Alien* and *The Shining*; the cultural histories *The Mummy's Curse* and *Zombies*; and, most recently, *Corridors: Passages of Modernity.*

Leslie Megahey has written, produced, and directed many TV arts and drama films since the late 1960s. His filmed version of Bartok's opera *Bluebeard's Castle* won the Italia Prize, and his three-hour documentary *The Orson Welles Story* is regarded as the definitive filmed interview with Welles. He was one of the first editors of *Arena*; served twice as editor of BBC1's Omnibus series, for which he won a BAFTA award; and was head of BBC Music and Arts programs from 1988 to 1991. He wrote and directed the 1994 feature film *The Hour of the Pig* (US title *The Advocate*), starring Colin Firth, Donald Pleasance, and Ian Holm. He also directed the Olivier Award-nominated stage play *Jack,* which he co-wrote with its star Nicol Williamson, in London's West End and on to a Broadway run. The *Montreal Festival international du film sur l'art* (FIFA) ran a retrospective of his films in 2001 and presented him with their lifetime achievement award. His apparently "lost" cult film, the ghost story *Schalcken the Painter,* was rediscovered and restored by the BFI in 2013 and released as a DVD/Blu-ray.

Robert Miles is Professor of English at the University of Victoria, Canada. He is a past president of the International Gothic Association. His teaching interests include Nineteenth-Century English and American

Romanticism, the Romantic-era Novel, Gothic Writing, and Jane Austen. He has published in the journals *Studies in Romanticism, Eighteenth-Century Fiction, The Eighteenth-Century: Theory and Interpretation, Novel: A Forum on Fiction, Gothic Studies, Essays and Studies, Women's Writing: The Elizabethan to Victorian Period, ELH,* and *Texas Studies in Literature and Language.* His book publications include *Romantic Misfits* (Palgrave, 2008); *Gothic Writing, 1750–1820: A Genealogy,* 2nd edition (Manchester UP, 2002); and *Ann Radcliffe: The Great Enchantress* (Manchester UP 1995).

Michael Newton teaches film and late nineteenth- and early twentieth-century British, Irish, and American literature at Leiden University. He is the author of *Savage Girls and Wild Boys: A History of Feral Children* (2002) and *Age of Assassins: A History of Conspiracy and Political Violence, 1865–1981* (2012), both for Faber & Faber. On the subject of cinema, he has written two BFI Film Classics, *Kind Hearts and Coronets* (2003) and *Rosemary's Baby* (2020), and for Reaktion Books, *Show People: A History of the Film Star* (2019). He has also edited *The Penguin Book of Ghost Stories* (2010) and, for Oxford World's Classics, *Victorian Fairy Tales* (2015).

Michelle O'Connell is a lecturer in Romantic literature at the School of English, Drama, and Film, University College Dublin. She has published essays on women's poetry and the fiction of the Romantic period, and is working on a full-length study on the construction of the public persona of the woman poet in the nineteenth century in poetry, fiction, and the press.

Rahel Sixta Schmitz is a PhD candidate at the Justus-Liebig-University in Giessen, Germany. She is a fellow of the International Graduate Centre for the Study of Culture as well as a member of the International PhD Programme "Literary and Cultural Studies." Her main fields of interest include gothic and horror fiction across all media. She has published articles on the apocalypse in fiction, Gothic and globalization, and uncanny media technologies. In her current research project, she focuses on virus and network metaphors in gothic fiction from the 1990s onward.

Tuğçe Bıçakçı Syed completed her PhD in English at Lancaster University with a full scholarship from the Ministry of National Education in Turkey. She currently works as a Post-Doctorial Teaching Assistant in the Department of English Literature and Language at Namık Kemal University in Tekirdağ, Turkey. Her research theorizes Turkish Gothic as a national mode intimately linked to the concept of globalgothic as well as to the ideological processes of Turkish national identity construction. She has published journal and magazine articles on Western and Turkish Gothic literature and cinema in both

English and Turkish. Her most recent publication is entitled "Turkish B-movie Gothic: Making the Undead Turkish in Oluler Konusmaz Ki" and was published in *B-Movie Gothic: International Perspectives* (2018) by Edinburgh University Press.

Sue Zlosnik is Emeritus Professor of English at Manchester Metropolitan University, UK. Working alone, she has published on a range of fiction by writers as diverse as: George Meredith; Robert Louis Stevenson; J. R. R. Tolkien; Chuck Palahniuk; and Patrick McGrath, on whose work she published a monograph in 2011 (*Patrick McGrath*). With Agnes Andeweg, she co-edited *Gothic Kinship* (2013). With Avril Horner, she has published six books, including *Daphne du Maurier: Writing, Identity and the Gothic Imagination* (1998); *Gothic and the Comic Turn* (2005); and, most recently, the co-edited *Edinburgh Companion to Women and the Gothic* (2016). They have also written numerous essays and articles together, recent examples being "Gothic Configurations of Gender" in *The Cambridge Companion to Modern Gothic,* edited by J. E. Hogle (2014), and "The Apocalyptic Sublime: Then and Now" in *Apocalyptic Discourse in Contemporary Culture,* edited by M. Germana and A. Mousoutzanis (2014).

1 Introduction

Michael Newton and
Evert Jan van Leeuwen

From *Frankenstein* to *Dracula*, from Sheridan Le Fanu's 'Carmilla' to *Don't Look Now*, from *The Mysteries of Udolpho* to Thorold Dickinson's *The Queen of Spades*, Europe has haunted the British and Irish – turning the experience of the continent into a rite for terror, for bewilderment, into an encounter with the uncanny and strange. The Europe found in these books and films is not merely a geographical region; it is a zone of various and contradictory ideas, aspirations, and, this book suggests, narratives: as Anthony Pagden (2002) declares, Europe is "a construction, an elaborate palimpsest of stories, images, resonances, collective memories, invented and carefully nurtured traditions" (33). If "Europe" is an imagined place, then it is striking how often Anglocentric writers have imagined it in terms framed by the Gothic—a literary mode in any case understood to emerge from sites within a specifically European terrain. A specter has, as Karl Marx and Friedrich Engels divined, been haunting Europe. In these terms, Europe has been hallucinated into a place of nightmare, but also of allurement, enchantment, and mystery. It has stood as an essential elsewhere, a realm beyond the seas, separate and distinct, and dreamed.

In order to explore these complex visions, this book offers a collection of diverse, but interconnected accounts of a specifically British and Irish gothic vision of continental Europe. It tracks the transformative effect of those visions on English-speaking intellectual life from the fall of the *ancien régime* to Brexit. By focusing on the development of the relationship between "the north-western archipelago" and continental Europe over more than two-hundred years, this collection marks an important departure from standard literary critical narratives, which have tended to focus on a narrow time-period and have missed continuities and discontinuities in the ongoing relationship with the mainland. This collection of essays shifts attention to the central place that Europe has occupied in the gothic imagination. It uncovers the diversity of forces that enabled and structured an engagement with a vision of Europe as a haunted locale. The book hones the usual normative, narrowly evaluative, account of the development of Gothic as enmeshed in purely local concerns through a broader inter-cultural approach that focuses on the meeting and merging of cultural traditions, and the germinative force of concepts and images concerning our European neighbors.

Moreover, this book exposes the ways in which British and Irish writers played a central role in portraying mainland Europe as a gothic landscape and a ghostly site, a place haunted in itself and also one that has actively haunted our imagination. Not only was study of German literature and the image of the Catholic south transformative for the development of Gothic, but writers have also used mainland Europe both to construct notions of a demonic double and to provide a beguiling image of other cultural, intellectual, and imaginative possibilities. This volume also addresses the question, explicitly in Robert Miles's opening essay, how Europe came to see itself as "haunted," and how it could begin to turn out representations of a dark "spectrality."

Sense of place has proved central to Gothic, with its predilection for haunted precincts characterized by intrusion, intervention and the coming into correspondence of discrete times and spaces, of home and abroad, the past and present. Above all, Europe has long constituted different kinds of narrative space, a set of contradictory concepts, and an exemplary near-"other."

In the case of Europe as a location for British and Irish gothic texts, the question of national identity is particularly acute and centers on a number of potentially creative paradoxes. While understanding that they too were part of Europe, British gothic writers imagined themselves in distinction from continental cultures. This duality of not belonging and belonging is typical of the European experience, as Luisa Passerini (2002) has written: "most peoples have experienced and continue to experience Europe as something to which they belong, but where they also feel they represent something separate" (205). At the same time, writers have reconstructed and reimagined continental cultural identities, though always ones in the service of an understanding of the home territories. In Britain, the long-standing relation to Europe through the lens of Gothic has intertwined with contemporary politics and the impact of historical events. In this way, gothic texts trace a history of relations to the continent. In this volume, many of the essays demonstrate how the ever-present past of Gothic—of Europe—has become simultaneously a British past. It is the presence of history—of the persisting foregone—that renders the European scene so Gothic, in a literary and cinematic form anyway dedicated to the survival of the past, in the ghost, the undead, the uncanny traces of past cultures.

The political crisis of the French Revolution, the advent of Napoleon, the era of reaction, the years of revolution, the two World Wars, the rise of continental fascism, and the new post-war development of a European community—all invoked reactions and debates in Britain. Haunted Europe mirrored, negated, or transformed domestic agendas and disputes.

Almost invariably, continental Europe, already burdened by its own considerable ideological considerations, was interpreted through the prism of issues and debates at home in Ireland or Britain. The continent was thereby constrained to serve competing aesthetic and social agendas, which, when taken together, call into question the possibility of a single or even dominant mode of reception. The extent to which such agendas shaped and even distorted our understanding of an entire continent is vital for the understanding our present cultural moment.

Where Is Europe?

Tracing Britain's relationship with continental Europe inevitably entails considering just what ground is covered by the word "Europe" and who is, or is not, a European. Even the question of where Europe is may turn out to have provisional and ambiguous answers. Is Britain part of Europe? Where is the heart of the continent? What are its limits and borders?

Over the last centuries, "Europe" is a word whose meaning has shifted and still shifts, counting for different things depending on the intentions of the speaker. Among the grander impact of politics and alliances, the British traveler and the tourist fostered a self-consciousness about "Europe" as a place, a distinct culture, a complex fabric of landscapes, histories, and identities. Such travelers were not simply visiting Europe; they were encountering its various nations and locales, places as distinct as Paris and Berlin, the Alps and the Aegean islands, diverse in custom, climate, and language. Yet some sense that these disparate settings constituted a greater whole persisted. According to the OED, it was only in 1714 that the word "European" was first used in distinction to "English," so that (in the example quoted) plants might be one or the other. The word "European," in use in English from the sixteenth century onward, was often used in order to designate an identity to be contrasted with the "barbarian," whether the African or Asian or American; as such the word took on a specific intensity of demarcation in an Imperial context, becoming synonymous with "whiteness," where "natives" elsewhere and "Europeans" here stood in opposition. In this sense, the British and Irish felt themselves to be certainly European. Some marked changes in the use of the word appear at the end of the eighteenth and the beginning of the nineteenth centuries, as coinages such as "Europeanised" (1786), "Europeanity" (1805), "Europeanise" (1821), "Europeanism" (1824), "Europeanly" (1831), and "Europeanisation" (1845) caught on, expressing both a sense of some set of qualities deemed specifically European, and also the possibility that these qualities might (or might not) be inscribed onto the people of borderline zones and colonial territories. The idea of Europe signaled modernity, Enlightenment, a belonging to a dynamic civilization at the center of power; later, as the term "Eurocentric"

(1927) arrived, it meant also a place, self-regarding and rapacious, an imagined center-point offering a perspective on the world that belittled or marginalized other perspectives. Usually equally negative, since the 1970s in British minds "Europe" has come to stand for that part of Europe (by no means the whole) identifiable with the institutions and the project of the European Union, a specific "community" of nations to which we might or might not want to belong.

From antiquity, Europe existed in opposition to that which it was not, differentiated from the Asia to the East, and the Africa to the south. From the early modern period, it was balanced too against the Americas to the west. Beginning with Montesquieu, moving into the writing of the later eighteenth-century French *philosophes*, such as Condorcet or Turgot, Europe stood for reason, progress, and dynamism, contrasted especially with the supposed superstition and stultification of Asia. This sense was in some regards a long-standing one—as far back as Periclean Athens, luxurious, tyrannical Asia (embodied in Persia) opposed democratic Europe (identical to Greece) (Hay 1968, 3). The place of liberty faced the kingdom of despotisms. Yet in Guillaume Raynal and Denis Diderot's *Philosophical and Political History of the Two Indies* (*Histoire des deux Indes*) (1780), Europe comes into existence precisely through its barbaric invasion and oppression of people living in territories oceans away; for Raynal and Diderot, the idea of Europe emerges not from reason and science, but from conquest (Pocock 2002, 64–65).

Gothic locates perplexity in the porous boundary; its borderline states are precisely marked as such because they are prone to invasion, and the rational mind, the physical world, the nation all find themselves penetrated or plagued by forces from outside. Étienne Balibar (2004) has argued that under contemporary conditions the border has moved from the outer edge of territories and is now dispersed everywhere, locatable in interactions within the cosmopolitan city. For over two centuries, Gothic has preemptively sketched this transferal. The stories in this book unveil the ways in which Gothic has long been preoccupied by tourists, travelers, and journeying researchers. David Punter (2016) has described the Gothic as a literature of "the in-between" (3)—it is precisely this that underlies the relation to Europe, an elsewhere that is a here, an over-there that comes to us, an ancestry, a place for desire.

In a reversal of things, it is the visiting Briton who crosses the border, journeying from a space that is both within Europe and outside it, an island adjunct to and immersed within a culture. In contrast to Ireland, writers in Britain imagine themselves as both fully European and possessing a liminal kingdom beyond the meanings inscribed into the continent. Yet, in 1796, Edmund Burke, that great standard-bearer of tradition and common law, declared that "No European can be a complete exile in any part of Europe" (quoted in Hay 1968, 123), asserting a belonging to a community that transcends national borders. The traveler enters into the heart of another locale, one in which he or she might be thought to share (in the traditions and histories of "Christendom") and yet that is simultaneously a foreign "elsewhere." Here the spirits and supernatural presences, the elementals and horrors, are also just as much autochthonous and local, though the locality is strange to its temporary visitor.

The Europe that formed the locale for the gothic fictions scrutinized in this book was at once a home to a set of languages, a set of nations, and a variously (and ideologically) understood set of concepts and traditions, with religious underpinnings and ideas of law and government that were both shared and distinct (Emerson 1998). But it is also, of course, a real, if loosely defined place, a geographical space delimited by watersheds, rivers, and the sea—a region that Winston Churchill was angry to hear demystified as the western "peninsula of the Asiatic land-mass" (Hay 1968, xvii). Its borders were pervious and uncertain. It incorporated democracies, tyrannies, monarchies, Empires. Over the last two-hundred-and-thirty years covered by this book, there were various attempts to consolidate European difference by conquest into a kind of Empire (by Napoleon, by Hitler); the land-mass too experienced the presence of actual empires (such as the Austro-Hungarian, the Ottoman). Yet a sense of the disparate and incompatible characterized these political unions. Europe was at once secular, Christian (though divided between the Protestant, Catholic, and the variously Orthodox), and, in the southeast, Islamic. Did the "Orient" begin in White Russia or at Moscow, or even within Vienna (as Metternich had declared, "Asia begins at the Landstrasse"). The position of Russia was especially bewildering, a country so vast as to seem in two places at once; Catherine the Great could affirm that "Russia is a European power," but from the Don, or the Volga, or the Urals (the boundary shimmered evanescently around those permanent features), it went deep into Asia (Pagden 2002, 46–47). The southeastern borders of Europe were just as smudged, with the Balkans, Albania, Turkey, and the Eastern Mediterranean seeming, depending on your perspective, either inside or outside the fold. In this volume, Tuğçe Bıçakçı Syed's essay on the Turks in vampire narratives investigates some of the products of this particular blurring. Otherwise, further west, in the eyes of some a cultured north faced an alien and indolent south, with Africa reputedly starting at the Pyrenees (Stock 2010, 10). Internal boundaries and borders rendered this mappable space of Europe even more nebulous. It proved impossible to say where Europe's limits lie. To take only one example, Greece was understood to be a center of European culture and indeed the root of it, yet at the start of our period the country was under Ottoman control, and its culture had anyway been mediated for seven hundred years or so through Muslim scholars. As a place, Greece was both marginal and central, and in this it shared much with other locales gathered under the name of Europe. Similarly, as Evert Jan van Leeuwen addresses in his essay in this volume, the Jewish peoples of Europe represented for some writers an anomalous case, both emphatically and to some, like Dennis Wheatley, suspiciously European, while seeming, in the writings of anti-Semites, "Asiatic" and extraneous. Even the Bible, that basis of the image of Europe as "Christendom" came from a liminal zone, centrally British, centrally European, and yet hailing from an "alien" Middle Eastern domain.

As suggested already, the archipelago of Britain and Ireland and the other islands might mark a space beyond the continental zone, or could, contrariwise, be included within its cultural and political frame. The United Kingdom could feel itself unique in not having to worry about borders (being an island and therefore happily independent and non-contingent), though the relations between England and Scotland, England and Wales, and the inclusion or exclusion of all or part of Ireland—given an internal border, in 1922—would rather complicate that assertion (Stock 2010, 22). Indeed, Britain was as riven with contradiction and complexity as the continent it faced, the idea of the nation as fractured as that of Europe. Britain itself is not a single thing but is rather a divided place with histories that are counter, controversial, and as much marked by disharmony as continuity—as most recently the Brexit vote and the surrounding debates have reminded us. Moreover, despite the fact that they formed one political unit for more than a century, the complex, fraught relation between Britain and Ireland similarly brings up the provisional status, the unstable meanings, and the interwoven ambiguities of the cultures and countries in question.

The query as to who was a European was complicated by the rise of Nationalism and the nation state. Beginning with Herder, a fascination with localism and folk roots spread across the internal borders of Europe. Professors of folklore found that those deep roots of place had analogies in other nations' traditions. Beside the tribal basis of identity, there were other forces at work, transnationalism and transcultural exchanges. Regarding the relation between Britain and continental Europe, Gerard Delanty (2018) has explored the idea of entanglement, stressing not separateness, but reciprocal involvement, thereby understanding national traditions (including literary ones) in transnational context. At its heart, Gothic itself was transnational, a movement understood to be of Germanic heritage that found itself in Britain, Ireland, the United States, France, and pretty much everywhere. This fact of the transnational, the transcultural, in diverse ways informs all the essays in this volume.

Haunted Europe and the Gothic Field

A sense of place and the construction of national and cultural identities are themes that have received increasing attention within Gothic Studies of late. Catherine Spooner's and Emma McEvoy's *Routledge Companion to the Gothic* (2007), Marie Mulvey-Roberts's *Handbook of the Gothic*

(2009), and Glennis Byron and Dale Townshend's recent volume *The Gothic World* (2014) specifically address gothic cultural and linguistic nationalities: American, German, French, Australian, and regional identities: Anglo-Caribbean, Southern American. Byron's *Globalgothic* (2013), as its title suggests, is concerned with the Gothic's engagement with the breakdown of traditional geographical, cultural, and linguistic boundaries. In his seminal study of the Gothic's relation to nationalist discourse, *Alien Nation: Nineteenth-Century Gothic Fictions and English Nationality*, Cannon Schmitt (1997) argues that "Gothics pose as semi-ethnographic texts in their representation of Catholic, Continental Europe or the Far East as fundamentally un-English, the site of depravity" (2). The "threat of invasion from without produces Englishness within" (Schmitt 1997, 3). Similarly, Robert Miles has argued that in the era of the first gothic wave,

> Britain's identity was of a modern, progressive nation transforming itself, and the world, through commerce and science, a process guided by the advanced condition of its constitution and government, in sharp contrast to Europe, figured as despotic, backward, feudal, Catholic and Gothic.
>
> (2007, 15)

Toni Wein's *British Identities, Heroic Nationalisms, and the Gothic Novel, 1764–1824* (2002) deftly foregrounds the extent to which notions of Britishness and non-British otherness are central to classic gothic fiction. Whilst classic Gothic is often associated with key English and American writers such as Ann Radcliffe, Matthew Lewis, Edgar Allan Poe, and Nathaniel Hawthorne, the genre can be understood as a European literary import of sorts. Angela Wright (2013) has shown that "the work of the Gothic is specifically indebted to a French tradition of writing, and is often either appropriated, translated or adapted from French authors of the long eighteenth century" (12–13), and Dale Townshend (2014) has presented concrete historical evidence for a late eighteenth-century British concern about an invasion of continental fictional terrors. He explains that for the moralist Hannah More,

> the Gothic romance is a monstrous hybrid formed by the conjunction of non-neoclassical taste and depraved morality, swarming into Britain from both Germany and France with a fury that enacted the original invasion of the nation by the Barbarian Goths.
>
> (xxxvii)

In the opening essay of this volume, Robert Miles highlights the significant role played in the development of the Gothic by dark-Romantic

German imports. In his essay, "Seeing Ghosts: The Dark Side of the Enlightenment," Miles employs the Canadian philosopher Charles Taylor's thoughts on the "modern Western social imaginary" to point out how the explosion of ghost-seeing in the period was directly connected to the rise of secularization and the "Enlightened" democratic project that characterizes Western modernity. His close-textual analysis of Friedrich Schiller's *Der Geisterseher* (1787–89) explains how the influential German poet, playwright, and philosopher draws a structural link between political conspiracy and the phantasmagoria (the meeting ground of haunting and technology). He concludes that this most influential German *Romanfragment* is in fact "a prophetic work about power in the modern age." Continental Europe was not only considered a site of the irrational and a source of political anxieties for British readers. As James Kelly (2014) argues, "Ann Radcliffe's Gothic novels can be read as continental travelogues" (44), allowing British readers imaginatively to visit the exotic wonders, as much as the potential terrors, mainland Europe has to offer. Michelle O'Connell carefully historicizes and critically analyzes the positive presence of European, notably French fairy mythology in the much-overlooked poems in Radcliffe's *The Mysteries of Udolpho* (1794) and Landon's poem "The Fairy of the Fountains" (1835) through the lens of feminist-psychoanalytic theory. In doing so she unearths the significance of this continental connection to the development of a female gothic mode not only concerned with the form and function of the supernatural within the genre but also busy with the fashioning of original female poetic voices and identities in the final decades of the eighteenth and the first decades of the nineteenth century.

Radcliffe has long been known as a talented word-painter of gothic scenery, and, in *Gothic Landscapes: Changing Eras, Changing Cultures, Changing Anxieties*, Sharon Rose Yang and Kathleen Healy (2016) point out that "landscape is more than a physical entity, it is a canvas upon which cultures paint their world, their desires, and their cultural and political beliefs" (5). One significant locale that has remained understudied within gothic scholarship, however, is the sea. In "Slavery as a National Crime: Defining Britishness in Encounters with the Flying Dutchman," Agnes Andeweg highlights the fact that the Otherness of the "Dutchman" in this popular story not only played a role in the development of British national identity, in the nineteenth century, but also in the development of an ideology of Empire that included problematic attitudes toward slavery and race. Later in this book, Dutchness in relation to the Gothic is also the subject of Michael Newton's interview with film director Leslie Megahey concerning his BBC ghost-film, *Schalcken the Painter* (1979). But this time the focus lies on very different themes, the gothic potential in the aesthetics of golden-age Dutch painting and the commodification of the painter's subjects.

Of course, not all nineteenth-century British writers of gothic and fantastic fiction perceived the continent as an inherently unsettling place and instead drew it in terms of chiaroscuro. Edward Bulwer Lytton's idealistic hero Percy, in the supernatural satirical romance *Godolphin* (1833), like various real-life British Romantics, flees from the daily struggle and strife in Britain to an idyllic Italy, in order to find solace and peace of mind, but where he also comes into occult knowledge about his own and his beloved's tragic demise. In his essay "Walking Abroad: Strange Exhibitions in M. R. James," Scott Brewster explores the ambiguous attractions of continental travel in some of the most influential turn-of-the-century ghost stories, arguing that "James's ghost tales of European travel recall the passions of discovery, and the allure of new, often less-trodden places, that are similar to those expressed in his autobiographical reflections: yet...often reveal the equivocal benefits of sojourns in mainland Europe." Michael Newton's essay, "Haunted Hotels and Murder Inns: Travelers' Tales from Europe and the Gothic Short Story from the 1820s to the 1940s," extends the analysis of the theme of gothic holidays by revealing that next to the labyrinthine gothic castle and ruinous family mansion, "hotels and inns" also "act as sites of disturbance or terror, places that frame a strange doubling"; in doing so these foreign abodes expose "the anxiety induced by temporarily living alongside strangers" and map out Britons' relationships to their continental neighbors.

Since *The Castle of Otranto* (1764), Italy has been one of the favorite continental settings in British gothic fiction. Writing about Radcliffe's *The Italian* (1797), Justin D. Edwards argues that "the narrative expresses what is improper and un-English when it comes to social conventions, communal responsibilities, gender roles, as well as matters of conduct and deportment" (2014, 56). Much has been made within gothic scholarship of British Gothic's representation of continental Catholic institutions (see, for instance, Hoeveler 2014). However, as early as 1979, Elizabeth MacAndrew pointed out that Radcliffe's continental settings were also landscapes of the mind. In *Udolpho*, "Emily's travels are symbolic journeys between different worlds that represent different states of mind she must confront and understand, whether they are in herself or in others" (132). In their essay "Daphne Du Maurier: Sex and Death the Italian Way," Avril Horner and Sue Zlosnik explain how the twentieth-century mistress of English Gothic turned toward Italy "to represent a haunted self," building on the gothic tradition in which Italy "signif[ies] a malign 'otherness'" to unravel the construction of male gender identity and sexuality in relation and contrast to models of femininity. Du Maurier's "Don't Look Now" is probably the most famous "tourist gothic" (Hughes 2013, 242) story; in his essay "Robert Aickman and the English Abroad," Nick Freeman positions several strange tales by this influential twentieth-century writer, detailing how Aickman both builds on and transforms this gothic tradition

as he turns Europe into "a place of enigmatic invention where strangeness and estrangement could intertwine, leaving characters by turns
frightened, bewildered, and even, at times, ecstatic."

While Freeman's essay foregrounds the important concept of estrangement in Aickman's strange tales with continental connections, David
Punter's ground-breaking critical study, *The Literature of Terror* ([1980]
1996) cemented the idea that at the heart of gothic fiction lies "a very
intense, if displaced, engagement with political and social problems"
(54). The twentieth-century writer who most overtly turned to gothic
conventions to express and explore such political and social problems,
and above all his own fears, was the best-selling author Dennis Wheatley. In "Dennis Wheatley's Satanic Continent," Evert Jan van Leeuwen
highlights the extent to which the ex-wine merchant and one-time military strategist utilized the most sensational aspects of the occult revival
in the post-war era to express his own highly conservative ideals of the
British way of life and to defend Great Britain from that specter Marx
had claimed haunted Europe: Communism. Wheatley pictures continental Europe as the playground of the Devil and the feeding ground
for all his fiendish plans to topple the institutions of monarchy, aristocracy, empire, the Church of England, parliament, and British society's
entrepreneurial spirit. As such his works build on the nineteenth-century
gothic fictions that Cannon Schmitt points out are often "marked by
the most virulent sorts of xenophobia" (1997, 13). In "'This Lonely and
Primitive Place:' The Visualization of Eastern Europe in the Web Series,
Carmilla," Rahel Schmitz continues the focus on ideological critique by
showing how Sheridan Le Fanu's classic vampire tale "uses its particular
fictionalization of Styria as a reflection of and response to the West's
supposedly superior cultures." She explains how the recent online drama
based on this story "detaches the fiction from such themes of national
identity" and by contrast moves from themes of nationality to gender
and sexuality "foreground[ing] its positive take on queer representation
by rendering the topic a non-issue in light of the dangerous supernatural
happenings within the region."

Undoubtedly the most famous continental gothic region is Dracula's
haunt of Transylvania. Roger Luckhurst (2014) explains that in colonial
times, the Gothic "invoked its fearful Others by displacing melodramatic menaces backward in time and sideways in space, always over the
border, always somewhere else" (62). In "Haunted by the Ottomans:
Imperial Gothic and the Image of 'the Barbar-Turk' in Dracula Narratives," Tuğçe Bıçakçı-Syed builds on Maria Boletsi's theories concerning
barbarism to highlight the significant role that images of and ideas about
Ottoman and Turkish identities and cultures have played historically in
the construction of gothic nationalist discourses, as well as discourses
of savagery versus civilization that have been so central to gothic culture since the mid-eighteenth-century gothic revival. Significantly, she

traces the othering and demonization of the Ottoman Turk in Dracula narratives such as Elizabeth Kostova's *The Historian* (2005) and Gary Shore's film *Dracula Untold* (2014) produced in a post-9/11 American culture marked by fear and anxieties concerning international threats on a global scale.

Finally, in "Losing Our Heads (European Edition)," Roger Luckhurst comes to grips with the versatile symbolic power of one of the most graphically gruesome gothic tropes: the severed head. Just as Robert Miles, at the outset of this volume, unpacked the continental connections between the irrational and the revolutionary in the comprehensive context of late eighteenth-century European discourses of Enlightenment, free-thinking, and "ghost-seeing," Luckhurst takes the reader on a scholarly world tour of headless narratives as he asks the question "why Europe remains so haunted by this decapitated figure"; he concludes at the close of this volume "that the Gothic remains a privileged register for addressing the overdetermined wounds of contemporary European identity," a closing statement that perfectly sums up the collective critical endeavors represented by the twelve essays in *Haunted Europe*.

Erotic Europe and the Atavistic Continent

Very often, when it comes to "haunted Europe," the British and Irish writers who reimagined the continent as a gothic space turned to the privileged viewpoint of the traveler, a someone moving from anywhere to anywhere, and not bound, as the locals must be, to the constraints and community of a somewhere. The figure of the traveler and the wanderer infiltrate Gothic, and the presence of motifs and elements of travel literature in Gothic, and of Gothic in travel literature are everywhere. Repeatedly, the imagined European Gothic finds its place in such temporary precincts as the inn or the hotel, the train or coach. The uncanny clings to border territories, to hidden places, and to cities that make a space for secrecies—such as Venice, Paris, or Prague. Frequently, an erotic element creeps into these tourist's tales, the allure and threat of the continent manifest in the sexualized figure of a woman or a man. The American writer, Thomas Russell Sullivan's "The Lost Rembrandt" (1890) expresses these darkly romantic energies. Sullivan's version of "tourist Gothic" has The Hague represent another possibility for life, strange and promising: "Here are acres of superb branches, with mossy trunks and gnarled roots, recalling some enchanted forest of the brothers Grimm, and that picture of it left over in your memory from the pantomime of childhood" (2). Realism dissolves into a reminiscence of magic. The traveler discovers both a lost Rembrandt painting (a female companion to the male corpse dissected in the famous painting, "The Anatomy Lesson") and an inviting female stranger, ready to offer the simple tourist a strange initiation into a hidden place. The Rembrandt painting brings the dead to life—even as it has death at its center: "All those that look have become even as the thing they look at; their very dust is now unrecognizable" (4). The tourist finds himself linked with death—in art, in haunting—where the mortality that seduces him belongs to a Europe that itself is both a site of death and a scene of sexual enticement. In such tales as these, the ghost, the dead, appears peculiarly alluring, the woman standing as a Circe wishing to transform the visitor into the permanency of sharing in their deathliness.

Similarly, Algernon Blackwood's tale, "Ancient Sorceries" (1908), concerns Vezin, a bachelor Englishman, "the timid, gentle, sensitive soul" (45). He behaves as a typical middle-aged hero of the period, an unheroic man drawn into an adventure—invited into strangeness, destabilized, and then returned to who he used to be. This Englishman of French ancestry becomes involved with the Satanic mysteries of a small Northern French town. Characteristically, once again it is sexual desire for the European woman that shakes his soul, his longing for the French daughter of the inn turning his life upside-down. The French language permeates the tale, on some occasions untranslated—another tongue disturbing and troubling his own (72). It is a potently recapitulatory horror story, with the stolid Englishman returning to a primitive self—and on this occasion, a medieval self, one bound to a continental origin. The European stands for desire, for something atavistic within; Vezin's "recognisable personality" for a while weakens and is all but overwhelmed (63). Similarly, in another of Blackwood's *John Silence* tales, "Secret Worship" (1908) the English protagonist, Harris finds himself involved in German, a language that is his own, but that was also imposed on him when he was sent as a boarder to a German-speaking school, "'an English boy…dropped down into a school of a hundred foreigners'" (148). On his return to that school as a sentimental tourist, the horror of the story turns on his inability to remember how to translate the word "*Opfer*" (sacrifice), a word soon to be applied to himself (162–63). When rescue comes, it is John Silence who saves him, coming as someone who is "'English too, thank God'," and not one of those "'German devils'," someone who is strikingly an "un-German figure."

If the British were represented by tourists and travelers, by expatriates and migrants, in the English-language gothic tale, the Europeans themselves were students, magicians, monsters, seducers, and seductresses. The German student in particular stands as an archetypal gothic figure of the early nineteenth century, combining the introspection of Hamlet and the overreaching ambitions of a Faustus. Via Mary Shelley's *Frankenstein* (1818), the European student embodies the idea of metaphysical excesses and speculations, as opposed to the stout certainties of English or Scottish empiricism. In Robert MacNish's tale, "The Metempsychosis" (1838), set in the University of Göttingen, we find a bizarrely comic instance of the studious type, a fellow so absent-minded as literally to lose himself. Similarly, in Richard Harris Barham's "Singular Passage in the Life of The Late Henry Harris, D.D" (1831), we encounter a story of malign influence from the continent, as two students at "Leyden University" murder an English girl, Mary Graham, using sympathetic magic aided by a lock of her hair. The Dutch university emerges as a shadier place than the Oxford where the villain, one Frederick S--- began his studies, before being asked to leave after some unnamed misdemeanor. Europe becomes the fitting home for such reprobates.

In Washington Irving's "The German Student" (1824), the story's hero is someone given to those "wild and speculative doctrines which have so often bewildered German students," and is living, like Swedenborg, in "an ideal world of his own," "a literary ghoul, feeding in the charnel house of decayed literature" (32). In a story preoccupied with the decapitations that have seemed characteristically continental, at the height of the French Revolution Irving's student unwittingly spends the night with a guillotined beauty. This beheaded woman stands as a Parisian relation to another of Irving's famous spooks, the headless horseman of Sleepy Hollow, though the enticing *femme fatale* acts as a figure of cosmopolitan myth, rather than of parochial legend. However, pertinently, the local spook in Sleepy Hollow is the spirit of a German (Hessian) mercenary, an invading European linked forever to local American ground, a locale that Irving also describes as being characterized by "retired Dutch valleys," with Ichabod Crane's schoolhouse having been designed by the very Dutch-sounding architect, Yost Van Houten (274). In any case, again the erotic obsession with a European woman that motivates "The German Student" resides at the very heart of many English-language evocations of Europe's hauntedness. The student cohabits with a corpse, his night of passion discovered to be perverse, the context of the assignation being a revolutionary Europe that has overturned old values and traditions. On waking beside the corpse, her sad, beguiling beauty turns to repulsion and she becomes a "fiend" (36).

Some atavistic, perverse desire motivates such tales, and aptly the hauntings that continental Europe contained often signaled a journey backward, returning to childhood or savagery, to lost guilts and fugitive desires. In Algernon Blackwood's "The Willows" (1917), the protagonists journey into "a separate little kingdom of wonder and magic" (129), a geographically in-between region that acts as part of a dissolving Empire, and somehow not a national territory at all. The story's two travelers sail down the Danube, as the river traverses nations and territories, crossing borders and entering a wilderness Europe, an unsettled place. The narrator's Swedish companion, "a man I considered devoid of imagination" (138), hailed as "the imperturbable Swede" (139), turns out to be far more eerily imaginative than he was supposed to be. The European territory the two men enter lives as somewhere that "belonged to some sort of beings outside man's world" (141), as they make a journey into a place understood only through superstitions: "I suppose they believe in fairies and elementals, possibly demons too" (142). Here they encounter the soul of a place, ancient and pagan: "the spirits and deities of places that have been acknowledged and worshipped by men in all ages of the world's history" (153). The imagination itself becomes a key into the unknown— for the narrator as for the reader. They are haunted by a presence that returns them to the dark encounters of childhood dreaming: "I dreaded the night as a child lost in a forest must dread the approach of darkness" (174). Adrift in this alien place, the narrator concentrates on the London shop where he bought his sand-shoes—recalling the normal world as comfort—"I thought of roast beef and ale, motor-cars, policemen, brass bands, and a dozen other things that proclaimed the soul of ordinariness or utility" (191). On the edge of this terrifying Europe, he returns in thought to familiar London, the city of Empire, to home.

It is the imagination itself, Blackwood suggests, that opens the portal into the alien realm. During the childhoods and adolescences of the editors of this volume, there was a time when continental Europe could be imagined as a place of enticing mystery, when David Bowie and Iggy Pop were hanging out in Berlin, when John Foxx, Paul Weller, and Simple Minds sang paeans to European travel, when in Merchant-Ivory's *A Room With A View* (1985) Helena Bonham Carter might lose herself among fields of Italian violets. That period when Europe seemed a place of romance belonged to a world ready to find romance in many locales, the attenuated end of an impulse that stretches back to Ann Radcliffe and Mary Shelley, to Sheridan Le Fanu and Bram Stoker. Besides the gothic accounts reconnoitered in this book stand Nathaniel Hawthorne's and Elizabeth Bowen's beguiled expatriates, Powell and Pressburger's Monaco in *The Red Shoes* (1948), *The Third Man's* glamorously corrupt Vienna, the Italy of *Brideshead Revisited*, and the central Europe of Stephen Poliakoff's *Caught on a Train*. Few British writers or filmmakers would paint such romanticized images of Europe today; a yearning, an idealizing sense of glamor and regret has gone. Also in our childhoods and teenage years, a new set of words entered the language – "Eurofanatic"(1967) and "Europhile" (1971) were swiftly matched by "Europhobia"(1967), "Eurosceptic" (1971), "Eurorebel" (1975), "Europhobe" (1978) and "Eurotrash" (1980). That entrancement was always the obverse of the dark gothic sense of Europe, even as that dense longing, that wistful charm, found its way into those gothic imaginings too. Once possessed by Europe, the impulse for a savage exorcism follows. It is curious how at this historical moment, "Brexit" has been understood as a loss of romance, a falling out of love, and how often the political break with "Europe" has been imagined as a divorce–the money owing a divorce settlement-the complex disenchantment that sets in with the end of a long, passionate affair. Europe once evoked the pull of mystery, the alternating currents of attraction and repulsion, and this book bears testament to that powerful enchantment.

References

Balibar, Étienne. 2004. *We, the People of Europe? Reflections on Transnational Citizenship*. Princeton: Princeton University Press.

Barham, Richard Harris. 1885. "Singular Passage in the Life of the Late Henry Harris, D.D." In *The Ingoldsby Legends or Mirth and Marvels*. 1842 ed., 118–38. London: Frederick Warne and Co.

Blackwood, Algernon. 1997. *The Complete John Silence Stories*. Mineola: Dover.

Blackwood, Algernon. 1917. "The Willows." In *The Listeners*, 127–203. New York: Alfred A. Knopf.

Byron, Glennis, and Dale Townshend, eds. 2014. *The Gothic World*. Oxon: Routledge.

Byron, Glennis, ed. 2013. *Globalgothic*. Manchester: Manchester University Press.

Delanty, Gerard. 2018. *The European Heritage: A Critical Re-Interpretation*. New York: Routledge.

Edwards, Justin D. 2014. "British Gothic Nationhood, 1760–1830." In *The Gothic World*, edited by Glennis Byron and Dale Townshend, 51–61. Oxon: Routledge.

Emerson, Michael. 1998. *Redrawing the Map of Europe*. New York: St. Martin's Press.

Hay, Denys. 1968. *Europe: The Emergence of an Idea*. 2nd ed. Edinburgh: Edinburgh University Press.

Hoeveler, Diane Long. 2014. *The Gothic Ideology: Religious Hysteria and Anti-Catholicism in British Popular Fiction, 1780–1880*. Cardiff: University of Wales Press.

Hughes, William. 2013. *Historical Dictionary of Gothic Literature*. Lanham: Scarecrow Press.

Irving, Washington. 1987. "Tales of a Traveller, by Geoffrey Crayon, Gent." In *The Complete Works of Washington Irving*, Vol. X, edited by Judith Giblin Haig. Boston: Twayne.

Irving, Washington. 1978. "The Legend of Sleepy Hollow." In *The Sketch Book of Geoffrey Crayon, Gent. The Complete Works of Washington Irving*, Vol. VIII, edited by Haskell Springer, 272–97. Boston: Twayne.

Kelly, James. "Gothic and the Celtic Fringe, 1750–1850." In *The Gothic World*, edited by Glennis Byron and Dale Townshend, 28–50. Oxon: Routledge.

Luckhurst, Roger. 2014. "Gothic Colonies, 1850–1920." In *The Gothic World*, edited by Glennis Byron and Dale Townshend, 62–71. Oxon: Routledge.

MacAndrew, Elizabeth. 1979. *The Gothic Tradition in Fiction*. New York: Columbia University Press.

MacNish, Robert. 1838. "The Metempsychosis." In *The Modern Pythagorean; A Series of Tales, Essays, and Sketches*, Vol. II – *Tales*, 1–55. Edinburgh: William Blackwood & Sons.

Miles, Robert. 2007. "Eighteenth-century Gothic." In *The Routledge Companion to the Gothic*, edited by Catherine Spooner and Emma McEvoy, 10–18. London: Routledge.

Mortenson, Peter. 2004. *British Romanticism and Continental Influences*. London: Palgrave Macmillan.

Mulvey-Roberts, Marie, ed. 2009. *The Handbook of the Gothic*. 2nd ed. Basingtoke: Palgrave Macmillan.

Pagden, Anthony, ed. 2002. *The Idea of Europe from Antiquity to the European Union*. New York: Cambridge University Press.

Passerini, Luisa. 2002. "From the Ironies of Identity to the Identities of Irony." In *The Idea of Europe from Antiquity to the European Union*, edited by Anthony Pagden, 191–208. Cambridge: Cambridge University Press.

Pocock, J. G. A. 2002. "Some Europes in Their History." In *The Idea of Europe from Antiquity to the European Union*, edited by Anthony Pagden, 55–71. New York: Cambridge University Press.

Punter, David. 2016. *The Gothic Condition: Terror, History and the Psyche*. Cardiff: University of Wales Press.

Punter, David. 1996. *Literature of Terror, Vol. 1: The Gothic Tradition*. London: Longman.

Schmitt, Cannon. 1997. *Alien Nation: Nineteenth-Century Gothic Fictions and English Nationality*. Philadelphia: University of Pennsylvania Press.

Spooner, Catherine, and Emma McEvoy, eds. 2007. *The Routledge Companion to the Gothic*. London: Routledge.

Stock, Paul. 2010. *The Shelley-Byron Circle and the Idea of Europe*. New York: Palgrave Macmillan.

Sullivan, Thomas Russell. 1890. "The Lost Rembrandt." In *Day and Night Stories*, 1–40. New York: Charles Scribner's Sons.

Townshend, Dale. 2014. "Introduction." In *The Gothic World*, edited by Glennis Byron and Dale Townshend, xxiv–xlvi. Oxon: Routledge.

Wein, Toni. 2002. *British Identities, Heroic Nationalisms, and the Gothic Novel, 1764–1824*. London: Palgrave Macmillan.

Wright, Angela. 2013. *Britain, France and the Gothic, 1764–1820: The Import of Terror*. Cambridge: Cambridge University Press.

Yang, Sharon Rose, and Kathleen Healey, eds. 2016. *Gothic Landscapes: Changing Eras, Changing Cultures, Changing Anxieties*. Cham: Palgrave Macmillan.

2 Seeing Ghosts

The Dark Side of the Enlightenment

Robert Miles

The ghost-seeing I mean is the kind we encounter in Friedrich Schiller's much under-appreciated *Ghost-Seer; or, Apparitionist* (*Der Geisterseher—Aus den Memoires des Grafen von O***), written and published in installments over a period of three years (1787–89) and left unfinished, as a fragment. As Walter Scott notes, the ultimate mark of success in the field of novel writing is to become known as the founder of one's own school of fiction (quoted in Williams 1968, 230). By this criterion, *The Ghost-Seer* was wildly successful, as it did, indeed, initiate a new sub-genre: that is, the conspiracy novel. It was also the impetus for another modern sub-genre, what one might call the "big con," by which I mean the kind of elaborate scheme of deception one finds in, say, George Roy Hill's *The Sting* (the Paul Newman/Robert Redford film from 1973), or the *Oceans 11* franchise. The confidence trick goes back to the very origins of the novel, to Petronius's *Satyricon*, and to the picaresque tradition that emerged out of it; though in the picaresque, the "con" is largely restricted to an artful dodger passing himself off as something he isn't—generally a wealthy aristocrat, temporarily incommoded by fortune, ripe for the plucking—and where the plucking actually happens, behind the scenes, in the reverse direction. This is quite remote from the baroque elaboration of the *Ghost-Seer*, whose set piece of coney-catching is a masterpiece of wheels within wheels within wheels: an agent of the Inquisition passes himself off as an Armenian during the Venice carnival in order to flip a gullible, Protestant, German prince back to the Catholic cause; in order to do so the Armenian employs a confederate to impersonate a Cagliostro-like magus, significantly known as the Sicilian, ostensibly to shake the Prince's Enlightenment beliefs through the showing of a private phantasmagoria, complete with magic lantern, disembodied voices, spectral appearances, and electric flashes, all designed to convince the Prince of the Sicilian's supernatural powers. The Armenian then unmasks his confederate—Wizard-of-Oz like, pulling back the arras to expose the Sicilian's chicanery—in order to convince the Prince of the Armenian's even more preternatural sagacity. But that is not the sting. The sting is far more cunning, and subtle, as I will shortly explain.

The conspiracy novel internalizes the confidence trick, but it differs from those works falling within the "big con" sub-genre because it additionally includes two essential features first encountered in *The Ghost-Seer*. First, the "sting" is the work of a powerful institution that aims to defend or entrench its power, whether as the establishment or as an insurrectionary, revolutionary force. Second, it employs "high-tech" as an instrument of persuasion. In *The Ghost-Seer*, as its title indicates, the kind of persuasion the Inquisition has in mind is facilitated through the seeing of ghosts. The question my essay asks is: why did late Enlightenment Europe come to be haunted? My essay makes three main contentions relative to this question. The first is that Schiller's largely overlooked *Ghost-Seer* is a logical place to start in looking for an answer. Logical, because *The Ghost-Seer* is not simply part of a fashion for ghost-seeing, a minor though collateral line of what we generally call the rise of the Gothic: rather, it constitutes, in itself, the substance of an answer. That is my second contention. The third is that Schiller's answer is best seen through the framework of the already rich critical discussion on why late Enlightenment Europe suddenly discovered itself to be haunted. As E. P. Thompson (1994) long ago observed—and here he merely echoes Thomas Carlyle—in the late Enlightenment there was "something like an explosion of anti-rationalism, taking the form of Illuminism, Masonic rituals, animal magnetism, millenarian speculation, astrology (and even a small revival in alchemy), and of mystic and Swedenborgian circles" (xiv). As Thomas Carlyle (1869) puts it, it was "As if Bedlam had broken loose; as if, rather, in that 'spiritual Twelfth-hour of the night,' the everlasting Pit had opened itself, and from *its* still blacker bosom had issued Madness and all manner of shapeless Misbirths, to masquerade and chatter there" (vol. v, 83).

Of course, saying that there was an explosion of ghost-seeing during the late Enlightenment is not itself an answer, and neither is the common explanation that it was because one thing begat another. I believe David Punter ([1980] 1996) was the first critic seriously to take issue with "the commonplace of literary history" (I, 10) that explained why the Gothic erupted in the early Romantic period; the narrative, that is, that Enlightenment reason begat an irrational reaction against it. There are many things to be said against this once standard thesis. To begin with, arguing that the recrudescence of the supernatural was a reaction to, say, the French Encyclopedia, is not in itself a coherent explanation. As John Fleming (2013) points out, in his own highly entertaining *Dark Side of the Enlightenment: Wizards, Alchemists, and Spiritual Seekers in the Age of Reason* (whose title I've purloined), there was, from the start, a thin line between the rational and irrational during the period we think of as the Enlightenment (2); accordingly, one could as easily say the Gothic was a reaction against the irrational as it was against reason (at which point the "reaction" theory has become gibberish). Further, if we keep to this common-sense view of literary history, where opposites allegedly beget each other, what are we to make of the fact that it turns Romanticism into a reaction against irrationalism? The renewed interest in the supernatural precedes the Romantic period; Carlyle, as much as Wordsworth or Coleridge, was a transcendentalist setting himself up in explicit opposition to the dark side of the Enlightenment, to its "bed-lam" of phantasmagorical fantasies, its "frantic novels" and sickly and stupid German tragedies, as Wordsworth puts it in his preface to the *Lyrical Ballads.* In other words, one school of irrationalism (Romantic Transcendentalism) is here pitted against another (late Enlightenment ghost-seeing), as if they were somehow opposites. Nor does the "reac-tion" thesis allow us to make a very important distinction between, on the one hand, the idea that during the late eighteenth century, "haunting" became a ubiquitous trope in European art and, on the other hand, the idea that a subset of this trope was itself the trope of haunted Europe; that even in far off America, when one began to consider literary haunt-ing (and here one might as well think of Edgar Allan Poe), haunting as often as not was imagined in a particular, European way: a castle (or facsimile), an act of (usually murderous) usurpation, and a dead hand emerging out of the grave, or tomb, or crypt.

Fortunately, beginning with Punter himself, there have been a number of scholars who have thought more critically, and more productively, about the issue than was evident in common versions of the "reaction thesis." In Gothic studies, in my view, the main names would be (in chronological order) David Punter, Terry Castle, Jerrold Hogle, and E. J. Clery. To these I would like to add a voice from outside Gothic Studies, the Canadian Philosopher Charles Taylor.

In the concluding, theoretical chapter to *The Literature of Terror,* Punter ([1980] 1996) advanced a thesis for the emergence of the Gothic that largely set the critical agenda for the following decades of gothic criticism. He argued that the Gothic was a symptom of a deep rupture in the European imagination occasioned by the rise of capitalism in the period we now call the late Enlightenment; that this rupture went all the way down, so to speak, to the very foundations of the Western psyche; and that the Gothic neurotically recycled imagos of the old, fractured order (the father, patriarchy, Oedipus), as symptoms of a new, perpetual, melancholia. Capitalism enfranchised acquisitive individualism, hence the need to break free from the old, aristocratic, patriarchal order, which had placed constraints on the legitimacy of upward bourgeois striving. But by the same token bourgeois acquisitiveness froze aristocratic mate-rialism as the acme of the desirable. The consequence was the modern, gothic, mental traveler, the psyche that both repudiates and perpetuates the imagery of a vanished order it chases, but cannot secure.

In "The Spectralization of the Other in *The Mysteries of Udolpho,*" Terry Castle (1987) built on the theories of the historian Phillipe Ariès to argue that the ubiquitous habit of ghost-seeing in the late Enlightenment was also the result of a fundamental shift in cultural practices brought about by the rise of capitalism, where the shift in question focused on burying the dead. In the old, enchanted, pre-modern consciousness, death was a mundane occurrence where the newly dead were shepherded across the threshold into another world, through wakes, bodies lying in state, and other festivities of transition, whereas in our modern, frag-mented lifeworlds, dead bodies are never seen, let alone psychologically accommodated, having been discretely whisked off, and dealt with, by dedicated professionals. The paradoxical result, says Castle, is that in the old, animistic world of ubiquitous spirits, the dead stay dead, having been successfully laid to rest through the magic performed by rites of transition, whereas in the modern world, of *mortus interruptus*, as it were, the dead (as we see in Edgar Allan Poe) just will not stay dead: they re-emerge as specters, as spectralization, as Castle calls it, where the dead don't so much haunt as plague the living: as with Emily St. Aubert, in *The Mysteries of Udolpho* (1794), everywhere one turns, one sees retreating out of the corner of the eye the specter of, not just the recently dead, but any other "other" who might happen to be physically absent. In what became a series of essays on spectralization, Castle went on to draw our attention, influentially, to the spectral entrepreneur Gaspard Etienne-Robertson (Castle 1988, 1995). While Robertson did not in-vent the phantasmagoria (a point to which we will return when we con-sider *The Ghost-Seer* in more detail) he did popularize its name while also producing its most sensational iteration: light and sound shows ar-ranged, *á la* Radcliffe, in the crypts of the Capuchin, in a Paris still living the aftermath of the terror and its mass deaths. Castle's really interesting point, though, was that no sooner did Robertson coin the term "phan-tasmagoria" for the technological bedlam of a magic lantern show, sur-rounded by bones, diaphanous webs, and spooky music, where the dead rematerialized—no sooner did the word emerge to denote a canny com-mercial development—than it served as the immediate *mot juste* for con-temporary experience: the world itself had become phantasmagorical; or rather, the phenomenon was internalized so that the mind itself became a phantasmagoria, a theater of constant spectralization. One awoke to find Robertson's macabre sound and light show going off inside one's head. To see the point one can jump immediately to Edgar Allan Poe, the great codifier of the Gothic (what else is Castle describing by spec-tralization than Roderick Usher's haunted cranium, as depicted in "The Haunted Palace"?); but it is more instructive to stay with the immediately succeeding period to Robertson's coinage, to catch a sense of how fast, and how systematically, the new sense caught on: thus, again, Thomas Carlyle, that great codifier of modernity, who picks up the term to de-scribe the damage wrought by Schiller's Sicilian, a.k.a. Count Caglios-tro: in the Count's mixed-up world of mystic mumbo jumbo, Egyptian mysteries, crystal balls, and hocus pocus, experience had become, says Carlyle (1869), in his great essay on the Diamond Necklace affair (1837), in which the "Sicilian" principally figures, a "black-magical phantasmagory" (172). So naturalized had the coinage become, that by 1850, that otherwise astute historian, Nathaniel Hawthorne (1978), unconsciously commits the anachronism of using the word (in exactly the way Castle posits) to help realize Hester Prynne's mental experience of finding herself radically isolated, and exposed, when pilloried in the public square for the sin of fornication:

> Reminiscences, the most trifling and immaterial, passages of infancy and school-days, sports, childish quarrels, and the little domestic traits of her maiden years, came swarming back upon her, intermingled with recollections of whatever was gravest in her subsequent life; one picture precisely as vivid as another; as if all were of similar importance, or all alike a play. Possibly, it was an instinctive device of her spirit to relieve itself by the exhibition of these phantasmagoric forms, from the cruel weight and hardness of the reality.
>
> (46–47)

The sense data that are memories, and the sense data that are real presences, have become indistinguishable for Hester Prynne, who stands here for the isolated modern consciousness, athwart traditional authority, irredeemably haunted by images of an unrecoverable past, each as vivid as each other, and each as vivid as waking experience. Experience and memory alike were now "phantasmagorical," a schism in experience rooted in Empiricism's Lockean, associationist model, as Jerome McGann (1998) notes in *Poetics of Sensibility* (13–18).

In *The Rise of Supernatural Fiction*, E. J. Clery (1995) also begins with the commercial bedlam of the late Enlightenment race for specters, as outlined by Carlyle: that is to say, like him, she takes the "Ghost of Cock Lane"—the sensation of its season—as an indicative starting point. Clery's originality was to be the first critic to focus, systematically, on the following point: what had previously been matter for serious theological discussion was now a hot commodity. Going back to *Hamlet*, the question of spectral evidence—that is to say, whether specters were the ghosts of the damned, and therefore unreliable, or the reliable emanation of a liberated soul, and therefore testimony verifying Christian beliefs—had previously exercised devout minds such as Dr. Johnson's. It was now the stuff of popular entertainment. Spectralization was as much a part of the capitalist project as Smith's "invisible hand" (Clery 1995, 66), a spectral trope as weird and all controlling as the one that inspired Walpole's *Castle of Otranto*, but now naturalized, and thus an invisible part of the "modern social imaginary" (Taylor 2004). Writing around the same time as Clery, Jerrold Hogle also recurs to *Hamlet*.

In *Hamlet* the ghost may very well be a counterfeit, but by the time we get to *Otranto*, or the modern ghost story, we are dealing, not with a possible counterfeit, but with the counterfeit's ghost, a spectral simulation that nostalgically reminds us of the good old days when the question of a counterfeit ghost was a serious one for theologians, rather than a picayune one for the entertainment industry (Hogle 1994).

These accounts of the rise in ghost-seeing in the late eighteenth century have a number of things in common. They all agree that something happened in the late eighteenth century that fundamentally altered the social imaginary; they link this change to the rise of capitalism, to the triumph of modernity, to (and here I am adopting the period's own sense of itself) the advent of the present day "age of commerce"; they identify a rift in the semiological system, so that key signs fundamentally change in "value," as Saussure would put it ("death," "ghosts," the "father"); and they posit a troubling alteration in the very notion of the real, hence the immediate usefulness, and ubiquity, of "phantasmagoria" as a trope for the spectralization of everyday experience, the ubiquitous dematerialization of the material world. As Carlyle (1869) puts it in "The Diamond Necklace," his present was an Age of Romance, meaning a destabilized period where from a "an all-encircling mysterious tide of Force" in "perpetual change, the lordliest Real-Phantasmagory, which men name Being" rises and vanishes (v, 134). In these accounts, Europe comes to be haunted at the close of the Enlightenment, as haunting is an epiphenomenon of modernity, of a certain kind of "emptying out," whether Hogle's ghost of the counterfeit, Punter's imagos, Castle's specters, or Clery's commercialized supernatural.

The reason I want to add Charles Taylor to the mix (principally *Sources of the Self*, from 1989, and *A Secular Age*, from 2007, but for an introduction see *Modern Social Imaginaries*, 2004) is that his work provides the intellectual scaffolding that helps make sense of what these accounts have in common. Like them Taylor (2007) sees the late-Enlightenment/early-Romantic period as the moment when modernity was instantiated, not at the level of the elite, the intelligentsia, but the mass (175); and like them he sees issues of transcendence, or ghost-seeing, if you will, as taking on an endemic characteristic within modernity, one best characterized by instability (303–4).

Taylor (2007) is a great believer in Weber's disenchantment thesis (24–25). While the work of disenchantment was protracted, highly involved, and purely accidental (Taylor is a militant anti-teleologist), it was largely complete around the time of the explosion in European ghost-seeing, and was characterized by a number of features we now take absolutely for granted, but which were, at the time of their mass instantiation, historically unique. These would include the valorization of ordinary life, where mundane flourishing came to be the standard measure of human happiness (Taylor 1989); a linear rather than circular sense of time (Taylor 2007, 54–59); a punctual self (1989) buffered against the chaos of a magical or enchanted world (2007, 37–42), shored up by natural rights, including to property. This modern Western social imaginary, as Taylor calls it, was further distinguished by the belief that sovereignty, and therefore legitimacy, flowed from the people (rather than some notion of divine order, or "*ontic logos*," as Taylor describes it); that this popular will should come to be known through a public sphere; and that the economy, as the source alike of our prosperity and security, is a natural organism—a self-regulated system guided by an invisible hand—that ought to be left to its own devices (Taylor 2004).

These assumptions form part of what Taylor (2007) calls "background." By "background" he means assumptions that must be held for our everyday actions and reactions to make any sense. In the course of our daily lives, this background is so deeply buried, as to be, in effect, invisible (Taylor 2007, 173). I can best illustrate the force Taylor attributes to the notion of background by adapting the words of Nathaniel Hawthorne, from his story "The New Adam and Eve" (1843), with a few of Taylor's:

> We who are born into the world's artificial system can never adequately know how little in our present state and circumstances is natural, and how much is merely the interpolation of *cultural practices*...It is only through the medium of philosophy that we can lessen those iron fetters, which we call truth and reality, and make ourselves even partially sensible what prisoners we are.

As much as for Hawthorne's artificial system, Taylor's (2007) background assumptions are an "iron cage" we mistake for truth and reality, and he indeed uses this same metaphor (59).

While ubiquitous, and all-enveloping, the modern, Western, social imaginary is not uniform, static, or totalizing. On the contrary, it is unstable, contingent, and ever mutating. At its core we find what Taylor calls the "nova," by which he means a super-charged fissiparousness at the very center of Western secularization. Taylor defines secularization, not as the decline in religious belief (which he in any event disputes); not as the separation of church and state (which exists more in theory than practice); but as the background assumption that belief is a lifestyle choice: that it is up to each individual to choose what it is they base their notions of human flourishing on, whether the possibility of transcendence or what Taylor (2007) calls the "immanent frame" (542); whether on a conventional notion of God, or ecological tree-hugging; or, finally, in the case of militant anti-immanence, on a Nietzschean "cheerful" nay-saying (Taylor 2007, 599). His large claim is that this assumption, about the electivity of belief, was unique in the wide sweep of human history at the time of its mass instantiation—as a reflex given—during the Romantic period. One might take as an example the driving point behind *A Secular Age.* So if one asks, what does Taylor mean by background, by assumptions that have come to seem unquestioned aspects of the way things are, a good place to start, by way of an example, would be the assumption that religious belief is a matter of personal choice. Taylor (2007) argues that for much of non-Western humanity, and until fairly recently in the history of the West, this natural fact would be received as an utterly outlandish, and, indeed, incomprehensible, notion (25).

As G. K. Chesterton famously quipped, a man who believes in nothing will believe in anything. While not exactly what Taylor (2007) means by the "nova," the remark nevertheless brings out the chaotic quality of the charged spiral of modern secularization, where belief and unbelief both undermine and reinforce each other (299). Carlyle's sense of the dark side of the Enlightenment, as an unholy witching hour, an unbridled orgy of ghost-seeing, alchemy, Egyptian wizards, pantheism, spiritualism, and technological chicanery, is of a piece with Taylor's nova, and its first efflorescence coincides exactly with its initial mass instantiation, in Taylor's view. At the heart of Taylor's take on Western modernity lies a paradox: at the very moment the possibility of enchantment was truly over, as an authentic expression of deepseated background understandings, it flares up again (as Susan Sontag [1964] long ago noted) as kitsch, pastiche, as something self-consciously understood as finished, and unrecoverable, other than through irony, which is no recovery at all. In other words, Taylor takes at face value Schiller's fundamental distinction between the naïve and sentimental, which was itself a reworking of an English, eighteenth-century cliché: think Richard Hurd and his faux lament for the era of fine fabling we've lost (the naïve) even as we've gained the inestimable blessing of our present, self-aware, "commercial age" (the sentimental) (Clery and Miles 2000, 77; Warner et al. 2010, 304).

With the essential elements of the critical conversation in place I now want to turn to Schiller's novella in order to investigate what it is that Schiller, in particular, has to tell us about the rise of haunted Europe. Or to put it differently, when we look closely at Schiller's text, to what extent does it confirm, extend, contradict, or alter the conversation I've just outlined?

But before I do so I want to draw attention to one of the iconic images of European haunting, an image frequently misunderstood: I refer to Goya's self-portrait of himself slumped at his desk, in apparent sleep, while a crowd of totemic animals swarm behind him: owls, bats, a strangely alert lynx. "The Sleep of Reason Produces Monsters" is one of the two or three most iconic images of the gothic imagination; so familiar has it become that we doubtless don't stop to consider its meaning, which seems abundantly clear: when reason sleeps, when the artist drifts into unconsciousness, and the super-ego nods, the id's fantasia comes upon us. The Gothic, says the image, begins with the suspension of reason, perhaps as a reaction against it.

But that is not the meaning of Goya's image. Painted as part of a set of sketches Goya called his "caprichos" (or caprices, recalling the root word—capreolus—is Latin for goat, itself a byword for lechery as well as the hyperactive, unfocused, mind), "The Sleep of Reason" pivots on a crucial ambiguity: "*sueno*"—the Spanish for "sleep"—can mean either dream or reverie. The artist in the image (we can see his dropped pen and sketchbook) is either asleep, and the images are his nightmare, or he is awake, but fantasizing, in which case the images are not the antithesis of reason, of the waking self, but its product. In Freud's terms, the monstrous is here seen to emanate, not just from the id, but also from the ego, from the waking, reasonable, self. The images themselves are chosen with studied ambiguity. There are bats, meaning superstition, the old feudal order of the church with its repressive mumbo-jumbo, but also owls, meaning Minerva, wisdom, reason. Except the name of the particular kind of owl depicted is also, in Spanish, a byword for a prostitute (Ciofalo 1997, 433).

The image dates from between 1797 and 1799. It is a pivotal moment in Spanish and European history. Like Wordsworth, Goya had found it blissful to be alive in that Revolutionary dawn, where the old Feudal order was to be swept away, with the empire of reason emerging in its place; but by the decade's end, post the Terror, and its aftermath, matters looked much different. Is the unreadable chaos of wisdom, superstition, lust, and repression—signified by the cloud of totemic images rising behind the sleeper—the product of the unconscious or of reason, the id or the rational self? The horrific idea Goya is raising here, is that reason, itself, is a form of destructive madness, and that Goya's own art is compromised by his lofty ideals. The image is fundamentally ambiguous: it is strenuously pro-Enlightenment (the sleep of reason produces monsters), while being, at the same time, the reverse (reason's dreams are monstrous, a critique later to be echoed, famously, indeed, notoriously, by Horkheimer and Adorno in their *Dialectic of Enlightenment*).

As Goya's image reminds us, Europe comes to be haunted around the end of the eighteenth century, not because it is reacting against a surfeit of light, illumination, and rationality; the haunting itself is part and parcel of what we have come to call the Enlightenment. Superstition comes again, not because people have suddenly become bored with reason. As Carlyle intuits, the phantasmagorical is itself a symptom of modernity, and the rise of reason.

While written a decade in advance of it, Schiller's *Ghost-Seer* is built on precisely the same ambiguity as Goya's image: the ghost-seer in question (or rather, the most ready candidate) is the German Prince that the Inquisition is looking to flip. He has been chosen, in part, because "A fondness for the marvellous had ever been his prevailing weakness" (388).[1] (This is a point that Ann Radcliffe reworks when describing Vivaldi in *The Italian* (1797), her version of a ghost-seer [347].) The Prince is both a

Protestant and an apostle of reason. The first thing we are told about him is that he "avoided all kinds of dissipation." He lives modestly and is devoted to knowledge, to the modern project. That is his weakness, his Achilles heel; believing nothing, he is ready to believe anything, as Chesterton would put it. Or as Taylor would say, he is already living the "nova" as the unconscious condition of his life. Ready to be haunted, the Prince is fertile ground on which the machinations of the Inquisition may be set up, and set going. By the time they are through with him, haunted he is. And it is through his dreams of reason that they ensnare him.

The Ghost-Seer is both a fragmented, and a fragmentary, text, being both incomplete and discontinuous. Written in installments, it seems that at some point Schiller either lost interest, or lost the plot. The latter conclusion is, I think, the most likely, much as Coleridge did in "Christabel," and for much the same reason: while following a compelling logic, the logic in question is one that inherently resists closure. There is no neat conclusion to be drawn, only a state of affairs to be delineated. The novella comes in two parts. In the first, Count Von O--- tells us the story of the affairs of his close confidante, referred to only as the Prince, beginning in Venice during carnival. Apparently owing to the deep game set afoot to ensnare the Prince in the toils of the Inquisition, Count Von O--- is recalled to Germany, mid-plot, thus leaving the Prince exposed. Instead, Baron von F--- is delegated by Count Von O--- to keep an eye on the Prince, and to assist him where possible. The second half of the novella is comprised of the letters sent by Baron von F--- to Count von O---, keeping him informed of the Prince's affairs. Letters go missing or are intercepted; the bias of the somewhat unimaginative Baron von F--- is gently reproved by the mysterious editor, presumably Count von O--- himself, who is equally limited in his understanding. In other words, Schiller takes care to locate the unreliability, and ambiguity, of his narrative. As a narrative it is partial, patchy, and incomplete.

The only way one can begin to make sense of the complex plotting—in both senses of narrative complication and conspiracy—is to follow the old narratological trick of distinguishing between discourse and history, the order in which information is relayed, and the putative history of the events depicted. Given the ambiguity of the novella's discourse, its manner of unfolding history, the history I present here is necessarily somewhat speculative. Perhaps our best anchor point occurs in the second sentence of the novella, where the Count von O--- assures the reader of the veracity of his narrative, being, as he was, an eyewitness: "The few who are acquainted with a certain political event will, if indeed these pages should happen to find them alive, receive a welcome solution thereof" (377). The political event seems to have been this: the Prince, now second in line to the throne of an unnamed German principality, had converted to Catholicism, an act threatening the Protestant establishment of his principality. In the second English translation of

1800 that is how matters are left, whereas the first, truncated, English translation of 1795 completes Schiller's story for him, with the Prince consenting to "the murder of the Prince who barred his ascent to the throne" (242). The plot misfires and the Prince's confederates dispatch him with poison.

The history related by the *Ghost-Seer*, then, is the history of how the German Prince came to be turned, from Protestant to Catholic, during his time in Venice, with grave political consequences. The conspirators appear to have been the Inquisition, through their agent, the Armenian, although a somewhat different complexion may be placed on this, if one believes the Sicilian. The Prince is initially hooked when the Armenian mysteriously appears, as he and the Count von O--- stroll through Venice, whispering to the Prince: "'Congratulate yourself, my Prince... he died at nine'" (379). Several days follow before the meaning of this mysterious communication is revealed: a letter arrives for the Prince informing him that his kinsman died (indeed, at 9:00), and that he is now second in line to the throne. The event naturally piques the Prince's curiosity, and his love of the marvelous. The plot is thickened by a series of ominous events that lead up to the Sicilian's seance. In the first, a Venetian who plotted to murder the Prince following an altercation over a card game has his head severed from his body in the presence of the Prince and Count von O---, by the Inquisition acting on a mysterious tip-off over the Venetian's intent to hire a bravo. Later, on a trip to the country:

> A troop of young girls and boys, dressed in theatrical habits, welcomed us in a pantomimical dance...the principal actress, who represented a queen, stopped suddenly, as if arrested by an invisible arm. Herself and those around her were motionless. The music ceased. The assembly was silent. Not a breath was to be heard...On a sudden she started from her reverie with the fury of one inspired, and looked wildly around her. "A king is among us," she exclaimed, taking her crown from her head, and laying it at the feet of the prince.
>
> (384)

Even stranger, the Prince wins a snuff box at a booth through a lottery; when he opens it he discovers a key he had previously lost. The event has the desired effect on the Prince:

> "How is this?" said he to me, as we were left for a moment alone. "A superior power attends me, omniscience surrounds me. An invisible being, whom I cannot escape, watches over my steps. I must seek for the Armenian, and obtain an explanation from him."
>
> (386)

It is at this point the Sicilian steps in. The Prince wonders what these portents could mean, and when one of the company scoffs at the tricks of jugglers and con-artists, the Sicilian steps forward to prove them wrong:

> Who had the key? The Sicilian, throwing back his cloak, took
>   out a looking-glass and held it before the prince. "Is this the
>   man?"
> The prince drew back with affright.
> "Whom have you seen?" I inquired.
> "The Armenian."

(387)

Now hooked, the Prince asks for a demonstration of the Sicilian's occult powers: "'You see in me,' said the prince," sounding like Dr. Johnson attending the exhibition of the Cock Lane ghost (Clery 1995, 18),

> a man who burns with impatience to be convinced on this mo-
> mentous subject. I would embrace as a benefactor, I would cher-
> ish as my best friend him who could dissipate my doubts and
> remove the veil from my eyes. Would you render me this import-
> ant service?

(388)

The Sicilian promises to bring back the dead spirit of Lanoy, an old army friend of the Prince, so that he might learn the rest of his last words, which had unfortunately been cut short as the Prince attended his friend's death bed:

> We found in the middle of the room a large, black circle, drawn
> with charcoal, the space within which was capable of contain-
> ing us all very easily. The planks of the chamber floor next to
> the wall were taken up all round the room, so that we stood as
> it were upon an island. An altar covered with black cloth was
> placed in the centre upon a carpet of red satin. A Chaldee Bible
> was laid open, together with a skull; and a silver crucifix was fas-
> tened upon the altar. Instead of candles some spirits of wine were
> burning in a silver vessel. A thick smoke of frankincense darkened
> the room and almost extinguished the lights. The sorcerer was
> undressed like ourselves, but barefooted; about his bare neck he
> wore an amulet, suspended by a chain of human hair; round his
> middle was a white apron marked with cabalistic characters and
> symbolical figures.

(391)

Readers will instantly recognize, not just the usual *modus operandi* of the real life Sicilian—the notorious Count Cagliostro—but the initiation ceremonies of the masons, especially the illuminati[2]:

> On a sudden we all felt at the same instant a stroke as of a flash of lightning, so powerful that it obliged us to quit each other's hands; a terrible thunder shook the house; the locks jarred; the doors creaked; the cover of the silver box fell down and extinguished the light; and on the opposite wall over the chimney-piece appeared a human figure in a bloody shirt, with the paleness of death on its countenance.
> "Who calls me?" said a hollow, hardly intelligible voice.
>
> (392)

The scene was to be frequently repeated by Gaspard Etienne Robertson, a few years later, in his phantasmagoria, the difference being that Robertson would pre-empt accusations of juggling by excusing his shows as a demonstration of the dark arts of con-artists such as Cagliostro: his phantasmagorias were in the public interest, as he exposed the machinery of deception; meanwhile, lost in the magic of a simulated reality, his audiences would scream, moan, and faint, when the magic lantern did its spectral business.

At this point a key moment of ambiguity occurs in the text. As the Sicilian conjures the apparition of the Prince's dead friend, a second ghost appears, upbraiding the first as a fake:

> The house again trembled; a dreadful thunder rolled; a flash of lightning illuminated the room; the doors flew open, and another human figure, bloody and pale as the first, but more terrible, appeared on the threshold. The spirit in the box began to burn again by itself, and the hall was light as before.
>
> (393)

The Sicilian falls down in terror before the second ghost, suggesting the second one is, indeed, real—not least, because the Sicilian tries to shoot the second ghost, only for the ball to roll "slowly upon the altar" (393). The Prince recognizes the second apparition as the ghost of Lanoy:

> "Can I render thee any further service in this world?"
> "None but to think of thyself."
> "How must I do that?"
> "Thou wilt learn at Rome."
>
> (393)

At this point the Armenian steps in, confronting the Sicilian:

> "Juggler," said he to him, with a terrible countenance, "Thou shalt summon no more ghosts."
> The Sicilian turned round, looked steadfastly in his face, uttered a loud shriek, and threw himself at his feet.

(390)

In short order the authorities arrive: the set is torn apart revealing an electrical machine, a clock, a little silver bell, a magic lantern, several drums, "to which large leaden bullets were fastened by strings; these had probably been used to imitate the roaring of thunder which we had heard" (396). A shot is fired up the chimney by the authorities, as a quick test for locating any confederates, and sure enough a wounded man tumbles out. After the Armenian disappears, one of the officers informs the Prince that the Armenian is "of the Inquisition," and it was he who arranged for the raid in order to arrest the "Sorcerer" (397).

After his arrest the Sicilian is imprisoned under the lead roofs of St. Marks, where the Prince and Count von O--- visit him. The Sicilian reveals the secrets of all the tricks I've mentioned—as tricks they were—but insists that the Armenian acts on his own, is an immortal magus, which was why he fell down in terror before him. To prove his assertion he tells another story, about a Neapolitan family, where Jeronimo, the oldest brother, is abducted by Pirates just before his wedding to his childhood sweetheart, herself a beautiful princess, in a dynastic marriage between two wealthy houses. Seven years have passed, and the families, now despairing of the Jeronimo's return, hire the Sicilian's dark arts to determine Jeronimo's whereabouts, and whether he still lives. The younger brother desperately wants to find his brother, to put an end to the agony of his own disappointed love for the Princess. The Sicilian agrees to help, and on his own recognizance, organizes the apparition of Jeronimo, proving his death: in the clincher Jeronimo drops his wedding ring, which the Princess recognizes. All now accept that Jeronimo is dead; and after a suitable bout of fainting, fasting, and convent-considering, the Princess agrees to dynastic fate and marries the younger brother. At the wedding the Armenian unexpectedly appears, and conjures a second ghost, this one correctly accusing the younger son of murdering his brother, and hiding his body in a well, where his moldering bones are duly discovered. The Sicilian flees in horror.

The Prince seizes on the detail of the ring. The Sicilian claims it was a counterfeit, forged after hearing a description of it. The Prince dismisses this as highly improbable, and on that basis deduces that the Sicilian is a root and branch liar; that he was in cahoots with the younger son as well as the Armenian. He concludes that the trick of the second ghost, at the first séance with the Prince, was part of the Armenian's repertoire of juggling tricks, and on that basis becomes a fully paid up member of the Enlightenment, having put the supernatural behind him, forever.

At this point the reader has a choice to make: either we conclude that the Armenian's fiendish plot has backfired, and that he's been rumbled; or we decide that the Sicilian artfully stumbles over the detail of the ring, in order to lure the Prince deeper into the trap. The evidence suggests the latter. The Prince soon finds himself exposed. Count Von O--- is recalled to Germany; a faithful servant apparently converts to Catholicism and becomes a monk, to be replaced by the ambiguous Biondello, a man of too many resourceful parts. The Prince saves the life of the Marquis Civatella, who repays the Prince by bankrolling him into debt and dissipation, as the Prince's family back in Germany—hearing alarming reports of his lifestyle, and rumors of an impending conversion to Catholicism—cut off his funds. Meanwhile the Prince falls in with the Bucentauro, a lodge of free-thinking masons and libertines. He seems to be adrift until he falls in love at first sight with a beautiful young woman he sees at a Catholic church, known as the Greek. Except it is not quite first sight, as she bears a remarkable resemblance to a picture of the Madonna, with which he had become enamored (a piece of coney-catching shortly to be purloined by Matthew Lewis in *The Monk*). Apparently by coincidence they meet up after a long fruitless search; it transpires that she is not Greek at all, but the illegitimate daughter of a German aristocrat. But at this point the narrative has become especially fragmented. We learn that she dies, having been poisoned; following a period of mourning and despair, the Prince is discovered, under the wing of the Armenian, a recent convert to Catholicism. The key moment in his conversion seems to be this (here Count Von F--- writes to Count Von O---): "She departed like a saint, and her last strength was spent in trying with persuasive eloquence to lead her lover into the path that she was treading in her way to heaven" (482), that path being the Catholic faith.

What are we to make of all this, and how does it key into the debates about the rise of haunted Europe, that I earlier set out? The first thing I would say is that Schiller seems to have cunningly anticipated most of my critics: he certainly comprehends Taylor's nova, as we see in the Prince, the skeptical visionary intent on ghost seeing, who combines in himself, both Enlightenment doubt, and the desire to believe, with each destabilizing the other. Clery starts her argument noting the desperation felt by old-style believers, such as Dr. Johnson, who greeted sensations such as the Cock Lane ghost as specimens of theological proof, a scenario Schiller reprises in the unbelieving Prince's eagerness to witness the Sicilian's spectral prowess. There is even a reference to *Hamlet* that Hogle could easily slot into his argument: "There are more things in heav'n and earth, / Than are dreamt of in your philosophy," quotes the

Prince, when the Armenian's divination that "he died at nine," proves true. Finally, it is not so much that the phantasmagorical material fits Castle's thesis as it is that much of what we come to think about the phantasmagoria is already here anticipated in Schiller's text.

But there is a final side to Schiller's novella that is not touched upon by my critics, apart from Taylor, and that aspect of the text is to be found closer to Schiller's motivating purpose in writing his novella. That purpose may be divined by the subsequent history of Schiller's text, by the uses other writers put it to. This purpose may be found in the sub-genre of the novel for which Schiller's work became the model: that is, conspiracy fiction. Schiller's formula was quickly adapted in Germany, in works such as Cajetan Tschink's *The Victim of Magical Delusion: or, the Mystery of the Revolution of P----l; A Magico-Political Tale* (1795) and Carl Grosse's *Horrid Mysteries* (1796); and in American works, such as Charles Brockden Brown's *Wieland* (1798) and *Ormond: or, the Secret Witness* (1799). Lying behind these works were the Illuminati conspiracy theories, loudly shrieked from the rooftops by the likes of the Abbé Barruel and John Robison (see Hofstadter [1964]; Wood [1982]). In other words, Schiller presciently provides a model for a bout of public paranoia, the occasion for which (the French Revolution) had not yet happened. Schiller's prescience may be somewhat diminished when we realize that his followers flipped the conspiracy, from the Inquisitional Armenian back to the Masonic Sicilian, but the key element for Schiller was the impossibility of any kind of political progress when the German public sphere was dependent upon the rationality of individuals in high places, such as the Prince. No matter how enlightened such an individual might be, they were no match for a set of conspiring bad actors. Schiller understood his historical moment to be dangerous, because new political institutions had not yet developed to match the ostensible enlightenment of the court; without a mature public sphere to manage rational belief, to manage ghost-seeing, the acts of conspiratorial agents were always going to be a danger. The same was true for the American Brown: in the present moment of revolutionary uncertainty, where the tenants of materialism were now foundational, danger lurked in haunting, in the new marketplace of spectral experience.

In asking the question, "why did late Enlightenment Europe come to be haunted?," Schiller offers a different kind of answer from the ones we have been used to, as he locates his analysis in his moment's revolutionary politics. Consider the problematic appearance of the second ghost that brings the Sicilian's phantasmagoria to its (apparently) disastrous close. The ghost's appearance is never directly explained, in the manner of Radcliffe.[3] Neither is it left as a religious sport, in the manner of Lewis, where belief in God may be in doubt, but malevolent spirits remain. We may conclude from the Prince's turn to free-thinking, along with his rejection of the Sicilian's explanations, that he deduces that the second ghost was another confederate in the conspiracy orchestrated by the Armenian-Sicilian tag-team. But if so, the deduction is just the bait for the trap. It is one wheel inside another; for if so, the Prince is meant to unmask the unmasker. The Prince is at his most vulnerable when inflated with a sense of his own Enlightenment, his own prowess in free-thinking as he cavorts with the Bucentauro, libertines who have gone beyond conventional understandings of good and evil. The Inquisition wants to feed his free-thinking vanity, as he becomes a more easily manipulated mark without the traditional supports of family, country, or religion. That is not to say Schiller's *Ghost-Seer* is a Counter-Enlightenment work extolling the benefits of a pre-Revolutionary order; rather, it is a prophetic work about power in the modern age. The Prince is a stand-in for the autonomous, Enlightenment subject. And that, for Schiller, was the problem. Unlike, say, England, in the small-scale principalities of Germany there was not yet an advanced print culture supporting the public sphere as a metatopical space where opinion might be aired, tested, and formed. The fate of the Prince's "nation" depended on the opinion of a single isolated, autonomous subject, who was, by that fact alone, vulnerable to the dark arts of established powers. Thus the Inquisition, involved in its deep conspiracy—with its wheels within wheels—to turn the Prince from Protestant to Catholic. We go through the rigamarole of the Sicilian's phantasmagoria because Schiller wants to stress the technological modernity of the conspiracy. The plot is not to return the Prince back to a state of easily manipulated superstition; it is to encourage his emancipation as an Enlightened subject. It is through the fantasies of reason—through the free-thinking of the emancipated subject who believes he is in possession of a rationally apprehended truth—that the Inquisition find their opening for their deeper, psychological games (prosecuted through the Greek honey trap). As such *The Ghost-Seer* speaks directly toward our present, where yet another transformation in the technology of the public sphere has created the unstable political situation of isolated, autonomous subjects falling prey to conspiratorial beliefs, to ghost-seeing.

Notes

1 All quotations are from the 1853 edition translated by Henry Bon. This translation is used by Project Gutenberg (www.gutenberg.org/files/6781/6781-h/6781-h.htm). All subsequent references are to this volume unless otherwise indicated.

2 For an image of Cagliostro with his cabalistic apron holding a Masonic meeting, see James Gillray's 1786 satire, "A Masonic Anecdote" on Wikimedia Commons.

3 Render interpolates a passage in which the Armenian takes responsibility for the second apparition and everything else of a supernatural nature in the romance (Schiller 1800). There is no such passage in Bohn's translation.

References

Carlyle, Thomas. 1869. *Critical and Miscellaneous Essays*. 7 vols. London: Chapman and Hall.

Castle, Terry. 1995. *The Female Thermometer: Eighteenth-Century Culture and the Invention of the Uncanny*. New York and Oxford: Oxford University Press.

Castle, Terry. 1988. "Phantasmagoria: Spectral Technology and the Metaphorics of Modern Reverie." *Critical Inquiry*, 15, no. 1 (Autumn): 26–61.

Castle, Terry. 1987. "The Spectralization of the Other in *The Mysteries of Udolpho*." In *The New Eighteenth Century: Theory, Politics, English Literature*, edited by Felicity Nussbaum and Laura Brown, 231–53. New York and London: Methuen.

Ciofalo, John J. 1997. "Goya's Enlightenment Protagonist—A Quixotic Dreamer of Reason." *Eighteenth-Century Studies* 30, no. 4 (Summer): 421–36.

Clery, E. J., and Robert Miles, eds. 2000. *Gothic Documents: A Sourcebook 1700–1820*. Manchester and New York: Manchester University Press.

Clery, E. J. 1995. *The Rise of Supernatural Fiction, 1762–1800*. Cambridge: Cambridge University Press.

Fleming, John V. 2013. *The Dark Side of the Enlightenment: Wizards, Alchemists, and Spiritual Seekers in the Age of Reason*. New York: WW Norton & Company.

Hawthorne, Nathniel. 1978. *The Scarlet Letter*. Edited by Sculley Bradley, Richmond Croom Beatty, E. Hudson Long, and Seymour Gross. New York: Norton.

Hofstadter, Richard. 1964. "The Paranoid Style in American Politics." *Harper's Magazine* (November): 77–86.

Hogle, Jerrold E. 1994. "The Ghost of the Counterfeit in the Genesis of the Gothic." In *Gothick Origins and Innovations*, edited by Allan Lloyd Smith and Victor Sage, 23–33. Amsterdam and Atlanta, GA: Rodopi.

McGann, Jermone. 1998. *The Poetics of Sensibility: A Revolution in Literary Style*. Oxford: Oxford University Press.

Punter, David. [1980] 1996. *The Literature of Terror: A History of Gothic Fictions from 1765 to the Present Day*. 2 vols. London: Longman.

Radcliffe, Ann. [1797] 1981. *The Italian; or, the Confessional of Black Penitents*. Edited by Frederick Garber. Oxford and New York: Oxford University Press.

Schiller, Friedrich. 1853. The Ghost-Seer; or, Apparitionist. Found among the Papers of Count O*****. In *The Works of Friedrich Schiller, Early Dramas and Romances*, translated by Henry G. Bohn, 377–482. London: Henry. G. Bohn.

Schiller, Friedrich. 1800. *The Armenian; or, The Ghost-Seer. A History Founded on Fact*. 2 vols. Translated by W. Render. Dublin: Printed by William Folds, for P. Wogan, H. Colbert, J. Rice, B. Dornin, G. Folingsby, and P. Moore, 1800.

Schiller, Friedrich. 1795. *The Ghost-Seer; or, Apparitionist. An Interesting Fragment, Found among the Papers of Count O*****.* Translated by William Render. London: Vernor and Hood.

Sontag, Susan. 1964. "Notes on Camp." *Partisan Review* 31, no. 4 (Fall): 515–30.

Taylor, Charles. 2007. *A Secular Age*. Cambridge, MA: Belknap Press of Harvard University Press.

Taylor, Charles. 2004. *Modern Social Imaginaries*. Durham, NC: Duke University Press.

Taylor, Charles. 1989. *Sources of the Self: The Making of the Modern Identity*. Cambridge, MA: Harvard University Press.

Thompson, E. P. 1994. *Witness Against the Beast: William Blake and the Moral Law*. Cambridge: Cambridge University Press.

Warner, Michael, Jonathan VanAntwerpen, and Craig Calhoun, eds. 2010. *Varieties of Secularism in a Secular Age*. Cambridge, MA: Harvard University Press.

Williams, Ioan, ed. 1968. *Sir Walter Scott on Novelists and Fiction*. New York: Barnes and Noble.

Wood, Gordon S. 1982. "Conspiracy and the Paranoid Style: Causality and Deceit in the Eighteenth Century." *The William and Mary Quarterly: A Magazine of Early American History and Culture* 39, no. 3 (July): 402–41.

3 "Such strains as speak no mortal means"

Melusine Voices in Radcliffe's *The Mysteries of Udolpho* and Landon's "The Fairy of the Fountains"

Michelle O'Connell

A recent development in Gothic Studies is an acknowledgment of the importance of the popular supernatural on which early romances draw. In employing the romance form for *The Mysteries of Udolpho* ([1794] 1998), Ann Radcliffe also drew on the romance-world's fairy mythology, in poems ascribed to the invention of the novel's heroine, Emily St. Aubert. Eighteenth-century scholarship began "rigorous scholarly engagements with medieval English texts," specifically the romance form (Haugen 2000, 45). With this came a renewed awareness of the importance of the genre's European developments. Concomitantly, fairy lore was embraced by *salonnière* Madam d'Aulnoy who circulated her first hybrid novel/fairy tale *Histoire d'Hippolyte, comte de Duglas* in 1690, "set[ting] a trend in France that became epidemic," as women writers considered the fairy tale a female genre (Zipes 2012, 34). D'Aulnoy's foundational text was quickly translated into English, and in 1855, *The Athenaeum* hailed a new edition of her fairy tales as embedded in British culture: "[she] has been for the last century and a half the great treasury of juvenile romance" (*The Athenaeum* 1855, 637). Radcliffe gestures toward d'Aulnoy's continental, proto-feminist fairy mythology, and to the tradition of female elemental spirits, water nymphs, in creating her poetic voice in *Udolpho*, which develops signification in counterpoint with the narrative's more conventionally constructed gothic world of sixteenth-century France. As Wright (2013) observes, despite the "hostility to all things French" in British popular culture, gothic literature is "nonetheless sprung from French sources, [and] nurtured by French culture" (10). Radcliffe's discourse expands to include both the symbolic order and the world of certainty and a more Kristevan semiotic mode of conveying meaning, in a carefully composed and presented series of poems, which both readers and critics have found difficult to accommodate in their reflections on her novel.

Anne Williams succinctly explains the importance of Julia Kristeva's "semiotic" to the Gothic, particularly its link to characterizations of terror and horror, and the Romantic sublime. She argues that "Gothic conventions of plot and character also represent various modes of disruption within the Symbolic," through which "they facilitate the high Romantic aim of 'fresh' vision, of seeing with an eye not dulled by habit or custom" (Williams 1995, 71). While Williams locates breaks in the symbolic order in gothic conventions, I argue that the poetry is an equally disruptive force within Radcliffe's *Udolpho*. Though commonly characterized as a collection of discrete interruptions which disrupt the narrative momentum, the poetry actually forms a coherent strand itself; there is, in fact, continuity between the individual poems of *Udolpho*, which both challenges and reverberates with the prose narrative by accessing an earlier and more universal supernatural. The alternative yet complementary reality created in these poems is a world where women become female elemental spirits, a sisterhood without borders, who sing in a sort of semiotic *chora*: "a nonexpressive totality formed by the drives and their stases in a motility that is as full of movement as it is regulated" (Kristeva 2002, 35). This contrapuntal voice engages with emerging conceptions of the female poet, anticipating the figure of the Regency and Victorian "poetess" as outlined in Mellor (1997). Echoing her French predecessors, who "called on the fairies they created to arbitrate on their behalf" (Zipes 2012, 35) and drawing on the self-characterization of another, Francophile novelist and poet, Charlotte Smith, Radcliffe's poetic figure anticipates Germaine de Staël's *Corinne, or Italy* ([1807] 1998) and her semiotic "music" is echoed uncannily in the most fully realized figure of the poetess: Letitia Elizabeth Landon. Landon returns to the medieval romance, and to d'Aulnoy's fairy land, in her excavation and revision of the legend of Mélusine in her late poem, "The Fairy of the Fountains," which reflects upon the polyvalent female poetic voice.

Ever since the publication of *The Romance of the Forest* (1791) and *Udolpho*, both subtitled *Interspersed with some pieces of poetry*, the original poetry presented in the novel, and indeed at times even the epigraphs and quotations from other poets, has been seen as problematic and disruptive. Contemporary critics were worried that the common novel reader, suffused with agitation and narrative desire, would skim or simply skip the original poetry. Anna Letitia Barbauld famously states that:

> The true lovers of poetry are almost apt to regret its being brought in as an accompaniment to narrative, where it is generally neglected; for not one in a hundred, of those who read and can judge of novels, are at all able to appreciate the merits of a copy of verses, and the common reader is always impatient to get on with the story.
>
> (1994, 98)

There have been a number of different contemporary critical approaches to assessing the poetry in both *The Romance of the Forest* and *Udolpho*, each of which offers new insights into Radcliffe's practice, and into her literary legacy. Nathaniel Paradise (1995) fittingly includes Radcliffe in his account of women novelists' engagement with poetry in their work, from Jane Barker to Charlotte Smith. Olivia Loksing Moy (2015) suggests that Radcliffe's heroines find in their imprisonment safe spaces for "reflection and elegiac expression" and contends that Radcliffe's imprisoned heroines became a template for the later poetess figure (378). Mary A. Favret (1994) argues that readers found the poetry in its different forms, original lyric, epigraph, and quotation, to be "random intrusions" which "parade their own ephemerality, their artificiality, their portability, their redundant and essential nature" (166). This chimes with Paradise's argument, and supports Leah Price's (2000) characterization of Radcliffe's mixture of prose and poetry as self-conscious anthologizing:

> Radcliffe's epigraphs and inset poems allow *Udolpho* and *The Romance of the Forest* to juxtapose as many different signatures as any epistolary novel. By studding third-person narration with descriptive set-pieces and lyric epigraphs, Radcliffe substitutes the collection of beauties for the collection of letters as a model for the novel's composite structure.[1]
>
> (93)

Beatrice Battaglia (2007) describes the poetry which appears throughout *Udolpho* as "acquir[ing] the evocative force of the chorus in a play," and explores the musicality brought to the novel (143). Writing about the poetry of *Udolpho*, Ingrid Horrocks (2008) asks, "If we endeavor not to skip over the poetry within these novels but to read it as a genuine and vital complement to the prose narrative, will these novels read differently?" (508). My response is emphatically "yes." Not only does the novel yield more when the poems are read, individually, in their prose settings, but the novel expands to include an altogether different female voice when those poems are read as a coherent collection, in addition to the competing voices of Enlightenment and superstition encoded in the plot of the novel.

Furthermore, Radcliffe's poetry engages with her contemporary literary context in establishing qualities associated with the female Romantic poet by drawing on European feminocentric fairy myths in her poetry, giving her female characters poetic voices and subjects distinct from the patriarchal worlds of danger depicted in the prose of her novels. It is significant that Madame d'Aulnoy and her contemporaries used their fairy characters to challenge, through fancy, Louis XIV's autocratic rule, and the misogyny and religious persecution prevalent in his court (Zipes 2012, 37). Echoing Charlotte Smith, Radcliffe envisions the nascent poetess figure as a troubled, besieged, and solitary figure, who exists in liminal, borderline landscapes. Smith looks always toward Europe, literally, as she gazes from the South Downs and Beachy Head across the English Channel toward France, and sees in England-bound French émigrés her own sense of exile and abandonment. That gaze is returned in 1807 when Madame de Staël publishes *Corinne; or Italy*, a novel centering on an English-Italian poetess/improvisatrice, who became the inspiration for a generation of female European poets (Vincent 2004; Lokke 2006) as well as embodying Francophobic fears for some in Britain, of the wild power of the female voice.[2] Reading the poetic voice in *Udolpho* as another strand of Emily's consciousness extends our understanding of *Udolpho*—not in place of but in addition to the many readings that assess Emily's psyche in terms of religion, modernity, and English fortitude in the face of invasion from Europe. In fact, Emily's voice is suffused with European culture.[3]

Radcliffe's poems were twice collected and published (without permission) in one volume.[4] The 1816 volume collects poems from *The Romance of the Forest* and *Udolpho*, but not her other romances. Jane Stabler (2014) reads this collection as a "[response] to the regret voiced by Barbauld and others that the poems included in the novels would not be appreciated by a 'common reader' who was bound to be hurrying onwards for the plot" (187). Despite the fact that Radcliffe did not authorize this publication it is instructive to read Radcliffe's poems initially as a collection in its own right, comprised of two parts (*The Romance of the Forest* and *Udolpho*), as well as considering how the poetry functions in its original prose context.[5] The volume opens with a sonnet: "The Visions of Fancy" (Radcliffe 1816a). Radcliffe's muse, "Fancy," is personified as a magical figure of command. The "wild illusions of creative mind" "arise to Fancy's art,/And by her *magic* force are swift combin'd/In forms that please" (ll. 1, 2–4, my emphasis). Fancy's "voice" becomes her instrument of power, and Radcliffe, in what becomes a defining feature of her poetry, assumes the speaker's power herself, when Fancy is elided and the "wild illusions" are called to the service of the poetic speaker in the final couplet of this sonnet: "O! still—ye shadowy forms attend my lonely hours,/Still chase my real cares with your illusive powers!" (ll. 13–14).

Radcliffe's choice of form is telling; Charlotte Smith was of course the contemporary poet then most identified with the sonnet form. Smith had already established a poetic persona which was very much based on her biographical circumstances. Her (untitled) introductory sonnet of *Elegiac Sonnets* exclaims: "Ah! then, how dear the Muse's favours cost,/ *If those paint sorrow best—who feel it most!*" (ll. 13–14, emphasis in original). Both speakers associate sorrow with creativity. Smith presents the poetic voice as simultaneously a burden and a curse, while Radcliffe's speaker sees poetry as a means of escaping from sorrow. Smith, famously, invoked her private sorrows in her public writing. In the prefaces to different editions of *Elegiac Sonnets*, she deplores the sorrowful tone of her poetry, invoking her real-world legal woes and financial difficulties. In Radcliffe's poetic collection, she too develops a melancholy persona, traversing Smithian liminal landscapes and settings: "Night," "Sun-set," "The first hour of the Morning," "Song of the Evening Hour," "To Autumn," all echo Smith's preference for landscapes between light and darkness, while Radcliffe also gravitates toward favored, liminal landscapes such as the sea and the seashore.

Within the discrete collections from *The Romance of the Forest* and *Udolpho*, the poems speak to each other internally, echoing verbal forms, poetic techniques, and treatment of subject matter. For instance, in the *Udolpho* subset, the third poem "Sonnet," takes for its subject matter the bat; the third-from-last poem is "The Bat;" "The Sea-nymph" is echoed in "To a Sea-nymph"; "The Mariner" links to "Shipwreck." This chiming is more than coincidence, and points to a careful consideration of the collections as a whole, rather than as occasional pieces crafted to suit the plot as needs be. Stabler (2014) suggests "that tropes of proliferation, repetition and refrain are characteristic of Radcliffe's poetic art and that within and between poems refrains become Radcliffe's way of pointing to the tension between masculine Romantic poetry and female experience" (189). At times, a line from a poem is even repeated in quotation marks, *within the same poem*, as though her own line becomes a borrowed quotation, adding to the proliferation of poetic voices described by Price (2000).[6] This repetition creates a different sort of uncanny encounter, a break which announces the presence of the semiotic, while momentarily destabilizing the symbolic order of language and disrupting meaning through its seemingly empty repetition and self-referentiality. Robert Miles (2015) has called for a more nuanced understanding of Radcliffe's technique of the "explained supernatural," arguing that "we need to resist the temptation of concluding, along with Scott, that in Radcliffe's kind of fiction we read for the explanation" (301). Instead, Miles posits that "holding in solution of antithetical possibilities" (305) or allowing more than one potential reality to exist simultaneously without a drive toward prioritizing one, is where the power of Radcliffe's enchantment lies. This awareness of simultaneously existing meanings is linked with what Miles calls "dream time," "a sense of time antithetical to the linearity that defines our modern notions of temporality" (Miles 2014, 122; 2015, 306).[7] He notes that:

> pre-modern subjectivity is embedded in nature, which is animated, alive with spirits that effortlessly cross spatial and temporal boundaries. This subjectivity is porous: the membrane between itself, and the world of spirits, benevolent or malign, is thin; such an exposed subjectivity is in need of prophylactics, incantations, magic, to keep out the bad and nurture the good.
>
> (2014, 126–27)

Understanding gothic subjectivity in ways beyond reality-mimicking characterization necessitates acknowledging a more inclusive supernatural, one that accesses a more ancient ontology, in addition to Enlightenment and religious forms of subjectivity. Diane Long Hoeveler (2010) argues that "The gothic was, in fact, extremely effective at keeping alive all of the *ne plus ultra* of the supernatural (ghosts, witches, necromancy, exorcism, the occult, and the devil)" (xv).[8] This supernatural lies behind inter-European literary exchange; Hoeveler details the complex interactions between Germany, Britain, and France in particular (xvii). Like Miles, she argues that the "explained supernatural" has been underestimated: "explaining away the supernatural in the gothic discourse is another way of privileging its talismanic force" (xviii).

Radcliffe's poems in *Romance of the Forest* and *Udolpho* notably abound in references to magic and creatures of popular supernaturalism. *Udolpho*'s "Sea-nymph" poems offer the most complete representation of accessing "dream time" by constructing a porous sense of subjectivity which co-exists with Emily's tyrannized Enlightenment self. That self stands in danger of falling victim to the "contagion" of superstition as a result of her imprisonment (Miles 2014, 127–28). The sea-nymph is aligned with the water-spirits in control of earth's seas *and* inland waterways, and thus with the fairy Mélusine, founder of the house of Lusignan. Zipes notes that "It is impossible to overestimate the significance of d'Aulnoy's embrace of…the Mélusine fairy tradition and folklore in France" (Zipes 2012, 38), as well as its adoption by her fellow women writers; the French literary fairy voice that emerges precedes Staël's *Corinne* as a literary avatar. In a glossary attached to a sixteenth-century translation of Paracelsus, nymphs are defined as follows: "*Nympha*, or *Nymphidecae*, are spiritual men or women, or corporeal spirits dwelling in waters, such an one was *Melusina*" (Sedziwój and Paracelsus 1664, 339). That fairies and nymphs were related is a commonplace. Indeed, as Melissa Ridley Elmes confirms, "Paracelsus characterizes Melusine as a nymph, [and] associated her with other water figures like the siren" (Elmes 2017, 99). Richard Hurd's *Letters on Chivalry and Romance* (1762) finds that parallels between ancient Greek and "Gothic" conceptions of "chivalry" account "for the constant mixture, which the modern critic esteems so monstrous, of pagan fable with the fairy tales of Romance" (39). "Pagan fable" here includes the classics. Later, Thomas Keightley's *Fairy Mythology* (1828) offers more than one etymological connection between the words (and conceptions of) "nymph" and "fairy" or "*fée.*" (Keightley 1828, 1: 8, 11–12).[9] Running through these early accounts of romance and fairy worlds is their common European (rather than national) heritage. Radcliffe's sea-nymph moves in a world with permeable borders, above and below water. She is a dream-like incarnation of the female poet, existing on the margins, being drawn again and again to liminal locations, on the cusp of night or daybreak, or on the seashore. However, there is a more direct link between nymphs and women writers; volume 1 of d'Aulnoy's *Fairy Tales* includes a frame-tale narrating her experience of a moment of inspiration:

> ...I suddenly perceived a Nymph by me, whose bright Eyes, lively Air, and genteel Behaviour, gave me as much Satisfaction, as they caused Surprise in me...I was going to speak to her, when she interrupted me by Verses which she repeated in favour of this Abode.[10]

(d'Anois 1721, 2)

The nymph herself is framed in a tale told to d'Aulnoy's companions, who had wandered off, and equally a representation of d'Aulnoy's writerly self. Radcliffe's nymph-figure clearly has established associations with creativity, and with French romance.

In "The Sea-nymph" (Radcliffe 1816b) Radcliffe's nymph relaxes on the ocean floor, watching the world from underneath:

> In coral bow'rs I love to lie,
> And hear the surges roll above,
> And, through the waters, view on high
> The proud ships sail, and gay clouds move.

(ll. 17–20)

This topsy-turvy perspective resonates with the paradox of this female sprite's power over the world of men; she guides ships, controls the waters and rivers, ensures fertile crops, and watches over the seas to protect sailors. Yet mischievously, she declares "I love to prove my charmful pow'r" (l. 23) by teasing mariners with her uncanny song, showing the power of her supernatural influence in simultaneously enchanting and frightening men, but acting always in a benevolent manner. The end of the poem explicitly connects the sea-nymph with the fairies that play on the shore, inviting the listener to "come, when the red sun-set tints the wave,/To the still sands, where fairies play;" (ll. 98–99), echoing the inshore nymphs who "Oft dance upon the flow'ry banks, /And sing my name, and garlands weave" (ll. 14–15); the nymph herself "dance[s] upon the lapsing tides" (l. 43). Boundaries are deliberately elided here, conflating nymphs and fairies in one collective magical and benevolent (though mischievous) force, which ties into much fairy lore across Europe. As Zipes (2012) observes, "During the Middle Ages, the images of the Greek and Roman fates were changed by different groups of people in popular culture throughout Europe" becoming "supernatural creatures" and mingling with pre-historic pagan divinities (40). That these creatures exist simultaneously in different cultures across Europe signifies their origins in a culture that pre-dates even the concept of individual nations. Significantly, Radcliffe's nymphs exist on what the mortal world recognizes as boundaries, particularly between land and sea, but also in the sense of existing in both the "dream time" (as outlined by Miles) and the mortal physical world. The nymph even hints that her presence is not confined to a singular subjectivity, when her voice is magically made choric:

> Sometimes a single note I swell,
> That, softly sweet, at a distance dies;
> Then wake the magic of my shell,
> And choral voices round me rise!
>
> (1816b, ll. 33–36)

Jane Stabler (2014) suggests that the repetition that characterizes Radcliffe's poetry is an extension of the repetition of language and plot points in the novels (189). The echoes between "The Sea-nymph" and the later "To a Sea-Nymph" (Radcliffe 1816c) are deliberate, and the poems are sometimes even in dialogue: "To a Sea-nymph" opens "O nymph! Who loves to float on the green wave" (l. 1), addressing the sea-nymph who describes herself in "The Sea-nymph" as "floating on the moon-light wave" (l. 24). The "pearly cave" (l. 4) of the later poem is an echo of the first, where the nymphs' (collective) cave is described as adorned with "pale pearl and sapphire blue" (l. 57). The power of the nymph's voice is acknowledged in the third stanza of "To a Sea-nymph," and the speaker imagines the power of the nymph's voice fading, to match her own mood, then swelling with the echoing power of the collective female voice evoked in the first poem, quoted earlier:

> Then, let thy tender voice at distance swell,
> And steal along this solitary shore,
> Sink on the breeze, till dying—heard no more—
> Thou wak'st the sudden magic of thy shell.
>
> (ll. 9–12)

A chorus and semi-chorus suddenly appear to repeat the invocation with which the poem closes, repeating the earlier line "O nymph! From out thy pearly care—arise!" (l. 16). This address to the sea-nymph signals much more than a superficial repetition of the earlier poem. Given that the speaker of this poem echoes the sea-nymph's original poem, she becomes one of the "sister nymphs" (1816b, l. 45) whose voices are represented in the chorus and semi-chorus of her own poem, this circular repetition lending itself toward almost supernatural, choric utterance.

Throughout "The Sea-nymph," the sea-nymph's greatest power is her voice: "such strains as speak no mortal means!" (l. 28). Her voice, individually, or collectively with her sister-nymphs, or enhanced by her magic shell, is supernaturally powerful, holds sway over "mighty rivers" (l. 6) and dolphins, the inland "spirits of the air" (l. 85) and mortal men. This voice metaphorically represents the female poetic voice, speaking to command, enchanting those who hear it, and soothing those who need it. In repeating the sea-nymph's phrases in her own poem, the speaker of "To a Sea-Nymph" invokes and expands the power of the fairy voice, as well as chiming with it, becoming one with the subject of the poem she speaks.

In *Udolpho*, Emily composes "The Sea-nymph" while left alone as Montoni revels with his companions in Venice. The poem comes to while watching a group of dancers and musicians and a procession below her window. Most significantly, however, is the fact that as well as declaiming from Petrarch, the group recites from Ariosto's *Orlando Furioso*, quietly signifying Radcliffe's allegiance to the romance form, and Ariosto's (perceived) low style. Decrying critics who measure all literary works against Aristotle's unities, Hurd (1762) states that "Ariosto ranks but little higher than the rudest romancer" in these terms (79). Emily's imagination finds this "rude" romance stimulating, transcending her present circumstances and reaching into the world of romance and fairy:

> … this spectacle, together with the grandeur of the surrounding palaces, appeared like the vision of a poet suddenly embodied, and the fanciful images, which it awakened in Emily's mind, lingered there long after the procession had passed away. She indulged herself in imagining what might be the manners and delights of a sea-nymph, till she almost wished to throw off the habit of mortality, and plunge into the green wave to participate them.
>
> (178)

Emily escapes in imagining the freedom and benevolent power of the sea-nymph, in direct contrast to the constraints of her situation at that point in time, subject to the will of Montoni. "To a Sea-nymph" appears much later in the novel, when Emily is given a brief respite from Udolpho, as Montoni prepares the castle for a siege. She is sent to Tuscany, where she observes a group of peasants circling round a girl "who held in her hand a chaplet of flowers" (420). The "invocation" is sung by the peasants and the garland of flowers is thrown into the waves. Emily's reaction exceeds the usual condescending curiosity of the elegant traveler: "'But they talked of a sea-nymph,' said Emily: 'how came these good people to think of a sea-nymph?'" (421). Emily's urgency is occasioned by more than her surprise that "[Florence's] taste for classic story should descend to the peasants of the country" (421). Rather than read this as a national tradition, Radcliffe emphasizes again the lack of division in culture that is transmitted to posterity in ways that cross national borders and class division. Emily is French, the peasant girls are Italian, yet they imagine the same sea-nymph. Her poem resurfaces in an uncanny repetition, and confronts her with her own fairy-persona embedded in a popular ritual, itself derived from a blending of classical and popular culture.

In Freud's ([1919] 2003) reading of the uncanny, he focuses on the etymology of the German word, *das Unheimliche*, discovering that the word can simultaneously refer to "two sets of ideas, which are not mutually contradictory, but very different from each other—the one relating to what is familiar and comfortable, the other to what is concealed and kept hidden" (132). Freud also refers to the role of the motif of the "double," "which can treat the ego as an object," and can result in the attribution to it of features which "seem to belong to the old, superannuated narcissism of primitive times" (142–43). Emily confronts a double of herself which existed only in an unspoken composition which was never written, and yet emerges in the address by a group of Tuscan peasants to the very elemental spirit which she imagined herself to be at the moment of composition. She repeats the word "nymph" as a talismanic word to protect her from this uncanny moment, a word associated with high culture which should therefore exclude young peasant girls from knowledge of it. However, she finds that the concept is more ancient than the word itself, and finds a connection to culture and nature which eludes language, and the symbolic order. The symbolism of the garland reinforces the connection between the sea-nymph, the female poet, and the bonds of female creativity if read from a semi-anachronistic perspective.

Following the publication of Madame de Staël's *Corinne* in 1807, the crown of bay, superseding the crowns presented to victorious military commanders for martial or political triumph, becomes a consistent trope in women's poetry. The poetic crown is brought to the fore in Charlotte Smith's *Elegiac Sonnets* as a mark both of creativity and sorrow. Smith's opening sonnet speaks of the "partial Muse" who "with sportive hand has snatch'd wild flowers,/To weave fantastic garlands for my head"; yet it is a "delusive art;/Which while it decks the head with many a rose,/Reserves the thorn to fester in the heart" (Smith 1993, 13, ll. 1, 3–4, 6–8). Letitia Landon's Improvisatrice includes a laurel wreath in her painting of a female poet (Landon 1997b, l. 118); Elizabeth Barrett Browning's Aurora Leigh crowns herself prematurely with a crown of ivy on her twenty-first birthday, making explicit a link with Dante, and her own Italian heritage; Aurora, like Corinne, is half-Italian, half-English (Barrett Browning 1996, 2:33–36). The crown becomes a synecdoche for poetry itself, as well as the vocation of poet. In Radcliffe's poems, the garland certainly does represent poetry, linking Emily both to Italian literary tradition, and more elemental and uncanny feminine powers. Emily's startled response to the sea-nymph suggests a more "dream-worldly" reading of this scene. The echoes of her own composition from Venice, earlier in the novel, indicate a correspondence between her poetic voice, and the figure of the sea-nymph who is invoked by the Tuscan girls. Emily sees her own chaplet floating on the waves, foreshadowing her threatened dissolution. Simultaneously, it reminds her of her own power, the power of poetry. It is this ambivalent, uncanny, and prophetic construction of the female poet that finds voice in later generations.

***

In 1798, the now infamous essay "Terrorist Novel Writing" composed a recipe for a gothic novel:

> *Take* – An old castle, half of it ruinous.
> A long gallery, with a great many doors, some secret ones.
> Three murdered bodies, quite fresh.
> As many skeletons, in chests and presses.
> An old woman hanging by the neck; with her throat cut.
> Assassins and desperadoes *'quant suff.'*
> Noise, whispers, and groans, threescore at least.
> Mix them together, in the form of three volumes to be taken at
>   any of the watering places, before going to bed.
>
> ("Terrorist" 2000, 184)

Just over three decades later, the Countess of Blessington wrote a similar recipe, this time directed to "Modern Poetesses":

> Beauties pining in their bowers;
> Broken harps, and untuned lyres;
> Lutes neglected, unquench'd fires;
> Vultures pecking at the heart,
> Leaving owners scarce a part;
> ...
> Loving one, and only one—
> Though he has that one undone;
> A Macedoine of good and evil,
> One part hero—three parts devil.
> "Stock in Trade of Modern Poetesses." [11]
>
> (Blessington 1997, ll. 12–16, 41–44)

Clearly women are still accused of faddish and formulaic writing. Ironically (most likely, intentionally so) this poem appeared in *The Keepsake* for 1833, a publication which did so much to popularize and commodify the sort of writing Blessington at which pokes fun. Yet *The Keepsake* for this year was edited by Frederic Mansel Reynolds, and approximately half of its contributors were men. It opens with an account of a real-life gothic marriage: a violent husband, a faked funeral, and a daring escape by a long-suffering (royal) wife who ends up in Louisiana, eventually finding love. Lord Dover's "Vicissitudes in the Life of a Princess of Brunswick" is presented as a factual account (1833, 1–7). Thus, the volume opens with a doubly male-authored endorsement of the relevance of gothic preoccupations, thirty-seven years after the "Terrorist" recipe and the editor's spiteful footnote attacking Radcliffe both predicted the genre's early self-consumption. The gothic has become a cosmopolitan genre, its pan-European reach justifying its universality in terms of women's experience and concerns.

Landon's "The Fairy of the Fountains" ([1834] 1997a),[12] published in a similar gift-book, takes on similar gothic concerns, but Landon choses European fairy lore as her source, drawing on William John Thoms's *Lays and Legends of France* (1834).[13] Thoms takes his tale "Melusine" almost verbatim from Keightley's *The Fairy Mythology*; Keightley's "The Story of Melusine" situates the tale in its greater context of European medieval romance. He stresses the communal, ever-borrowing, and ever-developing characteristic of European fairy lore and, by extension, its literature:

> Few will now endeavour to trace romantic and marvellous fiction to any individual source. An extensive survey of the regions of fancy and their productions will incline us rather to consider the mental powers of man as having an uniform operation under every sky, and under every form of political existence, and to acknowledge that identity of invention is not more to be wondered at than identity of action.
>
> (1828, 1:45)

Most instructive is Keightley's chapter "Middle Age Romance," which examines the Arthurian legend, the founding myth of England, as French in origin, tracing, for instance, Lancelot's existence back to "The metrical romance called La Charette,...begun by Crestien de Troyes, who died in 1191, and was finished by Geoffrey de Ligny" (1:49n). Where Richard Hurd defends the Medieval Romance from the imposition of classical rules, Keightley explores its continental European origins. When it comes to his French sources, Keightley quotes extensively in the original language (though he also quotes from translations of the Lays of Marie de France). Consequently, England's founding myths emerge from a shared European history. Keightley's history emphasizes the power of the fairy woman, or queen, and the frequency with which she would act on and fulfil her sexual desires through enchantment, particularly in his examples from the Middle Ages, such as "Tristan de Leonois," where "king Meliadus, the father of Tristran, is drawn to a chase...of a fairy who was in love with him, and carries him off, and from whose thraldom he was only released by the power of the great enchanter Merlin" (1:53).[14] Though Keightley states that any survey of medieval romance "will incline us rather to consider the mental powers of man as having an uniform operation under every sky and every form of political existence," and considers eastern fairy lore, he finds the origins of medieval romance in a mix of European cultures, most specifically ancient classical literature, and French and Celtic mythology (1:47–50). Keightley's focus on the importance of fairy mythology to medieval romance is endorsed by Scott, who finds in it a blend of the classic and the barbarian:

> These silvans, satyrs, and fauns, with whom superstition peopled the lofty banks and tangled copses of this romantic country, were obliged to give place to deities very nearly resembling themselves in character, who probably derive some of their attributes from their classic predecessors, although more immediately allied to the barbarian conquerors.
>
> (Scott 1831, 116)

Scott also declares that it is "to the Gothic race that we must trace the opinions concerning the elves of the middle ages [which...] were deeply blended with the attributes which the Celtic tribes had, from the remotest ages, ascribed to their deities of rocks, valleys, and forests" (120). Fairy mythology, and by extension the medieval romance, is a blend of the local and the universal; local customs and the universal nature of the human imagination.

Kari E. Lokke (2006) identifies two mythic themes which are embraced by Regency women writers "in response to their desires for the 'forbidden' knowledge so threatening to masculine authority: the female Prometheus or Satanic woman and the undine or Melusine figure" (78).[15] In writing *Corinne*, Staël herself, Lokke (2006) notes, "was inspired by an 1804 performance in Weimar of a dramatized undine legend, the Hensler opera *The Nymph of the Danube*" (79). With these, the undine/ Melusine and Promethean figures, is included the Sappho figure, and *Corinne* itself as the four self-reflective strands of writing available to Regency women writers as modes of self-fashioning, self-reflection, and meditating upon women's experience.[16]

Landon employs the Corinne-myth repeatedly, in major works such as *The Improvisatrice* (1824) and "A History of the Lyre" (1828), even assuming Corinne's voice, as Landon "translated all the versified portions of de Staël's novel for Isabel Hill's 1833 English translation" (Landon 1997, 276n). Landon also embraces the Melusine myth, in a lesser-known work, "The Fairy of the Fountains." Landon's poem opens in a rather conversational manner: "Why did she love her mother's so?/It hath wrought her wondrous wo" (ll. 1–2). This address is both contemporary and distancing; it has the flavor of gossip, but it also gives a sense of a tale framed, reproducing the distance which usually separates the contemporary hearer of romance or myth from the subject in the choice of archaic phraseology. Landon adds yet another narrative layer in her introductory note:

> The Legend, on which this story is founded, is immediately taken from Mr. Thoms's most interesting collection. I have allowed myself some licence, in my arrangement of the story: but fairy tales have an old-established privilege of change; at least, if we judge by the various shapes which they assume in the progress of time, and by process of translation.
>
> (225)

Like the possessor of a gothic manuscript or tale, Landon's "story" derives from Thoms's "Legend," which is itself founded on a "fairy tale."[17] What she does not acknowledge, but was probably aware of, was Thoms's appropriation of Keightley's text. While the poet-narrator asserts her own appropriation of this French material, she confidently claims "my arrangement" of the material as a thing unto itself. Yet her language undermines this confident control of the material, and like Mélusine, Landon finds that the substance of the tale is itself metamorphic, subject to "change" into "various shapes" by virtue of "time" and "translation," the latter of which must include translation into writing as much as translation from one language to another (225). This fairy quality of ethereal shape-shifting is one which Landon associates with female creativity, and which is exemplified in her own sometimes inscrutable but deliberate obfuscation of meaning, repetitive phrases and words creating confusing echoes, and confusing doubling-up of pronouns. These deliberate "errors" work to create an almost incantatory layer of language in Landon's poetry. A case in point is the opening line: "Why did she love her mother's so."[18] The implication is that the reader has been excluded from the substance of the conversation, rather than being addressed directly. In a rather characteristic gothic move, a conversation is partially overheard, the crucial element which might anchor meaning withheld, both including and excluding the eavesdropping reader.[19]

In its original form, the poem was printed in two parallel columns in *Fisher's Drawing Room Scrapbook*, and these lines (1–2) sit opposite lines 35–36: "Thy suspicion's vain endeavour,/Wo! wo! parted us for ever." These two couplets sit on top of their respective columns on page 57 of the *Scrapbook* (Landon 1835, 1:57). The insistent repetition of "wo" foretells Melusina's doom, even as the tale begins. Thus the poem opens with two overheard fragments of conversation: that between the speaker of the poem and their anonymous, silent interlocutor; and that between Melusina's parents, King Elinas and the Fay Pressine, overheard by the child as she stands on the castle wall, her mother inside, her father outside. This fragmentation of knowledge creates the desire for more, echoing Eve's original curiosity and sin. For Melusina, this overheard conversation becomes the means of her destruction, albeit resulting from her own actions.

In Thoms's version, Elinas seeks his wife out of joy after she gives birth to three daughters, forgetting her condition "that he should never visit her in her lyings in" (Thoms, 84). As Lokke (2016) notes, Landon represents Elinas's betrayal of Pressine, not in terms of his intrusion, but as eavesdropping (320). Pressine upbraids him:

> Wo for ever, wo the hour,
> When you sought my secret bower,
> Listening to the word of fear,
> Never meant for human ear.
>
> (Landon 1997a, ll. 31–34)

Landon *invents* his discovery of arcane knowledge, which results from his suspicious curiosity. Elinas is simultaneously Eve and the serpent, enticed by suspicion and jealousy to discover forbidden knowledge, his serpentine nature foretelling his daughter's fate. As the speaker laments: "alas, the serpent's skill/Is amid our gardens still" (ll. 456–57).

McGann and Riess point out that Landon gives special resonance to the words' "ring" and "scale" in the poem's opening (Landon 1997, 28). Elinas's "bright and golden" crown (or "round," a ring), which signifies his status and authority, also signals what Melusina has suffered for his betrayal of her mother: she is a princess—her mother is daughter of a king of Scotland and her father is king of Albania.[20] Yet she has been banished to a cave in the mountains. In Landon's shaping of the myth, Melusina's sisters are elided, thus giving greater emphasis to her isolation and disinheritance.

"Scale[s]" are first introduced as a facet of Melusina's *father's* identity: "Curiously inlaid, each scale/Shone upon his glittering mail" (ll. 25–26), thus linking her curse to her power and standing. "Scale" prefigures the scaly "serpent's shape" of Melusina's future identity: her hybrid, Scottish-Albanian nationality will become a hybrid fairy-serpent identity (l. 551). Yet her curse is also her martial strength in the mortal world. In the myth, after her banishment, she builds castles and towers to entice Raymond, offering him ready-made power and wealth, while helping him to conceal his accidental slaying of his beloved uncle during a boar-hunt (Thoms, 85–86). In Landon's version, there is no building. Neither does she refer to the ten sons that Melusina bore Raymond. Instead, when he intrudes on her on a Saturday, breaking the magical condition for their marriage, his loss is hers: "Hope and happiness are o'er,/They can meet on earth no more" (Landon 1997a, ll. 568–69). As always with Landon, the preposition does double-duty: "they" refers both to "hope and happiness" and to the lovers, so that "hope and happiness" are conflated with the existence of their relationship/marriage.

The most significant way in which Landon's version differs from Thoms's is in Melusina's foreknowledge and melancholy. Thoms's Melusina does not foresee the demise of her marriage and her family. Destiny is the source of the "attacks" on Melusina and Raymond, giving them deformed children, and finally having a cousin incite Raymond's jealousy (Thoms, 86). In Thoms, as in other versions of the myth, it is not when Raymond *sees* Melusina's serpent half that the curse is fulfilled. Instead, it is when he *speaks* to reveal his knowledge of it to her, revealing her secret in the presence of others, that Melusina is doomed to perpetual wandering and lamentation (Thoms, 86–87). The symbolic order cannot encompass or contain Melusina's amorphous nature, so she is expelled from it.

Landon remodels Melusina very much in the style of her self-reflecting poetesses. Lokke (2016) notes that Melusina is "a figure for the female poet," and that "The Fairy of the Fountains" is "a poem about female creativity, imagination and visionary powers" (319). Drawing on existing Romantic tropes of prophecy and foresight,[21] Melusina knows all even prior to her first engagement with Raymond. In her essay "On the Character of Mrs. Hemans's Writings" ([1835] 1997c), Landon's characterization of the female poet draws on a sympathetic understanding of mythic figures: "Genius places a woman in an unnatural position; notoriety frightens away affection; and superiority has for its attendant fear, not love" (183). Melusina's foresight here speaks equally to internal fears of repetition and failure, which she sees in her mother's fate. Following her initial meeting with Raymond, she delays him for a year and a day, departing radically from the myth where urgency dictates that she solve Raymond's dilemma, following the death of his uncle, to preserve his name and his inheritance. Here Melusina's reluctance is based on the war between her human desires and her fairy wisdom. Before she finally capitulates to her desires and Raymond's she sits in her echoing stately hall:

> Near her stands a crystal globe,
> Gifted with strange power to show
> All that she desires to know.

> (Landon 1997a, ll. 384–86)

However, it is not magic from which she takes her fears. Throughout this waiting period, "She was haunted with a dream/Of the knight beside the stream" (ll. 408–9). Raymond is a double of her father, King Elinas, standing outside the castle wall, subsequently invading her subconscious, a moment Lokke (2016) characterizes as "proto-psychoanalytic" (319):

> Who has not, when but a child,
> Treasured up some vision wild;
> Haunting them with nameless fear,
> Filling all they see or hear,
> In the midnight's lonely hour,
> With a strange mysterious power?
> So a terror undefined
> Entered in that infant mind;—
> A fear that haunted her alone,
> For she told her thought to none.
>
> (Landon 1997a, ll. 47–56)

In keeping with the forms of romance, her father's betrayal of her mother foretells Raymond's abandonment of Melusina. What Landon brings to this coincidence is the sense that Melusina tastes of the pleasures of mortal life *despite her foreknowledge of her fate*. She stands outside of time, where foreknowledge is and is not experience. Like the poetess, her gift of foresight ensures her suffering.

Radcliffe's early fairy-figures, whose powers are channeled into a contrapuntal *jouissance* foretelling the ultimate triumph of the gothic heroine, have, by this juncture, been collapsed into a different sort of revisiting, where Melusina simultaneously holds the possibility of love and betrayal in an ever-repeating circle, best figured in the (disembodied) banshee she ultimately becomes:

> Still is heard that lady's wail,
> Ever round that ancient tower,
> ...
> With a low and moaning breath
> She must mark approaching death,
> While remains Lord Raymond's line
> Doomed to wander and to pine.
>
> (ll. 571–72, 574–77)

Melusina is tied to her creations and her fate is bound to theirs: her buildings and her descendants. Her only release is their failure.[22] The poetess, built on fairy foundations, is doomed to the spirit world for her violation (intended or not) of the symbolic order. The gothic heroine/poetess here is spectralized, articulating Landon's sense of dislocation which she associates with the tendency to embody women's poetic voices in their biographical, physical selves. Staël's Corinne articulates the female poet's sense of cultural dislocation when she exclaims: "I have the definite feeling that the voice within me is of greater worth than myself" (46).

Landon follows in the footsteps of her French predecessors, exemplified in Madame d'Aulnoy, who choose to embody radical otherness in fairy form. Melusina's punishment is rather ironically to speak her pain; her voice becomes so powerful that it can prophesy the death of the French kings. Melusina's wails simultaneously articulate punishment and freedom; her voice is her power, and she is finally free of the serpentine weight of her mortal body; her ancient fairy self holds both power of death and life in her perpetual wandering in the dream world.

Notes

1 Interpreting the structure of the novel this way, by reading the gothic novel as "a hook to hang anthology-pieces on" foreshadows the way in which women's poetry, and with Letitia Landon's career in particular, indeed does market itself in the Regency period (93–94).

2 In a reactionary reimagining of the novel (Forster 2008) the misguided anti-heroine, Clarissa Moreton (who adopts the name "Corinne") wears a crown of flowers on her loose hair when she drives out with her companions, and unintentionally instigates a riot when she addresses a restless crowd, who believe that she is dressed as Lady Godiva (80).

3 Wright (2013, chapter 4) details Radcliffe's complex, subtle, and sophisticated engagement with French culture and literature in her novels, including her strategic use of epitaphs and quotation, though Wright's focus is not on Radcliffe's poetry.

4 Published 1815 and 1816; both were entitled *The Poems of Mrs Ann Radcliffe*. I use the 1816 collection. Rather opportunistically, the editor included fourteen of his own poems in the volume.

5 The poems from *The Romance of the Forest* are found on pages 9–43; those from *Udolpho* are found on pages 44–95. Each collection follows the order in which they appear in the novel, with the exception of "Stanzas" ("O'er Illion's plains...") which is the eighth poem in *Udolpho*, and is listed here as the twelfth.

6 This occurs in the *Romance* poems; see "Sonnet" (Radcliffe 1816, 15), "Sonnet" (29), "To the Nightingale," and "Air." In the *Udolpho* collection, repetition is less self-conscious.

7 Miles (2014) draws on Charles Taylor's *A Secular Age* (2007) in developing this argument.

8 Hoeveler (2010, xv). Hoeveler also draws on Taylor, and reading the gothic as part of the "secularising process" of Enlightenment-era Europe.

9 Therefore, Radcliffe's sea-nymph can be identified with the Melusine and the undine figures.

10 In the French original this preface is in volume 3. There was confusion regarding the spelling of "d'Aulnoy" in early English translations, as noted in *The Athenaeum* 1855 (637).

11 This poem was brought to my attention by Paula R. Feldman's anthology, *British Women Poets of the Romantic Era* (1997).

12 While it was first published 1835 in *Fisher's Drawing-Room Scrapbook*, McGann and Riess date the poem to 1834 (420).

13 McGann and Riess include this tale and note the origin in Keightley (Landon 1997, 286–88). Lokke (2016) also notes the origins in Thoms and Keightley (315).

14 This mode of the exercise of sexual power has obvious attractions for novelists like Charlotte Dacre; in *Zofloya* (1806), Victoria indulges in enchantment

in order to seduce Henriquez. Walter Scott too acknowledges that in Fairy Land, 'A King, more frequently a Queen of Fairies was acknowledged' (Scott 1831, 121).

15 Craciun discusses Landon in a related context in *Fatal Women* (Chapter 6).
16 Craciun (2009) discusses these satanic women in late eighteenth-century writers such as Mary Robinson, Anne Bannerman, and Charlotte Dacre.
17 "Translation" gestures toward gothic devices such as the frame narratives of Radcliffe's *The Italian* (1797) or Walpole's *The Castle of Otranto* (1764).
18 The puzzling nature of this "error" is noted by Craciun and Lokke (Craciun 2003, 284; Lokke 2016, 322 n.1).
19 It is important to note that Landon draws on the dramatic monologue, an element of her writing which has only relatively recently been excavated (Byron 2003, Chapters 2–3; Takiguchi 2007; Stephenson 1995, chapter 4). Baiesi (2009, chapter 4) details the connection between the dramatic monologue and romance.
20 Her hybrid nationality echoes Corinne and her poetic descendants, yet it also foreshadows her physical hybridity, when she is condemned to become part woman, part serpent every Saturday.
21 Smith (2013) links Radcliffe's gothic poet-heroines Adeline de Montalt and Emily St. Aubert to the prophetic in women's writing of the period.
22 In Thoms, after the fall of Lusignan she is doomed to foretell the deaths of the Kings of France (89).

References

The Athenaeum. 1855. "Fairy Tales. By the Countess d'Aulnoy." No. 1440, 637–38.

D'Anois, (sic) Madame [Marie-Catherine Le Jumel de Barneville, Baroness d'Aulnoy]. 1721. *A Collection of Novels and Tales, Written by that Celebrated Wit of France, the Countess D'Anois, in Two Volumes.* London: W. Taylor.

Baiesi, Serena. 2009. *Letitia Elizabeth Landon and Metrical Romance: The Adventures of a Literary Genius.* Bern: Peter Lang.

Barbauld, Anna Laetitia. 1994. "Mrs. Radcliffe." In *The Critical Response to Ann Radcliffe*, edited by Deborah D. Rogers, 96–99. Westport, CO and London: Greenwood Press.

Barrett Browning, Elizabeth. (1856) 1996. *Aurora Leigh.* Edited by Margaret Reynolds. New York: WW Norton.

Battaglia, Beatrice. 2007. "The 'Pieces of Poetry' in Ann Radcliffe." In *Romantic Women Poets: Genre and Gender*, edited by Lilla Marie Crisafulli and Cecilia Pietropoli, 137–51. Amsterdam: Rodopi.

Blessington, The Countess of. (1833) 1997. "Stock in Trade of Modern Poetesses." In *British Women Poets of the Romantic Era: An Anthology*, edited by Paula R. Feldman, 152–53. Baltimore, MD: Johns Hopkins University Press.

Byron, Glennis. 2003. *Dramatic Monologue.* London and New York: Routledge.

Craciun, Adriana. 2009. *Fatal Women of Romanticism.* Cambridge, Cambridge University Press.

Dover, Lord. 1833. "Vicissitudes in the Life of a Princess of the House of Brunswick." In *The Keepsake for MDCCCXXXIII*, edited by Frederic Mansel Reynolds, 1–7. London, Paris and Frankfurt: Longman, Rees, Orme, Brown, Green and Longman.

Elmes, Melissa Ridley. 2017. "The Alchemical Transformation of Melusine." In *Melusine's Footprint: Tracing the Legacy of a Medieval Myth*, edited by Misty Urban, Deva F. Kemmis and Melissa Ridley Elmes, 94–105. Leiden and Boston: Brill.

Favret, Mary A. 1994. "Telling Tales about Genre: Poetry in the Romantic Novel." *Studies in the Novel* 26, no. 1–2 (Fall): 153–72.

Feldman, Paula R., ed. 1997. *British Women Poets of the Romantic Era*. Baltimore, MD: Johns Hopkins University Press.

Forster, E. M. 2008. *The Corinna of England, and a Heroine in the Shade: A Modern Romance*. Edited by Sylvia Bordoni. London: Pickering & Chatto.

Freud, Sigmund. (1919) 2003. "The Uncanny." Translated by David McClintock. Introduction by Hugh Haughton. In *The New Penguin Freud*, edited by Adam Phillips, 123–62. London: Penguin.

Haugen, Kristine Louise. 2000. "Chivalry and Romance in the Eighteenth Century: Richard Hurd and the Disenchantment of the *Faerie Queene*." *Prose Studies* 23, no. 2: 45–60.

Hoeveler, Diane Long. 2010. *Gothic Riffs: Secularising the Uncanny in the European Imaginary, 1780–1820*. Columbus, OH: Ohio State University Press.

Horrocks, Ingrid. 2008. "'Her Ideas Arranged Themselves': Re-Membering Poetry in Radcliffe." *Studies in Romanticism* 47, no. 4 (Winter): 507–27.

Hurd, Richard. 1762. *Letters on Chivalry and Romance*. London: A Millar, W. Thurlbourn and J. Woodyer.

Keightley, Thomas. 1828. *The Fairy Mythology, in Two Volumes*. London: William Harrison Ainsworth.

Kristeva, Julia. 2002. "Revolution in Poetic Language." In *The Portable Kristeva*, edited by Kelly Oliver, 27–92. New York: Columbia University Press.

Landon, Letitia Elizabeth. 1997. *Selected Writings*. Edited by Jerome McGann and Daniel Riess. Peterborough, ON: Broadview.

Landon, Letitia Elizabeth. (1834) 1997a. "The Fairy of the Fountains." Landon 1997. 225–41.

Landon, Letitia Elizabeth. (1824) 1997b. "The Improvisatrice." Landon 1997. 51–80.

Landon, Letitia Elizabeth. (1835) 1997c. "On the Character of Mrs. Hemans's Writings." Landon 1997. 173–86.

Landon, Letitia Elizabeth. 1835. *Fisher's Drawing Room Scrapbook*; with Poetical Illustrations, by L.E.L. London.

Lokke, Kari E. 2016. "Letitia Landon's 'The Fairy of the Fountains' and Gothic Narrative." *Pedagogy* 16, no. 2 (April): 315–22.

Lokke, Kari E. 2006. "Woman and Fame: Germaine de Staël and Regency Women Writers." *Keats-Shelley Journal* 55: 73–79.

Mellor, Anne K. 1997. "The Female Poet and the Poetess: Two Traditions of British Women's Poetry." *Studies in Romanticism* 36, no. 2 (Summer): 261–76.

Miles, Robert. 2015. "The Surprising Mrs Radcliffe: *Udolpho*'s Artful Mysteries." *Women's Writing* 22, no. 3: 300–316.

Miles, Robert. 2014. "Popular Romanticism and the Problem of Belief." In *Ann Radcliffe, Romanticism and the Gothic*, edited by Dale Townshend and Angela Wright, 117–34. Cambridge: Cambridge University Press.

Moy, Olivia Loksing. 2015. "Radcliffe's Poetic Legacy: Female Confinement in the 'Gothic Sonnet.'" *Women's Writing* 22, no. 3: 376–94.

Paradise, Nathaniel. 1995. "Interpolated Poetry, the Novel and Female Accomplishment." *Philological Quarterly* 74, no. 1 (Winter): 57–76.

Price, Leah. 2000. *The Anthology and the Rise of the Novel: From Richardson to George Eliot.* Cambridge: Cambridge University Press.

Radcliffe, Ann. (1794) 1998. *The Mysteries of Udolpho.* Edited by Bonamy Dobrée. Introduction by Terry Castle. Oxford: Oxford University Press.

Radcliffe, Ann. 1816. *The Poems of Mrs. Ann Radcliffe, Author of "The Mysteries of Udolpho," &c. &c. &c.* London: J. Smith.

Radcliffe, Ann. 1816a. "To The Visions of Fancy." Radcliffe 1816. 9.

Radcliffe, Ann. 1816b. "The Sea-nymph." Radcliffe 1816. 56–62.

Radcliffe, Ann. 1816c. "To a Sea-nymph." Radcliffe 1816. 67–68.

Scott, Sir Walter. 1831. *Letters on Demonology and Witchcraft, Addressed to J.G. Lockhart, Esq. By Sir Walter Scott, BART.* 2nd ed. London: John Murray.

Sedziwój, Michal and Paracelsus. 1664. *A New Light of Alchymy Taken Out of the Fountain of Nature and Manual Experience: To Which Is Added a Treatise of Sulphur/Written by Micheel Sandivogius, i.e. An Agrammatically, Divileschi Genus Amo. Also Nine Books of the Nature of Things, Written by Paracelsus; also a Chymical Dictionary... All Which Are Faithfully Translated Out of the Latin into the English Tongue by J.F.* London: Printed by A. Clark, for Tho. Williams.

Smith, Charlotte. 1993. *The Poems of Charlotte Smith.* Edited by Stuart Curran. Oxford: Oxford University Press.

Smith, Orianne. 2013. *Romantic Women Writers, Revolution and Prophecy: Rebellious Daughters, 1786–1826.* Cambridge: Cambridge University Press.

Stabler, Jane. 2014. "Ann Radcliffe's Poetry: The Poetics of Refrain and Inventory." In *Ann Radcliffe, Romanticism and the Gothic,* edited by Dale Townshend and Angela Wright, 185–202. Cambridge: Cambridge University Press.

Staël, Madame [Germaine] de. [1807] 1998. *Corinne, or Italy.* Translated by Sylvia Raphael. Introduction by John Claborne Isbell. Oxford: Oxford University Press.

Stephenson, Glennis. 1995. *Letitia Landon: The Woman behind L.E.L.* Manchester and New York: Manchester University Press.

Takiguchi, Tomoko. 2007. "The Death of a Woman Artist: The Female Other in Letitia Landon's Dramatic Monologue." *Women's Writing* 36, no. 4: 251–67.

"Terrorist Novel Writing." (1798) 2000. In *Gothic Documents: A Sourcebook,* edited by E. J. Clery and Robert Miles, 183–84. Manchester: Manchester University Press.

Thoms, William J. 1834. *Lays and Legends of France.* [From his series] *Lays and Legends of Various Nations: Illustrative of Their Traditions, Popular Literature, Manners, Customs and Superstitions.* London: George Cowie.

Vincent, Patrick. 2004. *The Romantic Poetess: European Politics, Culture and Gender, 1820–1840.* Durham, NH: University of New Hampshire Press.

Williams, Anne. 1995. *Art of Darkness: A Poetics of Gothic.* Chicago and London: University of Chicago Press.

Wright, Angela. 2013. *Britain, France and the Gothic, 1764–1820: The Import of Terror.* Cambridge: Cambridge University Press.

Zipes, Jack. 2012. *The Irresistible Fairy Tale: The Cultural and Social History of a Genre.* Princeton: Princeton University Press.

4 Slavery as a National Crime

Defining Britishness in Encounters with the Flying Dutchman

Agnes Andeweg

In 1964, the African-American poet Amiri Baraka, then still known as LeRoi Jones, premiered his first play *Dutchman* in New York. The one-act drama, a searing dialogue between a white woman and a black man traveling a metro car ending in the woman coolly murdering the man, created quite a stir, and today is regarded as a landmark of the Black Arts Movement.[1] Even though the word "Dutchman" never actually appears in the script, many critics then and now have associated Baraka's title with the figure of the Flying Dutchman: the ghostly captain, or his ship, doomed to sail the world seas forever. Theater historian Errol Hill (2006), for instance, read Baraka's title as a clear reference to the history of slavery, and in Hill's interpretation the story of the Flying Dutchman becomes a wry myth of origin for African-Americans:

> The Flying Dutchman is an obverse metaphor for the horror of black slavery. We need only change the spectral vessel to a Dutch man-of-war; the venue from the Cape of Good Hope to Jamestown, Virginia; the date from eternity to the year 1619; and for the criminal white captain doomed to sail perpetually without ever reaching port we have a cargo of innocent starving Africans whose only crime was to be born black.
>
> (11)

According to Hill, Baraka rewrote this myth of origin with *Dutchman*, and his act of reclaiming black American history marked another stage in the history of black nationalism.

In the highly politicized context of the American 1960s, Baraka's allusion to the Flying Dutchman legend in order to invoke the history of the slave trade may seem an obvious one to make. But *Dutchman* is rather an exception when we consider the adaptations and remediations of the Flying Dutchman story, European or American, spanning more than two hundred years. As I have described elsewhere, in many of the stories, poems, and plays featuring the Flying Dutchman, the ship's cargo is not specified or even mentioned. Much more narrative energy is spent on his wandering, his inability to reach port or to contact loved ones. The name

Flying Dutchman has not only been used in texts but was also given to race horses, ink pens, ploughs, trains, and planes, transforming the ghost into another matter altogether: often detaching it from ship or cargo while stressing the supernatural power of these technologies (Andeweg 2015). Though the Flying Dutchman, first mentioned in a British travelogue around 1800, is a colonial ghost in two senses of the word—originating in the colonial period and as a character involved in colonialism—only rarely is he associated with slavery or the slave trade. An early British example of this is John Leyden's poem *Scenes of Infancy* (1803), which attributes the Flying Dutchman's doom to his being the first ship involved in the slave trade: "Stout was the ship, from Benin's palmy shore/That first the weight of barter'd captives bore" (91). Another is Thomas Hood's comical poem "The Demon-Ship" ([1826] 1871), which pits a horrifying past symbolized by a ship full of men as "black as Afric slaves" against a frightening but ultimately comforting modernity, where blackness is the consequence of shipping coal (Hood [1826] 1871, 213–17). In both Leyden's and Hood's poems, the information that the doomed ship is Dutch is relegated to the paratext (footnote and epigraph, respectively), and thus its nationality does not seem to carry much meaning.

However, Dutchness does become a significant category in relation to the slave trade and slavery in the two British Flying Dutchman adaptations I will examine in this essay: Edward Fitzball's *The Flying Dutchman, or the Phantom Ship* (1827), and a poem "Flying Dutchman" (1832) signed by a certain Clegg. Both texts had a long life in the nineteenth century: Fitzball's play was one of the most famous nautical gothic melodramas of its day, and the poem—which was most likely inspired by Fitzball—found a wide circulation through reprints up until 1878 at least.[2] I will argue that these two British representations of the Flying Dutchman engage in British self-definition, using the Dutch as a screen to denounce pro-slavery ideology and racist attitudes. These ideologies cannot be warded off completely however, and thus these texts attest to the often problematic "Doppelgänger dilemmas" (the term is Marjorie Rubright's) that the Flying Dutchman presents to a British audience: part of his frightening quality is that he is too close for comfort (Rubright 2014). Slavery, evoked as a marker of difference with the Dutch, does not suffice to keep the European continent at a distance, even long after British abolition.

Early British gothic fiction has often been analyzed in terms of the religious, political, and cultural oppositions it helped to construct between Britain and the European continent, in particular in Catholic countries like France and Spain. The cultural work that Gothic can be said to be performing in the works of for example Radcliffe and Lewis is to (re)define cultural differences between spaces that are geographically already separate. This division of territorial space is obviously much less clear at sea, and so this raises the question if and how national boundaries and identities are being upheld and transgressed in the nautical Gothic. Obviously, in Flying Dutchman texts the sea looms large in the staging of supernaturalism. As Emily Alder (2017) has convincingly argued in a recent special issue on nautical Gothic, the sea's gothic potential is almost self-evident yet hardly studied. In the two Flying Dutchman texts under scrutiny here, the sea is an active participant rather than merely the backdrop to action. I shall discuss how the sea now takes and then lashes out, as inscrutable but demanding depth, or as a natural and equally demanding force, respectively, affecting human protagonists— but not indiscriminately.

Edward Fitzball's *Flying Dutchman*

Gothic drama and tales of terror kept Gothic in the popular imagination during the early nineteenth century, after the first wave of gothic novels started to fall away (Cox 2002; Hoeveler 2012). The 1820s and 1830s not only witnessed many theatrical adaptations of gothic novels by well-known authors like "Monk" Lewis, Ann Radcliffe, and Mary Shelley but also original plays or plays adapted from less canonical gothic materials. Fitzball's *Flying Dutchman* is a good example of the second kind: it was adapted from a tale in *Blackwood's Edinburgh Magazine* which appeared in 1821, which, in turn, was the first extensive narrative about the Flying Dutchman, introducing stock elements such as the captain's name (Vanderdecken) and the motif of lost letters.[3] Combining elements from nautical and ghost melodrama proved to be a recipe for success. As Fitzball (1859a) would write in his memoirs:

> These sort of dramas were then very much the vogue. The Flying Dutchman was not by any means behind even *Frankenstein* or *Der Freischütz* in horrors and blue fire. The subject was a very fresh one, though it had so much of salt water in its composition.
>
> (1: 169)

The Flying Dutchman premiered in December 1826 at the Adelphi theater, one of the popular illegitimate theaters which were not allowed to stage serious drama or the classical narrative genres, and much more than their legitimate counterparts relied on music, pantomime, and special effects to support spoken text in their plays. Though scrutinized by the censor, illegitimate plays allowed for more responsiveness to actual events than legitimate plays with their set scripts (Gould 2011). A quote from a review of a much later adaptation of Flying Dutchman material, called *Harlequin Billy Taylor, or The Flying Dutchman and the King of Raritongo* (1851), may illustrate this: "The dialogue in the first part displayed a good amount of jokes and happy allusions, notwithstanding the Lord Chamberlain's interference" (*London Daily News* 1851).

Fitzball was the first to dramatize the ghostly Dutchman, and some scholarly attention has been devoted to the way various elements—special effects, acting, music—work together in his melodrama to stage the supernatural and help blur the boundaries between on- and off-stage, presence and absence, and good and evil. Gothic drama's use of technologically advanced machineries made the supernatural convincing in theater, as Diego Saglia (2015) has argued. The innovative and spectacular effects used in illegitimate ghost melodrama gained huge popularity and were soon copied by legitimate theaters, such as Drury Lane. Thus the "sensational proliferation" of ghost drama in the 1820s actually helped bring about the disintegration of legitimate theater (Moody 2007, 41–42). In the earlier quote, Fitzball mentioned blue fire, the conventional color used in the theater for ghost apparitions, but besides these, *The Flying Dutchman* also employed other technologies such as the so-called vampire trap, a trapdoor to make characters instantly disappear, and lighting effects culminating in a moving phantasmagoric image projected on the backscreen to produce the phantom ship (Saglia 2015, 286–87). Fitzball vividly describes how he preferred the phantasmagoria over having a real ship on stage.[4] Still in 1856, when the play was revived, *The Times* reviewer perhaps sardonically recommended its special effects to a younger audience: "the tossing sea is of a quality to satisfy the most severe judge of undulating carpets" (*The Times* 1856).

Besides the use of technology, the combination of acting and music importantly contributed to a convincing staging of the supernatural. The part of Vanderdecken, the Flying Dutchman, was played by famous actor and superintendent, T. P. Cooke. A master of pantomime, Cooke had had a previous career in the navy, which involved an episode of near-drowning (Moody 2007, 93). He was therefore cut out for the part of the non-speaking Vanderdecken, having already acquired fame as the vampire Lord Ruthven and as Frankenstein's monster. As Jane Moody (2007) observes, the combination in Vanderdecken of muteness and heightened sensitivity especially brought about by music gave him a sublime quality: "Supernatural monstrosity was depicted...as both human and alien, powerfully destructive and yet poignantly susceptible to tender feeling" (93–94). Concurring with Moody, and based on a close analysis of the musical cues and the surviving pieces of the score, Michael Pisani (2014) argues that "the music...should identify the Dutchman not as a villain but as a tragic figure" (91). In this nautical gothic drama which is ultimately a romance, the liminal and frightening Vanderdecken is able to garner sympathy through his genuine romantic feelings. Villainy is relegated elsewhere and motivated not via the supernatural but through different mechanisms of othering. This is relevant to my interest in the way that the play represents slavery. To appreciate how these mechanisms operate, we need to take a closer look at the narrative, even though, regarding the plot, a contemporary reviewer deemed that "consistency has been held in sufficient contempt by the author" (*Morning Post* 1826).[5]

There are many stock features from the Gothic in Fitzball's play, even though it is not situated in a medieval past but in the present-day, taking place at the Cape of Good Hope, in 1827. This setting is however connected to the doom of the past in the shape of a gothic fortress with turret and moat, identified as Vanderdecken's "previous habitation," in which a damsel called Lestelle Vanhelm suffers from her over-possessive uncle, Captain Peppercoal. He is about to marry her off to the son of a former sea mate, Peter von Bummel, who is described as a "cockney Dutchman, a dabbler in the Law," and therefore palpably not apt husband-material. Her true lover is the English lieutenant Mowdrey, who plans to elope with Lestelle, and the third suitor is Captain Vanderdecken who wants to abduct her in order to sacrifice her to Rockalda, "Evil Spirit of the Deep." Vanderdecken and this personification of the sea mutually exercise power: the play opens with Rockalda engaging in a "mystic dance" with the "silv'ry moon"; Vanderdecken's arrival disturbs this natural harmony ("this sudden discord"). She is however in charge: Vanderdecken pleads to have his service renewed for another century and asks Rockalda's permission to go ashore "to increase the number of thy victims" (11). Haunting the African shore, he is a captain who goes back and forth to the deep sea to snatch his victims away from their environment. This practice is firmly framed in terms of romance, evading associations with slave trade yet using the very word: "And now seek a bride to share thy stormy fate. Rockalda's fatal death book make her sign, and become my slave" (11). Before setting foot on land Vanderdecken receives an invisibility cloak and a protective spell which renders him invulnerable. This may sound rather illogical for a ghost, but can be read as indication of the difference between sea and land: on land his spectral qualities are less pronounced than at sea. Likewise, superstition is context-bound, restricted in terms of class and gender: only the sailors, servants, and women believe in the ghost's existence, not Peppercoal and Von Bummel.

Vanderdecken first appears on board the British ship on its way to the Cape with the Dutch lawyer Von Bummel. When he presents a love letter addressed to one Lestelle Vanhelm in Amsterdam, the crew immediately recognize him as the famous Dutch ghost—they know the street does not exist anymore, and do not dare to touch his letter. Vanderdecken seizes Von Bummel's letter of introduction from Lestelle's father to gain easy access to Captain Peppercoal. Von Bummel does not succeed in grasping Vanderdecken's love letter in return: it explodes, demonstrating that arranged marriage is tradable, but romantic love cannot be passed on. What follows is a comedy of errors, with many miscommunications and cross-dressings, familiar gothic and comical doublings of characters and of characters and paintings, all with the purpose to gain Lestelle, who herself remarkably resembles the deceased spouse of Vanderdecken. Of the male characters, only Mowdrey, the young British officer, is Vanderdecken's emotional equivalent—romantically moved, he represents the new generation. The play ends with a duel between Mowdrey and Vanderdecken in the cave, without Rockalda present. Mowdrey tries to rescue the abducted Lestelle, but falls wounded to the ground, hit by Vanderdecken. Mowdrey's cunning servant and marine painter Toby Varnish manages to burn Rockalda's magic death book; Vanderdecken cries out and, having broken his vow of silence, is forever doomed.

Like the ghostly Vanderdecken, the aforementioned Peppercoal is a (former) sea captain. While the play does not state Peppercoal's nationality explicitly, the jokes about his name, his acquaintance with Von Bummel's father, his possession of both the old fortress and the girl of Dutch descent indicate that he is Dutch, also because this former trade captain is clearly stuck in the wrong age: Peppercoal still addresses everyone around him in naval terms. Peppercoal is ridiculous and evil at the same time: he is compared to a "sea monster" and a "snarling sea griffin" by Toby Varnish, and therefore may be seen to be symbolically on a par with Rockalda. He has promised Lestelle, the only object of exchange in the play, to landlubber Peter Von Bummel, the "walking Dutchman," as Peppercoal calls him, who is equally out-of-place: continually sea-sick, and regarding everything and everyone in legal terms. Von Bummel and Peppercoal embody a merchant ideology and representation of the Dutch as perennial traders of goods and people, a familiar trope in British popular culture dating back to the early modern period (Rubright 2014). The Dutch men are ready to trade Lestelle according to contract, and only Mowdrey, with the aid of Toby Varnish, is able to break these contractual bonds through love. Lestelle also harbors these modern feelings, as evidenced through her wish to elope to England, the "land of liberty" as she calls it, even though her ancestor of the same name lived in Amsterdam. Lestelle's willingness to form bonds with the British symbolizes how the British Empire successfully finds itself at the Cape, ideologically and practically.

Contextualizing this spectacular and supernatural drama, it is clear that many elements of Fitzball's play point to a colonial context that would have been familiar to the London audience, starting with the setting. The South African Cape had only relatively recently become a British colony. It had been a Dutch settlement since the early 1600s, serving as a refreshment point on the journey to the East Indies. In 1795, when the Dutch Republic was occupied by the French, the Dutch entrusted the Cape Colony to the British in order to prevent it from falling into French hands, demanding that they would give it back afterward. And so the British did in 1803, only to take possession again in 1806. This situation was ratified by the Vienna treaty after Napoleon's defeat. *The Flying Dutchman*'s final scene, in which the Dutch Peppercoal and Von Bummel take the British lieutenant Mowdrey and his servant Toby Varnish from the Devil's Cave back to the shore, in a sloop flying the "British flag," as the directions read, can easily be read as a metaphorical rendition of Cape Colony changing hands (45). Likewise, the Dutch predecessors of the British have become the outlaws in the play, no matter how much they "dabble" with the law as Von Bummel does: the first appearance of Vanderdecken shows him "holding in his hand a black flag, emblazoned with a white Death's head and cross bones" (11).

By 1820 the British government initiated a settler policy for the Cape, mostly inspired by the economic crisis and huge unemployment at home, and in order to avoid having to introduce more radical reforms (Thompson 1996, 22). This settler policy provided people willing to emigrate to the Cape Colony with financial support. About 5,000 British emigrants used this opportunity to leave the country—4,000 selected from 80,000 applicants, and 1,000 who paid for their own journey. These incentives led to a sizeable new group of white colonizers at the Cape (around 1800, Cape Town had a population of about 14,000 burghers and 15,000 slaves). Over time, this influx of new settlers resulted in increasing ethnic tensions between the two white groups: between what the British would call the Boer population of earlier white settlers from Dutch descent, and the newly arrived British settlers. Besides linguistic and cultural differences, there was another difference between the two white colonizers' groups: the new British settlers were explicitly forbidden to hold slaves (Thompson 1996, 56).[6]

Fitzball's *The Flying Dutchman*, performed a few years after British settlement policy, stages the encounter between the old and the new colonial order, the British and the Dutch, attempting to mark clear distinctions between the two. Negative stereotypes of the Dutch had been abundant in English literature ever since the early modern period. As Marjorie Rubright (2014) has discussed regarding early modern representations of Anglo-Dutch relations, ongoing "Doppelgänger dilemmas" posed problems: "Often, English efforts to put distance between Englishness and Dutchness—attempts at dis-identification and differentiation—failed to produce distinct boundaries" (237). One way of marking the differences between the British and the Dutch in *The Flying Dutchman* is by gothicizing the Dutch, and relegating them to the past. Another is by unevenly handing out modern sensibilities: the Dutch Von Bummel and Peppercoal are treacherous, and they lack feeling and the value of liberty. The exception is the ghostly Vanderdecken: he can be really affected by Lestelle's song, and thus he represents a sensibility that Peppercoal and Von Bummel, the very material and present Dutch characters on stage, lack. Vanderdecken still haunts the African coast to snatch away his victims but has sublimated his trade into romantic feelings.

In *The Flying Dutchman*, the Dutch also have slaves, as opposed to the new British arrivals. Peppercoal is not only the possessive custodian of Lestelle, he is a slave owner as well. His personal slave Smutta is introduced when Peppercoal calls him an unfaithful dog. To compare: while

Mowdrey's servant Toby Varnish is at some point also called a dog by his master Mowdrey, unlike Smutta he gets to say something back. And whereas Toby saves his master Mowdrey, Smutta hinders his mistress Lestelle despite his best intentions, unintentionally impeding her when he cuts the rope of her lover's boat. At the same time Smutta is better informed than the rest about mysterious matters: he informs Lestelle about the sea cave and the Flying Dutchman's return. His misunderstandings of Von Bummel's legal jargon ("assault and battery") and the resulting wordplay ("no salt and buttery") both emphasize Von Bummel's misplaced use of legal discourse and Smutta's ignorance. Smutta's stereotypical language keeps him symbolically in his place even when the play temporarily grants him power. In one scene Von Bummel, cross-dressed as a young woman, is chased by a group of slaves, led by Smutta. Von Bummel addresses his capturers as if he is speaking to a jury in court:

> Oh! Gentlemen of the jury, pity and protect a lovely young creter... Conduct me to the nearest vessel please, I'm England bound, (*aside*) I wish they were bound neck and heels together. Pity me sweet gentlemen, good-looking, fair-complexioned gentlemen. I'm only a poor trembling, palpitating little damsel.
>
> (38)

Even though *The Flying Dutchman* attributes the desire to chase and bind the black characters to the Dutch, as happens in this passage, it does not disengage itself from representing Smutta and the other enslaved characters as the stereotypical butt of humor. From the valuable work of Hazel Waters (2007) and Jenna Gibbs (2014) on the representations of blacks in Victorian theater, we know that plays and poems played an important part in the development of the stereotypical black image, and in popularizing "scientific" prejudices as well as transforming/reifying popular beliefs about race. Though Gibbs (2014) and Waters (2007) do not discuss *The Flying Dutchman* or the figure of Smutta, the way his character is represented supports their analyses in many ways. Waters (2007), who traced a history of increasingly degrading representations of black characters in the course of eighteenth- and nineteenth-century theater, writes that "liberty was always invoked whenever slavery was" (38). In the scene discussed previously, the primal scene of bondage is parodied and existing racial and social hierarchies are temporarily overthrown. By recasting the scene of bondage into a legal setting, and by blurring slavery and romance (liberty pertains to white damsels only), potential dilemmas about existing power structures and black emancipation are averted.

Jenna Gibbs (2014) writes: "[B]lackface supplicant slaves in images, prose, and lyrics along with the theatrical jester, Harlequin Negro, were symbiotic counterparts to white Britannia in articulating subjecthood as white, masculine, and a prerogative of the bourgeois and the elite" 54).

As Gibbs (2014) describes, blackface could be seen on the Victorian stage well before the arrival of black minstrel shows in Britain around 1835, mostly in parts for black supplicant slaves (52–86). In *The Flying Dutchman*, Smutta's role as supplicant slave indeed functions to confirm white masculine subjectivity. But it would be mistaken to assume that his part was necessarily a blackface performance. Waters (2007) informs us that there were some black actors to be found on the London stage in the early nineteenth century, the most famous being Ira Aldridge (58–88). As I was able to ascertain, Smutta was played by a black actor, who was announced on the bill as Signor Paulo. Signor Paulo Jr. was a renowned clown, who had made his debut in 1815 in Sadler's Wells. As a later biographer wrote "The son of 'Le Petit Diable' and 'La Belle Espagnole' was born almost within the walls of Sadler's Wells, and became known to fame as Signor Paulo, a very popular clown for many years" (Cook 1883, 4). His real name was Paul Redigé, and he was the son of Paul Redigé, a French rope dancer who also performed under the name Signor Paulo, and Maria Garcia, a pantomime actress known as "La Belle Espagnole." From the scant information available it seems she was a black woman from Georgia ("La Belle Espagnole" 2017). The British Museum has a portrait of Signor Paulo from the 1820s in its collection (Zeitter 1820s), as well as one of his mother (Gillray 1796). This casting choice also shows the proximity of pantomime, harlequin, and melodrama, not just in the way these genres exchanged and borrowed features but also in the persons of the actors themselves (Figure 4.1).

The stereotype of the black slave lived on for many decades, persisting after slavery was abolished in 1833, though small shifts in the way Smutta was perceived can be registered by tracing newspaper reviews of later performances of Fitzball's *The Flying Dutchman*. When the play was revived in 1856 and performed in *The Adelphi* once more, Smutta is no longer called a slave, but referenced to as "the black" (*Morning Post* 1856).[7] In 1860, Smutta, without explanatory epithet—which suggests he is still a familiar character—is "amusingly rendered" (*Bedfordshire Times and Independent* 1860) and in 1865 a reviewer praised the actor who "played the part of Smutta exceedingly well" (*Sheffield Daily Telegraph* 1865). In 1887, Von Brunnel (sic) and Smutta are mentioned in one breath as the ones who "supplied the comicality and mirth" (*Yorkshire Gazette* 1887). Similarly, 1882 and 1886, Smutta, now called "a negro servant" is seen as a major source of comedy, creating "much merriment by his antics" (*The Salisbury Times* 1886; *Exeter and Plymouth Gazette* 1891).

Though Smutta would never become as popular as the figure of Mungo, the prototypical black slave originating from the late eighteenth-century play *The Padlock* (Gibbs 2014, 59–66), he does reappear in a number of later texts. As Fitzball's drama is the first source with a character of this name, and given its popularity, it is more than likely that later reappearances of Smutta were inspired by Fitzball. In Edward Stirling's *Sadak*

Figure 4.1 Signor Paulo by J.C. Zeitter c. 1820s. ©The Trustees of the British Museum.

and Kalasrade (1837), a pirated, comical version of Mary Russell Mitford's opera of the same title, Smutta also features as a slave—dressed in a "striped calico dress" just as in Fitzball's play—to "Mustapha, the Cadi," acting comically by aping his master (*Pattie's Modern Stage: A Collection of the Most Approved and Popular Dramas* 1839). Again, assigning the black slave to an "Other," in this case a Muslim magistrate, could help shore up the notion of British liberty for a home audience. Twenty years later, in William Hurton's novel *The Doomed Ship of the Arctic Sea* (1855), the character of Smutta has morphed into a black foster brother and steward to white Captain Larpent from the West Indies. Their affective bond is suggested by the fact that as babies they were both breast-fed by Smutta's mother, an enslaved woman at a plantation. Smutta and Larpent die more or less in each other's arms after having been attacked by mutineers. Though Smutta is put on an almost equal footing with his foster-brother, his inferiority is never really questioned, and his speech is as stereotypically rendered as ever. Though Smutta is no longer an enslaved character, he is a slave in romantic terms:

> Smutta felt the blood tingling all over him. Never before in his life had a real lady taken him by the hand, and spoken such honeyed words. I saw that Oriana had won the giant's simple heart in a moment, and that he was henceforth her slave.
>
> (Hurton 1855, 20)

In *The Doomed Ship*, as in Fitzball's *The Flying Dutchman*, the discourse of slavery easily shifts into the discourse of romance. Here the easiness with which he succumbs to his feelings marks him as the less masculine. Lastly, in a late prose adaptation of Fitzball's play in *The Boys of England Story Teller* (1878), published under the heading of "Our Chimney Corner at the old Village Inn" and thus clearly marked as nostalgic, Smutta still is the "servant" to Peppercoal, but the original dialogues from Fitzball in which Peppercoal belittles and ridicules him have now been left out. Apparently, by 1878, the association of the Dutch with the mistreatment of slaves had vanished. The Dutch had abolished slavery, finally, in 1863—thirty years after the British—and maybe that is why this could no longer be used as a distinguishing feature for a British readership, even within the context of nostalgia.

Smutta and the Flying Dutchman

Besides Smutta's reappearances in drama and prose I discovered a poem I will discuss at more length. It was published under the titles "The Flying Dutchman" and "Smutta and the Flying Dutchman" and appeared through various channels in the mid-nineteenth century. It is not included in Marcus Wood's vast anthology of Anglo-American poetry on slavery, perhaps overlooked because it was never published in a poetry collection, and it has received no scholarly attention so far. This is a pity, for "The Flying Dutchman" seems remarkable for its ambivalence about slave emancipation. Wood (2003) found very few poems after the 1780s displaying what he calls a "cultural confidence about accepting slavery" (xii), which he explains by the fact that by that time abolition had become a mainstream movement. Yet "The Flying Dutchman's" publication history demonstrates how anti-emancipation sentiments were felt and apparently voiced even decades after abolition. It was first published in 1832, the year before the Emancipation Bill would pass after a long period of intense societal debate and upheavals in Britain and in the colonies, and with the memory of dramatic Jamaican slave rebellions of 1831–1832 still fresh in the public mind. "The Flying Dutchman" appeared in William Hone's popular *Year Book*, an anthology of miscellaneous materials ("amusements"), and was later reprinted anonymously in magazines, *The Penny Satirist* and *The Ladies Cabinet*, respectively (Clegg 1832; *The Penny Satirist* 1846; *The Ladies' Cabinet of Fashion, Music and Romance* 1850). The *Year Book* itself would be reprinted over and over again, in Britain but also in the United States at least till 1878.[8] Whereas the poem was signed "Clegg" and "March 1831" in Hone's *Year book*, in later reprints author and date are no longer mentioned.[9] Though I have not been able to trace numbers of print runs, the poem's repeated publication implies that it kept a certain currency in British and American popular culture. That it was considered to be a piece of amusement like any other may be illustrated by the fact that *The Ladies Cabinet of Fashion, Music and Romance* published it amidst articles on the jealous husband, the language of flowers, and Modern Rome. As with other Flying Dutchman adaptations, the presence of the Dutchman in an English-speaking context evokes and negotiates tensions about British national values, most of all liberty.

This poem starts—as do most Flying Dutchman adaptations—with a ship in a storm, this time situated at a distance in time as well as in space, on the "Pacific Sea in August '87," which could either be read as 1787 or 1687. Its cargo is explicitly mentioned: the ship is "Brimful of negroes carried off by force,/And going to market to be sold in form." Even though the narrator has difficulty reproducing the captain's name, he knows it is a Dutch ship, with a black shipmate:

> The captain's name I cannot think of yet
> (These Dutch names 'tis so easy to forget),
> This much I know, his vessel was a cutter,
> His mate a negro of the name of Smutta.

The narrator elaborates on the sufferings of the enslaved—their being confined, beaten and force-fed—while maintaining his ironical tone ("dainty fish"):

> Who long had languished huddled up in coffins,
> Exposed to threats and stripes, and kicks and scoffings—
> Their food dried shark, and other dainty fish;
> But potted grampus was the standard dish,
> A pound of which was every day at noon
> Cramm'd down their gullets with a wooden spoon.

When worst comes to worst, the captain, "conscience-stricken by the angry waves," orders Smutta to release the enslaved men, so that he will not founder with a ship full of captivated people. Apparently, only natural forces, here personified as "angry," are able to imbue the captain with the value of liberty. However, the slaves call for revenge as soon as they are released and proclaim Smutta their chief. They throw the crew overboard, upon which the narrator temporarily discards his distant (external) position. He addresses the freed slaves directly, blaming them and Smutta in particular for what they have done: "Oh slaves, for shame! for shame! oh Smutta, fie!/They were in truth ill us'd, but Smutta had/No cause to grumble—Smutta, 't was too bad."[10] The narrator resumes his narration ("however, to my tale") and recounts how Smutta then sees the captain's ghost appear, rendering his speech in a stereotypical way often used for black characters: "him pale, him grim, him thin, him all in white." Like a prototypical slave-trader the ghost carries a whip, telling Smutta that he has called for reinforcements:

I have not lost my time, but made you over
To Vanderdecken, that eternal rover,
And this for making spectres of your betters;
Fool that I was to free you from your fetters!

The ghostly slaver captain bequeaths his cargo to Vanderdecken, the Flying Dutchman, who then sinks the ship in hellish fire: "A shower of brimstone shortly sunk the cutter/Drown'd the unlucky crew and smother'd Smutta."[11]

Paul Gilroy (1993) famously conceptualized the Black Atlantic as a fluid space of resistance and exploitation, and as a space beyond nationalism.[12] The poem does offer this space temporarily: as soon as the enslaved become physically mobile, resurrected into life when they are released from their coffins, they become socially mobile: demanding a voice and taking over the ship. Though the slaves cannot be blamed for their insurgence—for, as the narrator confirms, "they were in truth ill-used," Smutta's subversion of maritime hierarchy is poetically rejected. The narrator clearly puts all the blame on Smutta for leading this mutiny, for he had "no cause to grumble." Thus, the poem feeds white anxieties about black emancipation: giving freedom to one will result in a complete subversion of hierarchy. A significant feature of this Flying Dutchman poem is how it doubles the ghost: one ghost, even when armed, is not enough apparently to contain the threat of black insurrection. The societal order at sea, here briefly imagined as a potential space of liberty and of self-governance by blacks, can only be restored by a super-supernatural force, who does not just bring a whip, the slaver's tools, but hellish brimstone to restore the hierarchy.

A racist ideology is here both affirmed (see how the narrator judges), and simultaneously denounced by projecting it onto the Dutch, risible "others" from the past. That this poem remained a source of entertainment—horror by proxy—up until the 1870s, could be read as a sign of the continuing anxieties that occupied some members of the British public during the decades of intense debates about slave emancipation, first in Britain and then in the United States. First published in 1831, this poem can represent the slave trade—abolished by the British in 1807 and by the Dutch in 1814—as a despicable practice belonging to the past. But the step of black emancipation, here following directly from ending trade, is represented as a step too far. Through this poem British readers could contemplate the potential horrors of black emancipation and decide that haunting was to be preferred over black enfranchisement. Whereas, on the one hand, the Dutch captain is ridiculed as an unmemorable relic from the past, his slaver ghost and his devilish double are needed to ward off societal chaos. While one could argue that this poem only makes fun of the Dutch and enables the shoring up of a superior British sense of self, it does not succeed in completely projecting anxieties onto the Dutch other. The poem betrays its vested interest in current home affairs, and its inability to relegate anxieties to the past or to the Dutch through its use of the word "enfranchise." In the overall colloquial language the poem employs, this word stands out as a much more formal term. A simple search for word frequencies in British newspapers shows that the use of "enfranchise" in combination with "slave" increased tremendously around the time the poem was first published: 2,054 between 1830 and 1839 compared to 265 in the previous decade.[13] Until about 1870 the word would remain in as frequent use as in the 1830s. The hotly debated topic of enfranchisement ensured the poem's actuality for many years.

To conclude, in both texts, Dutch characters serve as a screen on which to project British ambivalences about slavery. Fitzball's play and the poem allow British and other English-speaking audiences to temporarily enjoy pro-slavery sentiments that have politically been left behind, as long as they can safeguard the distinctions with the Dutch, and the European continent at large. The cloak of humor rather than the "invisibility cloak," that is the supernatural, serves as a means to put these sentiments at a distance, and allows these texts to survive in Anglo-American popular culture for decades after the abolition of slavery. In both texts the ghostly Flying Dutchman is quite literally of a different order than the other Dutch characters. Not involved in the daily, material practice of slaver-enslaved relations, he can act as driven by sublimated feelings: in Fitzball's play his enslaving happens in the service of romance rather than for economic purposes; in the poem he acts as an instrument of justice, poetically justifying the slaver captain. Thus, supernatural haunting is seemingly "purified" yet made to work in service of a perniciously racist representational regime.

Notes

1 For an overview of *Dutchman*'s reception, see Carol Bunch Davis (2015).
2 In his memoirs, Fitzball estimates the number of performances at more than ten thousand; this is clearly an exaggeration as it would amount to thirty years of non-stop performances (Edward Fitzball 1859b, 14). The play was staged at the Adelphi, the Surrey, and—in a pirated version by Douglas

Jerrold—the Coburg. For the number of performances at the Adelphi, see "The Adelphi Theatre Project: All-Inclusive Index."

3 "Vanderdecken's message home" was published anonymously, but has been attributed to the Canadian writer John Howison. See Morrison (1995).

4 In his memoirs Fitzball cites his conversation with the theater manager who is afraid the ship will be too expensive: "Two hundred pounds!—for what sir?" "Timber" "Timber!" almost shouted I. "Timber for a Phantom Ship? My dear sir, that would be an absurdity indeed." "Of what would you compose it?" was the evidently sarcastic reply....."A shadow." "A shadow?" laughing incredulously (Fitzball 1859b*, Volume 2, 13–15).

5 The reviewer does not elaborate on his motivation, unfortunately. The relative unfamiliarity of the Flying Dutchman story at this point may be relevant here: several reviews extensively summarize the plot.

6 In practice British colonists owned slaves as well, see Worden (2017).

7 In the reception of the initial performance in 1826, Smutta is not mentioned once. In many reviews, the plot is summarized extensively, probably because the Flying Dutchman was not a familiar story yet.

8 That the poem kept a certain notoriety can also be supported by the fact that it was quoted in a local newspaper as late as 1880 (*Derbyshire Times and Chesterfield Herald* 1880).

9 Hone had acquired fame as a radical publisher when he was acquitted of blasphemy in 1817. His later works, such as *The Year Book* and other similar books (*The Table Book, The Every-Day Book*), were not satirical (Ledger 2004, 491).

10 If we read this little admonition of Smutta as a form of irony, because it is such a small one, the narrator could even be condoning his revolt.

11 The poem's satirical tone and deliberate subversion of a familiar narrative are reminiscent of Byron's popular poem *Don Juan*, of which parts were published in installments between 1819 and 1824. The rhyme here on "cutter" may be meant to recall the infamous "cutter/butter" rhyme in Canto II, Stanza 61 of *Don Juan*.

12 I believe the dynamics Gilroy describes applies here even though the poem is situated in the Pacific rather than the Atlantic. For a discussion of how to read the Atlantic and Pacific together, see Ganser (2018).

13 With the note that the number of pages archived roughly doubles in period (123,034 versus 70,511). Search conducted in the British Newspaper Archive, www.britishnewspaperarchive.co.uk/, 30 November 2018. In the first two decades, between 1800 and 1820, the term combination was only used 80 times in total.

References

Alder, Emily. 2017. "Through Oceans Darkly: Sea Literature and the Nautical Gothic." *Gothic Studies* 19, no. 2 (November): 1–15.

Andeweg, Agnes. 2015. "Manifestations of the Flying Dutchman: On Materializing Ghosts and (Not) Remembering the Colonial Past." *Cultural History* 4, no. 2: 187–205.

Bedfordshire Times and Independent. 1860. "Rifle Volunteers" (March 6). *British Newspaper Archive*.

Clegg. 1832. "Flying Dutchman." In *The Year Book, of Daily Recreation & Information: Concerning Remarkable Men, Manners, Times, Seasons, Solemnities, Merry-Makings, Antiquities & Novelties, Forming a Complete*

History of the Year; & a Perpetual Key to the Almanac, edited by William Hone, 479–80. London: William Tegg.

Cook, Dutton. 1883. "Pantomimic Families." *The Theatre* (January).

Cox, Jeffrey N. 2002. "English Gothic Theatre." In *The Cambridge Companion to Gothic Fiction*, edited by Jerrold E. Hogle, 125–44. Cambridge: Cambridge University Press.

Davis, Carol Bunch. 2015. "'A Ghost of the Future': Racial (Mis)Perception and Black Subjectivity in LeRoi Jones's Dutchman." In *Prefiguring Postblackness: Cultural Memory, Drama, and the African American Freedom Struggle of the 1960s*, 57–80. Jackson: University Press of Mississippi.

Derbyshire Times and Chesterfield Herald. 1880. "Local Historical Gleanings" (July 31). *British Newspaper Archive*.

Exeter and Plymouth Gazette. 1891. "'Pepper's Ghost' in Exeter" (March 6). *British Newspaper Archive*.

Fitzball, Edward. 1859a. *Thirty-Five Years of a Dramatic Author's Life*. Vol. 1. London: T.C. Newby.

Fitzball, Edward. 1859b. *Thirty-Five Years of a Dramatic Author's Life*. Vol. 2. London: T.C. Newby.

Fitzball, Edward. 1827. *The Flying Dutchman, or, The Phantom Ship, a Nautical Drama in Three Acts*. Phantom Ship. London: Lacy.

Ganser, Alexandra. 2018. "From the Black Atlantic to the Bleak Pacific: Re-Reading 'Benito Cereno.'" *Atlantic Studies*, 15, no. 2 (April), 218–37.

Gibbs, Jenna. 2014. *Performing the Temple of Liberty. Slavery, Theater, and Popular Culture in London and Philadelphia, 1760–1850*. Baltimore, MD: Johns Hopkins University Press.

Gillray, James. 1796. "La Belle Espagnole,-Ou-La Doublure de Madame Tallien." The British Museum.

Gilroy, Paul. 1993. *The Black Atlantic: Modernity and Double Consciousness*. Cambridge, MA: Harvard University Press.

Gould, Marty. 2011. *Nineteenth-Century Theatre and the Imperial Encounter*. London: Routledge.

Hill, Errol. 2006. *A History of African American Theatre*. Cambridge: Cambridge University Press.

Hoeveler, Diana Long. 2012. "Victorian Gothic Drama." In *The Victorian Gothic: An Edinburgh Companion*, edited by William Hughes and Andrew Smith, 57–71. Edinburgh: Edinburgh University Press.

Hood, Thomas. [1826] 1871. *Whims and Oddities, in Prose and Verse*. London: J.C. Hotten.

Hurton, William. 1855. *The Doomed Ship; or, The Wreck of the Arctic Regions*. London: Willoughby.

"La Belle Espagnole." 2017. *The Misfortune Club. Meanderings in 19th Century History* [blog] (September 22). www.themisfortuneclub.com/2017/09/la-belle-espagnole.html.

Ledger, Sally. 2004. "From Queen Caroline to Lady Dedlock: Dickens and the Popular Radical Imagination." *Victorian Literature and Culture* 32, no. 2 (September): 575–600.

Leyden, John. 1803. *Scenes of Infancy: Descriptive of Teviotdale*. Edinburgh: Printed by J. Ballantyne for T. N. Longman, and O. Rees, London: sold by Manners and Miller.

London Daily News. 1851. "Holiday Amusements, 'Boxing-Day'" (December 27). *British Newspaper Archive*.

Moody, Jane. 2007. *Illegitimate Theatre in London, 1770–1840*. Cambridge: Cambridge University Press.

Morning Post. 1856. "Adelphi Theatre" (June 5). *British Newspaper Archive*.

Morning Post. 1826. "Theatres" (December 5). *British Newspaper Archive*.

Morrison, Robert S. 1995. "John Howison of 'Blackwood's Magazine.'" *Notes and Queries* 42, no. 2 (June): 191.

P.D., ed. 1839. *Pattie's Modern Stage: A Collection of the Most Approved and Popular Dramas*. Vol. 3. London.

Pisani, Michael V. 2014. *Music for the Melodramatic Theatre in Nineteenth-Century London and New York*. Iowa City : University of Iowa Press.

"Results for 'enfranchise Slaves'" (Between 1st Jan 1800 and 31st Dec 1849). *British Newspaper Archive*. n.d. Accessed on 30 November 2018.

Rubright, Marjorie. 2014. *Doppelgänger Dilemmas. Anglo-Dutch Relations in Early Modern English Literature and Culture*. Philadelphia: University of Pennsylvania Press.

Saglia, Diego. 2015. "'The Frighted Stage': The Sensational Proliferation of Ghost Melodrama in the 1820s." *Studies in Romanticism* 54, no. 2 (June): 269–93.

Sheffield Daily Telegraph. 1865. "Local and District News" (April 20). *British Newspaper Archive*.

"The Adelphi Theatre Project: All-Inclusive Index." n.d. Accessed on 24 November 2018. www.umass.edu/AdelphiTheatreCalendar/msti.htm.

The Ladies' Cabinet of Fashion, Music and Romance. 1850. "SMUTTA, AND THE FLYING DUTCHMAN" (April 1). 19th Century UK Periodicals.

The Penny Satirist. 1846. "The Flying Dutchman" (April 18). *19th Century UK Periodicals*.

The Salisbury Times. 1886. "Local News" (December 11). *British Newspaper Archive*.

The Times. 1856. "Adelphi Theatre" (June 6). *The Times Digital Archive*.

Thompson, Leonard. 1996. *A History of South Africa: Revised Edition*. New Haven: Yale University Press.

Waters, Hazel. 2007. *Racism on the Victorian Stage. Representation of Slavery and the Black Character*. Cambridge: Cambridge University Press.

Wood, Marcus. 2003. *The Poetry of Slavery : An Anglo-American Anthology, 1764–1865*. Oxford: Oxford University Press.

Worden, Nigel. 2017. "Slavery at the Cape" (April 2017). *Oxford Research Encyclopedia of African History*. oxfordre.com, doi: 10.1093/acrefore/9780190277734.013.76.

Yorkshire Gazette. 1887. "Entertainments" (December 3). *British Newspaper Archive*.

Zeitter, John Christian. 1820s. "Signor Paulo." Printed by Godefroy Engelmann. The British Museum.

5   Strange Exhibitions

M. R. James, Europe, and the Phantom Museum

Scott Brewster

Ghosts, or, more strictly, troubling presences, artefacts and curios, in M. R. James's tales mainly inhabit the home-grown haunts of casual visitors: the seaside resort, the secluded country house, the cathedral close. The recurrent attraction, or solace, of "his calm environment" in which the "ominous thing" puts out its head (James 1924, vi), suggests that James's typical traveler follows a predictable, even insular, domestic itinerary. This image of the "safe," leisurely home tour, however, must be set against the enduring fascination with continental Europe in James's personal and creative life. Traveling in Europe, according to Richard William Pfaff (1980), was one of the principal pleasures of James's adulthood. His early excursions included an archaeological expedition in Cyprus in the winter of 1887, regular cycling trips to France, and a summer tour in 1899 to Denmark and Sweden with his illustrator James McBryde. In *Eton and Kings* (1926), James says of his friend Mark Sykes: "he was not that detestable thing, a cosmopolitan; he was very English, very robust, totally without affectation" (222). Yet this suspicion of the foreign is utterly at odds with James's account of his travels on the continent, including his first journey to "the sacred soil of France" (62), the Alps, and Italy. A cycling holiday in France in 1884, when he spent time deciphering and noting sculpture and glass in various cathedrals, is recalled as a moment where "I have not often been more acutely alive in mind and body" (152). James's encomium to cross-channel travel—leaving aside his frustration with the "muddleheaded, unintelligent, fussy, infernal imbeciles, all and every single person in the whole of France in any way connected with railways or luggage" (Pfaff 1980, 112)—evocatively captures this love affair:

> But what is comparable, after all, to the very first day in France? The passing of Abbeville and sighting the towers of St Wulfram—the church of Longpoint on the other side of the Somme valley—the great smell of Amiens—the thousand and one things that still make the train journey from Calais to Paris a delight to me.

(62)

The pleasures of the cycling tour in France during the years before the Great War, something James undertook on more than thirty occasions, underscore the more poignant recollection of his wartime experiences recounted in *Eton and Kings*:

> Typical of the background of one's thoughts during those years were the evenings when an air-raid threatened, and the lights went down, and you sat wondering what the next hour would bring forth. Typical also the summer days when, having bicycled out a few miles into the country, you lay on the grass by the roadside and listened to the throb of the guns in France.
>
> (263–64)

Far from marking a consolatory retreat, the act of cycling to the peace of the countryside, a place where conflict is nonetheless audible, brings back former delights even as it accentuates a present sense of disconnection and dis-ease. A space of seclusion and private contemplation— akin to a library or museum—becomes a place where one is exposed to a darkening continent where ignorant armies clash by night. The more ominous consequences of cross-channel traffic can be discerned in "Casting the Runes," where the malevolent occultist Karswell and his deadly curse are safely expelled at Dover. In a dark inversion of James's reminiscence about his visits to France, Karswell subsequently perishes at St. Wulfram's Church at Abbeville, whose incomparable towers are evoked in *Eton and Kings*.

James's ghost tales of European travel recall the passions of discovery and the allure of new, often less-trodden, places that are similar to those expressed in his autobiographical reflections; yet, like the wartime memory cited above, these stories often reveal the equivocal benefits of sojourns in mainland Europe. As we shall see, the journeys abroad in "Canon Alberic's Scrapbook" ([1895] 2011), "The Treasure of Abbot Thomas" ([1904] 2011), "'Oh, Whistle, and I'll Come to You, My Lad'" ([1904] 2011), "Mr Humphreys and his Inheritance" ([1911] 2011), "Number 13" ([1904] 2011), and "Count Magnus" ([1904] 2011) are forms of continental exchange that involve unsettling encounters with a past that is at once intimate and discomfortingly remote. Each tale stages a strange exhibition, or an exhibition of strangeness, that we might expect from a visit to what David Punter (2008) has called the "phantom museum" (219–41). Visitors to such a space may have earnest and focused intent, and even maintain orderly habits, but they tend to be led astray by eccentric or peculiar things that do not conform to any notion of shared heritage.

I have recently traced the peregrinatory habits of James's protagonists, particularly when traversing home ground: to ramble rather than proceed with devotional purpose places the traveler in peril, but permissive, even reckless, curiosity may be the hallmark of the dedicated scholar (Brewster 2017). Pilgrimages to sites of antiquarian interest undertaken by James's continental tourists similarly digress, diverted from their path by unobtrusive, but ominous, "things" that catch the eye. To dwell, and to indulge such reflective pursuits is to set free the unquiet spirits and forces of other times and places; the oddities repatriated by the tourist never seem at home in their new surroundings. This chapter charts the pilgrimage to James's phantom museum, considering the spectral qualities of the artefacts these travelers pursue, peruse, and (sometimes) purloin, and how his cultural tourists succumb to the lure, or distracting fascination, of collecting peculiar objects and remote histories.

In examining the "museological dimension" (Punter 2008, 222) of these tales, I am drawing on Punter's response to the collection of Henry Solomon Wellcome, and the book that accompanied the exhibition of a selection of Wellcome's material at the British Library in 2003. A vast store of archaeological, anthropological, and medico-scientific objects, the Wellcome collection is a lumber room of the bizarre and exorbitant, testament to a compulsive accumulation of the exotic and macabre not entirely distinct from the acquisitive instincts of James's antiquarians and curious scholars. Punter's discussion offers a different approach to familiar territory, "namely, the complex relations between the phantom, the relic, the museum, the nature of collecting and that type of Gothic which we have come recently to know as 'imperial Gothic'" (Punter 2008, 222). He recounts the recurrent fantasy in many ghost stories "of the museum at night, of what is left when the crowds have gone home, of what strange life might animate the relic, the talking head, the stuffed crocodile" (Punter 2008, 230). This spectral life resists attempts at classification, since labels and histories are "always rotting down, becoming detached, undergoing mysterious changes—perhaps especially in the night, when the museum is closed. This is when the things settle back into their customary disorder, relax into their customary gaze of mutual incomprehension" (Punter 2008, 231). Such a state of affairs would surely be anathema to M. R. James, curator of the Fitzwilliam Museum at Cambridge, cataloguer of its manuscripts, and renowned scholar of Biblical apocrypha and church architecture. Yet James faced precisely the challenge of establishing provenance, of deciphering texts in varying states of preservation, of reading and hearing distant tongues and voices. His ghost stories rehearse the problems associated with origins, attribution, and preservation; despite the best efforts of the frame narrator or protagonists, there are many loose threads, textual or physical evidence is partial or inaccessible, and so much remains unsaid or irrecoverable. Recurrent difficulties of ordering and comprehension in James's tales are exacerbated by the departure from home ground and its carefully curated space, particularly when embarking on travel in Europe.

This speculative step into James's phantom museum, moving from exhibit to exhibit and from room to room, bears a certain spatial affinity to Punter's approach, which visits Europe in virtual fashion but journeys back and forth between London, continental Europe, and beyond, before settling back "home" in England. As such, it conjures an array of ghostly remains that at once asserts and displaces the certainties of assembling and labeling. Punter's imaginative tour of the Wellcome exhibition traces the restless traffic of the collection that lies behind the public display, a commerce in which objects, mementos, and rarities acquired through travel find their "final" resting place on distant ground. The museological legacy (artefacts and experiences which return with the traveler) compiled in James's tales, particularly those that venture to Europe, represents a disconcerting rather than pleasurable exchange.

Our first vicarious circuit of the phantom museum is "Canon Alberic's Scrapbook." James first visited St. Bertrand de Comminges, where the tale is set, in 1892, or perhaps as early as Spring 1887, and he returned again in 1899 and 1901. The Cathedral sits, invitingly, on the pilgrimage route to Santiago de Compostela. The story catalogues the cathedral's exhibits (just as James had done after his first visit) and this catalogue—an odd assortment, appropriately enough for our theme—includes an ivory crozier wrought from a narwhal's tusk, and a stuffed crocodile (a typical inhabitant of the phantom museum). The latter relic is a souvenir brought back by a crusader, forming another connection to pilgrimage. The protagonist Dennistoun is fully intent on filling a notebook on "the objects in the treasure chamber" (4) and photographing every corner of the cathedral (James had sketched the crocodile in 1892). With its "remnants of glass and tapestry" (4), dilapidated organ, and various pictures, the cathedral is museum and gallery as well as place of worship. This sacred space assumes the shadowy character of a phantom museum particularly toward dusk. Dennistoun, and the nervous sacristan, grow increasingly uneasy as the light fades, and the "curious noises" of "muffled footfalls and distant talking voices" become "more frequent and insistent" (5). These are "the strange noises that trouble a large empty building" (4), when visitors or worshippers depart.

This faintly unsettling soundscape cannot diminish Dennistoun's evident thrill at uncovering the scrapbook, the cursed possession of the sacristan. It is not housed in the cathedral, but is nonetheless the central exhibit of the phantom museum over which the sacristan presides. Dennistoun's desire to bring the priceless artefact back to Cambridge, and to empty his bank balance if need be, suggests he has caught the collecting fever that provoked the Canon's original ransacking of illuminated manuscripts in the Chapter library to compile his scrapbook. Such illicit passions recall Dennistoun's real-life namesake, James Dennistoun

(1803–55). As A. S. G. Edwards (2011) has pointed out, the breaking up and reconstituting of medieval manuscripts were prevalent in the nineteenth century, and Dennistoun compiled

> a famous nineteenth-century album or scrap book of medieval man-
> uscript fragments that survived largely intact until 1984 when, as
> part of the estate of the late Kenneth Clark, Lord Clark of Saltwood
> it was sold at Sotheby's and broken up.[1]
>
> (104)

Both the real-life and fictional Dennistoun resemble another nineteenth-century collector, the "Book-Ghoul" identified in Andrew Lang's *The Library* (1881):

> The Book-Ghoul is he who combines the larceny of the biblioklept
> with the abominable wickedness of breaking up and mutilating the
> volumes from which he steals. He is a collector of title-pages, frontis-
> pieces, illustrations, and book-plates...he broods, like the obscene de-
> mon of Arabian superstition, over the fragments of the mighty dead.
>
> (52)

This invader of the ideal library reduces cultural value to a question of consumption. In contrast, it might seem that James's scholars are custodians of treasures, sanctioned inhabitants of the library rather than dangerous interlopers, but the hungry acquisition of the Book Ghoul is both abhorred and endorsed in James's tales.

Penny Fielding (2000) has read Lang's "conjuring up of the neo-medieval private library" (759) in relation to James's protagonists. This private, contemplative space symbolizes "ahistorical universalism" (756) as a bulwark against rowdy social divisions, but even here the objects sought by James's antiquarians summon up monstrosities "in the very attempt to contain, process or understand them" (751). Canon Alberic and Dennistoun are Book Ghouls, opportunistic collectors. One compiles, while the other inherits, a collection that is not a collection, an assortment that cannot be rendered internally cohesive. The Canon's truly monstrous scrapbook is a bibliographical treasure trove, but it is also plunder, "curated" from other texts. Dennistoun plans to repeat this larceny, but in closing the deal for a nominal sum and securing the book, he releases a more "obscene demon" than even the Book Ghoul. As Fielding (2000) suggests, Dennistoun's coveting of the Canon's scrapbook is thus self-defeating:

> A scrap-book is a collection that brings together and integrates dis-
> parate items, yet, as its name reminds us, is also an assemblage of bits
> of texts: scraps. As a metonym for the private library, the scrap-book

reminds us that this institution also is heterogeneous and fragmentary and that its project of establishing a complete *collection* will always be thwarted by the dynamics of *collecting.*

(763)

Perhaps, however, the story hinges on the desire to linger over the individual case, rather than to yearn for accumulation or completion (and the Canon's compilation is not, of course, whole in any meaningful sense, since the scrapbook is bound together by a form of violence). Dennistoun's attention is drawn by an idiomatic "bit," one item in the book that proves impossible to integrate with the rest of the scraps, and which refuses to accede to any acquisitive, classificatory design. It is a sepia drawing of King Solomon confronting a beast-like figure, akin to "one of the awful bird-catching spiders of South America translated into human form" (9). The picture tells a tale of mastery, of commanding vision, of a fearless confrontation with the exorbitant and grotesque, but all subsequent viewers of this figure are daunted. The drawing disturbs, dismays the gaze. Supposedly showing the legendary accumulator of treasure taming demons, facing up to, and overcoming, a horrifying spectacle, the effect on its viewers is precisely to thwart or confound the desire to categorize and contain the object of scrutiny. Vision is not overwhelmed, exactly: it is stricken, transfixed, and no observer—not even a "lecturer on Morphology" (9)—can forget the first sight of the demon: "I entirely despair of conveying by any words the impression which this figure makes upon anyone who looks at it" (9). It is a curious exhibition of a curious exhibition, one that cannot be framed by interpretive text. Laughing in the church and harrying the sacristan, this gruesome exhibit has been waiting for Dennistoun, a living portrait that produces and participates in the museum experience. Fielding (2000) sees the demon as another Book Ghoul since combining and ordering precipitate "the breakdown of social signification" (763), but arguably the demon, a creature both trapped and then set free by the assembling of fragments, confounds and rejects the very principle of collecting. Its violence is about pure disintegration and destruction, rather than restitution—a challenge to the wisdom and authority represented by Solomon.

That evening, "shut up alone with his acquisition" (10), Dennistoun has a fortunate escape when the creature materializes at his side, then flees before it is able to harm its unwitting deliverer. Portable exhibition or archive, the scrapbook loses much of its site-specific power when relocated to the Wentworth collection (a thinly veiled version of the Fitzwilliam). Not only is future viewing restricted, its most precious, idiosyncratic exhibit is no longer on display, either in printed or embodied form. While a photograph of the demon remains in the possession of the narrator—who may be another avid collector, in spite of the apparent moral of Dennistoun's tale—the original drawing is destroyed.

We might note, too, that the manuscript fragments are not restored to their rightful places, or appropriately repatriated. By moving across the English Channel, the collection is subject to further dispersal or disordering. The Wentworth represents a form of secular cathedral, an exclusive repository, with areas of restricted or heavily mediated access like the private library situated, say, in a country house. Is its purpose to preserve and protect the treasures of the past for the public good, or to satisfy rather more private pleasures? The process of exchange, or acquisition, ushers the creature into the phantom museum and, far from ensuring its classification, enables it to escape its frame, or perhaps its case, into some unknown kingdom.

The unanticipated consequences of acts of relocation and appropriation—of circulating, and claiming, valuable artefacts—underpin such exchanges with mainland Europe in "The Treasure of Abbot Thomas." The story opens with an initially reluctant act of translation—which is also a transportation, a bearing from one place to another—by the antiquary Somerton, a reading that reveals a tale of secreted treasure, itself a transfer from one place to another. Somerton's "pilgrimage" (96) to decipher the puzzle of the glass eventually unlocks the code that reveals the resting place of the hidden treasure. The glass is an enigmatic exhibit; the figures, each occupying a light in the window, are apparently randomly assembled with no historic, symbolic, or doctrinal "bond of connection" (96), and the writings associated with them differ from any "text of the Vulgate" (95) known to Somerton. Typically of James, the small deviation absorbs and intrigues. Damage from a rough broom discloses the first clue to cracking the Abbot's code; a failure of curation, a mishandling of a precious artefact but one that enables illumination. Somerton completes the process by removing all the black pigment that surrounds the mantles of the figures. Given this eager act of desecration, it is hardly surprising that when he arrives in Steinfeld in Germany to locate the treasure, Somerton is obliged to simulate interest in the Church in order to avoid raising suspicions. He is obsessed by the process of exchange and substitution that drives but also imperils the collector, and does not apprehend the very strangeness of the object that comes within his reach.

An apparent indifference to provenance, and to looking further afield, is threaded throughout the story. The painted glass that piques Somerton's curiosity was taken from the Abbey Church of Steinfeld to England, and moved from its original setting to adorn a "private chapel" (95) in England, a setting based on Ashridge, Hertfordshire, another site catalogued by James. As Darryl Jones notes, it is evident from James's *Notes of Glass in Ashridge Chapel* that he had never been to Steinfeld himself (James 2011, 437). The narrator shares the "grave disadvantage" of not having visited the site, but is content to dismiss it as unprepossessing, a place that offers "little, if anything, of first-rate interest to be seen" (98).

This decided lack of curiosity, or reluctance to retrace Somerton's steps, is striking, given how easily the rector Mr. Gregory, from his quiet Berkshire parsonage, can travel to Steinfeld via Antwerp and Coblentz. Perhaps the narrative hesitation can be explained by the fact that the antiquary's "short journey abroad" quickly turns sour. His valet Brown writes in "an uneducated but plainly an English hand" to Gregory for assistance, declaring that "it will be a Pleasure to see a Honnest Brish Face among all These Forig ones" (97), a residual suspicion emerging at a moment of vulnerability and displacement. The story, then, is one of disconnection, of failure to embrace the possibilities of translation and the opening it provides to other times and places. In this tale, the aversion to sharing operates on both sides of the Channel. Revealingly, on the well that conceals the Abbot's treasure, Gregory finds a label that reads "Depositum custodi" or "Keep that which is committed to thee" (110). Somerton has tried to steal from a private hoard, one that refuses to allow acquisition; assembled through plunder, this concealed collection at once teases and thwarts the ardent collector.

"'Oh, Whistle, and I'll Come to You, My Lad'" also revolves around an object that has undergone multiple acts of translation and importation. In the ruins of a Templar preceptory (which comes to function as a form of phantom museum), Parkins unearths a whistle whose origin, and relation to the east coast of England, remain unknown. As the Templars' influence was spread throughout the continent, including England, this instrument could have been brought to Burnstow from another part of Europe, but since the order was founded to protect pilgrimages to the Holy Land, then it may have been accidentally uncovered, bought or pillaged in a still more distant place. Although the inscriptions on the whistle are in Latin, a common point of reference for Christian religious orders and antiquarians, they are both difficult to decipher. "FUR FLA FLE BIS" can be rendered as "Fur Flabis Flebis," meaning "Thief, you will blow, you will weep;" "Furbis Flabis Flebis" translates as "You will blow, you will weep, you will go mad." The second marking, "QUIS EST ISTE QUI U/VENIT" ("Who is this who is coming?") appears more straightforward, but its purpose is ambiguous. Parkins's subsequent experience suggests the phrase is performative rather than denotative, serving as a warning to the one who has ill-advisedly tested the whistle while at the same time summoning the object's familiar. To sound out the enigma of the whistle, as Parkins discovers to his cost, is to open a strange commerce with other realms. As he blows the whistle, the noise it emits has "a quality of infinite distance in it and, soft as it was, he somehow felt it must be audible for miles around" (83). The redoubtable Colonel who later comes to the rescue remarks of the intemperate breeze excited by Parkins: "'In my old home we should have said that someone had been whistling for it'" (86). Although Parkins dismisses this "superstition" common amongst country-folk, he acknowledges that the whistle is a "rather a curious one" (87). Whatever his limitations, including his iras-cibility on the golf course, the well-traveled Colonel proves himself more alert to outside influences—indeed, perhaps, more cosmopolitan—than the Professor of Ontography, observing that the belief about a supernatu-ral wind is held in many countries: "'They believe in it all over Denmark and Norway, as well as on the Yorkshire coast'" (86). We will return to these connections across the North Sea later.

"Mr Humphreys and his Inheritance" is another exercise in transla-tion and curation. Humphreys takes unexpected possession of Wilst-horpe, a house that is a museum or shrine dedicated to European travel, although his uncle, its most recent inhabitant, appears to have been keen to conceal this continental legacy. The maze that Humphreys inherits was laid out by his uncle's grandfather, "old Mr Wilson," a "man of peculiar tenets" and "a great traveller" (206) according to the bailiff Cooper. A motto over the entrance reads "Secretum meum mihi et fi-liis domus meae" ("my secret is for me and the sons of my house"). The celestial globe at the center of the maze has occult decoration, and depicts an "assemblage of the patriarchs of evil, perhaps not un-influenced by a study of Dante." It seems "an unusual exhibition of his great-grandfather's taste" (213), but Humphreys suspects it had been acquired in Italy, prompted in part by a portrait of old Wilson, with the Colosseum in background, holding a roll of paper on which a labyrinth is discernible. A "Temple of Friendship" (203), constructed of Italian marble and based on the Sibyl's Temple at Tivoli, stands on a prominent mound in the garden. (The well in "The Treasure of Abbot Thomas" is constructed of Italian marble, with an Italian carving.) Like the portrait, the temple has about it "a pleasant flavour of the grand tour" (203). It contains what transpires to be marker stones for the maze, one of which bears the inscription "PENETRANS AD INTERIORA MORTIS," or "Penetrating to the inner places of death" (220). The globe feels hot to Cooper's touch, but not Humphreys's, implying that he has inherited his ancestor's temperament.

Humphreys dates the construction of Wilsthorpe to "1770 or there-abouts" (202), the very year, by coincidence, that William Beckford inher-ited Fonthill Splendens from his father. An avid traveler, like Mr. Wilson, and one drawn to the allure of the Grand Tour, Beckford wrote, then immediately suppressed, an idiosyncratic account of his travels in Italy, *Dreams, Waking Thoughts and Incidents* (1783), and later went into self-imposed exile in continental Europe as a result of the scandal sur-rounding his relationship with William Courtney. To strengthen this circuitous association, Wilson's will contained "a generous legacy to a servant who bore an Italian name" (220). Yet this peregrination may lead us astray. Tempting as it is to see James's tale as a cryptic acknowledgment of a "friendship" that dared not speak its name, all forays into the heart of this mysterious chapter of family history are thwarted, or prove perilous.

The private library at Wilsthorpe, which Humphreys aspires to catalogue, is the counterpart of the maze, inviting but frustrating attempts
to uncover its hidden pattern. He laments "the extreme unreadableness
of a great portion of the collection" (208), and its strangest holding has a
"blank and forbidding" exterior (208). This "mutilated" collection of ser-
mons and meditations, stuffed into a small quarto, piques Humphreys's
curiosity. Here we have another scrapbook, the deposit or bequest of a
previous Book Ghoul in the family. His eye falls on a marginal note, "A
Parable of this Unhappy Condition," which tells of an adventurer who
enters a gated labyrinth to reclaim a priceless jewel at its heart, only to
be menaced by shadowy pursuers on his return, a nightmare experience
that never leaves his mind. Although its purpose is ostensibly didactic,
warning against the quest for worldly treasure, the Parable immerses
and disorientates the reader, or visitor, in this ill-omened realm. As if
replaying the hide-and-seek logic of the maze, the book that harbors
this Parable of the labyrinth is never found again (198), one more lost
thread that could be used to lay out a trail. Humphreys makes several
abortive attempts to map the maze before he completes the task, and has
a perpetual sense of being observed when walking its overgrown paths.
These cartographical endeavors seem to open a portal whereby the heart
of the maze, and its "foreign" flavor, can reach out to Humphreys. In the
library, while surveying his plan of the maze, he has a nightmarish vision
of a "*burnt* human face" emerging from the paper, and of "waving black
arms" attempting to clutch his head (219). This impels Humphreys to
have the globe opened, revealing ashes—"a case of cremation" (220), it
is assumed—and subsequently to have the maze removed. To navigate
Wilsthorpe, to plot a route to its obscure past, is necessarily to digress
down alternative paths often hidden in plain sight.

James's other beloved European destination was Scandinavia. He
traveled in 1899 to Denmark, the southern tip of Sweden and then back
via Lübeck, Hamburg, and Bremen with James McBryde and Will Stone.
In *Eton and Kings* James remarks of his Northern tour with McBryde
that "[p]erhaps...the expeditions I made in his company to Denmark
and Sweden...were the most blissful of all that I ever had" (219). As with
his wartime memories of France, however, this blissful journey was soon
marked by loss and regret. Stone died of pneumonia in 1901, shortly
before McBryde produced his picture story *The Story of a Troll Hunt*, a
tale of three travelers to Scandinavia, their suitcases labeled MRJ, WJS,
and JMcB, who embark on a search for a troll. McBryde himself died
in 1904, a devastating blow for James. Northern Europe, and its oth-
erworldly traditions, nonetheless remained a source of fascination for
James; he arranged for the posthumous publication of McBryde's book,
and published a translation of Hans Christian Andersen tales in 1930.

His two ghost stories set in Scandinavia bear a number of traces of
his journeys north, both real and imaginative. "Number 13" is located

in Viborg, in Jutland, which James visited with McBryde and Stone in
1900, and its protagonist Mr. Anderson alludes unmistakably to Hans
Christian Andersen, who in James's words presented Denmark as "a
land of romance" (James 1926, 144). Stone may have suggested the idea
for the tale, but by the time James is thought to have performed the
story at Christmas in 1903, his friend was already dead. In its fleeting
allusions to trolls, the tale captures that element of romance, but there
are also ghostly legacies and phantom exhibits. James described Danish
people as "very un-foreign on the whole" (Cox 1987, 307n), and the
country's blend of peculiarity and homeliness had a lasting attraction,
as the canceled opening in the manuscript of "Number 13" indicates:

> Too few Englishmen travel in Jutland. Too few that is if we are tak-
> ing the unselfish view that the pleasantest parts of the world ought
> to be visited by the largest possible number of people: not one too
> few, on the other hand [.] if we are expressing what are most likely
> our genuine feelings that there ought to be certain parts of this earth
> kept sacred from the mass of tourists. Still I am not really appre-
> hensive that Jutland will ever become a crowded tourist resort. Its
> beauties are of a tranquil, a tame, a melancholy kind. Its literature
> is luckily not popularized by translations, and its sights in the way
> of [ ], galleries and museums are few. I am therefore the less afraid
> that I shall do it the disservice of bringing the curse of trippers and
> hotel coupons upon it by singing its praises. Perhaps the story that I
> am to tell may even have the opposite effect.
>
> (Cox 1987, 306n)

Jutland is attractive in its remoteness, its silence, and its resistance to
cultural translation. What treasures Jutland quietly displays seem peculiarly suited to the solitary, contemplative gaze and, as Anderson's experience in the story attests, those artefacts can ward off or even menace
the traveler, thereby preserving the exclusivity of the region.

"Number 13" is related to the frame narrator by Anderson in Up-
psala, where the pair had been amused by the contract, signed in blood
when he sold his soul to the devil, of Daniel Salthenius, who later became Professor of Divinity at Konigsberg. James had seen this contract
himself in 1901 (Cox 1987, 309n). Anderson is on the trail of arcana;
namely, papers on Viborg "relating to the last days of Roman Catholicism in the country" (48). His research discloses a dispute involving a
"blood-sucking *Troldmand* (troll man or sorcerer)," Nicholas Francken,
perceived by Protestant antagonists to be under the patronage of Bishop
Friis, the last Catholic to hold the see. Francken inhabited a house owned
by the Bishop, one whose location cannot later be found on the list of
town property. As Michael Newton also discusses elsewhere in this book,
this sinister, mysterious figure fleetingly becomes Anderson's spectral and

threatening neighbor in the Golden Lion Hotel, which we surmise was Francken's original abode; he inhabits room 13, which is not visible in the daytime, only late in the evening, when Anderson retires. At night, Anderson's room rearranges itself, growing smaller, a phantom space in keeping with the adjoining room 13. He initially regards this as a "very interesting experience" (54) for the casual tourist; his landlord indicates that his typical guests, commercial travelers, will not stay in a room 13 (55), and it seems to take a different type of visitor, one who notices and is not deterred by obscure things, to glimpse the door number. Perhaps appropriately, Anderson can only persuade the landlord to investigate the strange occurrence by inviting him to view photos of English towns in his room, turning his possessions into a form of exhibition (56). No physical trace of Francken is recovered; there is nothing but an indecipherable vellum parchment in a copper box, which ends up in the real museum in Viborg. Nothing is brought back in the tale, and this visit to the phantom museum produces only the mutual incomprehension suggested by Punter.

In "Count Magnus," critics have largely overlooked the close parallel between Mr. Wraxall, the story's doomed protagonist, and another English traveler who undertakes a Scandinavian tour. David Punter (2017) has recently linked the surname of James's protagonist to the owners of Tyntesfield, a Gothic Revival house in North Somerset; its last owner, the second Baron Wraxall, was a lifelong bachelor who died "leaving an impossible will" (Punter 2017, 185). Yet a more direct connection can surely be traced to Sir Nathaniel Wraxall, the travel writer, memoirist, baronet, and MP whose *Cursory Remarks Made in a Tour Through Some of the Northern Parts of Europe* ([1775] 1776) quickly went through four editions. In his selection of James's stories, Michael Cox (1987) notes the connection between Wraxall and James's character, but mentions only his *Historical Memoirs* (1815) and its account of Francis Dashwood's Hell-Fire Club at Medmenham, upstream from Eton (309n); there is no reference to *Cursory Remarks*. Nathaniel Wraxall's Scandinavian and Russian itinerary was unusual and intriguing in its time, just as it is for Mr. Wraxall in James's tale. The latter's expedition to Scandinavia takes him to "a region not widely known to Englishmen forty years ago" (64); it shares a sense of isolation with James's melancholy, neglected Jutland. To underscore the geographical associations, Wraxall's papers, in which his final days are recorded, are "a series of collections for a book of travels" whose character can be compared to "Horace Marryat's *Journal of a Residence in Jutland and the Danish Isles*" (63).

The narrator of "Count Magnus" declares Mr. Wraxall's style of travel narrative "chatty" (63); true to this portrait, on one occasion our unwise tourist tries, with only partial success, to elicit local lore about Magnus, a form of enquiry so different in character to his scholarly study of historical documents. Similarly "chatty," Nathaniel Wraxall has a penchant for diplomatic gossip, social, and romantic intrigue, and he takes an Enlightenment view of the barbarous underdevelopment of some parts of Northern Europe, but his travelogue also reveals a faintly gothicized sensibility, just over a decade after the publication of Walpole's *The Castle of Otranto*. Macabre curiosities and exhibits, such as the embalmed bodies in Danzig Cathedral, or the tomb of Margaret de Waldemar (an uncanny echo of Edgar Allan Poe's living corpse) in Malmö, catch his eye. There are also visits to claustrophobic spaces of confinement, and an experience of the sublime in an iron ore mine at Danmora: "I felt a pleasure connected with terror as I hung over this vast and giddy hollow to the bottom of which the eye attempts in vain to penetrate" (Wraxall 1776, 148). Nathaniel Wraxall is a traveler keen to experience the phantom museum of Northern Europe, just like James's unwary scholar, but he lives to tell the tale of its strange exhibitions.

"Count Magnus" also retraces the footsteps of other journeys. The story is set in Råbäck, which James visited with McBryde in 1901; Mr. Wraxall passes through Trollhatten in southern Sweden on his way back to England, its etymology as "Trolls' Hoods" alluding to Magnus's hooded familiar and suggesting a darker version of McBryde's fairy tale. His research visit to Råbäck involves a daily walk of around a mile between the manor house where he examines family papers, and the village inn, during which he passes the mausoleum of Count Magnus de la Gardie. Magnus is a savage, pre-Enlightenment figure, a reminder of the darker north that, in their differing ways, Nathaniel Wraxall and McBryde evoke. The church that houses the tomb is "a curious building to English eyes," its ceiling adorned with a "strange and hideous 'Last Judgement'" (65). Its most intriguing exhibition space, the mausoleum itself, can only be glimpsed through the keyhole on Wraxall's first visit. Granted access by the deacon, Wraxall is enthralled by the Count's sarcophagus, ornamented with images of warfare and an ominous hunting scene that recalls the desperate flight through the labyrinth in "Mr Humphreys and his Inheritance." Conveniently, he also notices a key that will allow him to enjoy out-of-hours admission to the vault. Diverted from his customary course later in the evening, in a state between waking and dreaming, Wraxall cannot resist visiting this phantom museum at night. Yet this private communion with the exhibits proves fateful, since they are not at rest: padlocks are loosened, and Wraxall is harried back to England, and a violent death, by Count Magnus and his shadowy counterpart. The frame narrator purchases the house where Wraxall died, and the story comes to light when his papers are found "in a forgotten cupboard under the window in the best bedroom" (75). The papers are neglected heirlooms, relegated to storage, but when returned to the light they offer a fugitive glimpse of the past, of concealed or occult knowledge. They are, in short, more perplexing but intriguing items in James's phantom museum, there to entice, as well as caution, inquisitive scholars.

It cannot be argued, of course, that the phantom museum is a property solely of James's ghost tales that visit Europe, but these stories
reflect acutely on the benefits and obligations, unseen influences, and
unacknowledged compulsions underlying the scholarly pilgrimages of
his protagonists. Exchange with Europe draws on a shared archive, but
it is an archive that necessarily houses incongruous, misplaced, and singular exhibits that trouble any collection. Although James's scholars
often founder in the face of the different, it is also this difference that
proves irresistible. At a time when Britain is contemplating the advan-
tages and costs of being an island nation, it is perhaps instructive that
the quintessentially English James is so willing (at times) to sojourn in
haunted Europe, and contemplate the attractions that its phantom mu-
seums place on display.

Note

1 There are further strange affinities to be traced here, if one had time to
  dwell; Clark's first book, published in 1928, was *The Gothic Revival*, and
  he was appointed Director of the Ashmolean Museum in 1931, recalling
  James's period as Director of the Fitzwilliam from 1893 to 1908.

References

Brewster, Scott. 2017. "Ghost Walking." In *The Routledge Handbook to the
  Ghost Story*, edited by Scott Brewster and Luke Thurston, 312–18. New York
  and London: Routledge.
Cox, Michael, ed. 1987. *M. R. James: "Casting the Runes" and Other Ghost
  Stories*. Oxford: Oxford University Press.
Edwards, A. S. G. 2011. "M. R. James, 'Canon Alberic's Scrapbook,' and
  'Dennistoun'." *Notes and Queries* 58, no. 1 (March): 104–5.
Fielding, Penny. 2000. "Reading Rooms: M.R. James and the Library of
  Modernity." *Modern Fiction Studies* 46, no. 3 (Fall): 749–71.
James, M. R. 2011. *Collected Ghost Stories*. Edited by Darryl Jones. Oxford:
  Oxford University Press.
James, M. R. 1926. *Eton and Kings: Recollections, Mostly Trivial 1875–1925*.
  London: Williams and Northgate.
James, M. R. 1924. "Introduction." In *Ghosts and Marvels: A Selection of
  Uncanny Tales*, edited by V. H. Collins, v–xvi. Oxford: Oxford University Press.
Lang, Andrew. 1881. *The Library*. London: Macmillan.
Pfaff, Richard William. 1980. *Montague Rhodes James*. London: Scolar Press.
Punter, David. 2017. "The English Ghost Story." In *The Routledge Handbook
  to the Ghost Story*, edited by Scott Brewster and Luke Thurston, 179–87.
  New York and London: Routledge.
Punter, David. 2008. "A Voyage through the Phantom Museum." In *Le Gothic:
  Influences and Appropriations in Europe and America*, edited by Avril
  Horner and Sue Zlosnik, 219–41. Basingstoke: Palgrave Macmillan.
Wraxall, Sir Nathaniel. [1775] 1776. *Cursory Remarks Made in a Tour through
  Some of the Northern Parts of Europe*. London: Cadell.

6   Haunted Hotels and Murder Inns

Travelers' Tales from Europe and the Gothic Short Story from the 1820s to the 1940s

Michael Newton

In gothic fictions from the Victorian period to the mid-twentieth century, it is as travelers and sojourners that most British, Irish, and Americans experience continental Europe. Consequently, hotels and inns are central to those travels and those tales. In this essay, I shall consider how when it came to the gothic imagining of the continent, these transient lodgings act as sites of disturbance or terror, places that frame a strange doubling. Taking key texts by Charles Dickens, Wilkie Collins, Amelia B. Edwards, Sheridan Le Fanu, M. R. James, and Karen Blixen as my examples, I shall explore one of the ways in which gothic short stories and tales have manifested the anxiety induced by temporarily living alongside strangers, and thereby consequently charted our relationship to our permanent neighbors in continental Europe. This essay responds to a set of coincidences—coincidences in fact about co-incidence, related to European travel, the hotel, and the unwanted guest in the room—whether that unbidden guest is a ghost or a writer.

The hotel as understood in these tales becomes one of the ways in which Gothic frames property relations. The entrance to the inn or the hotel operates as the threshold to the street, ushering you in to a domestic space that's simultaneously a public space. The hotel is, of course, a temporary living circumstance, designed by its very brevity not to be a lasting part of life. For a night or two we call it "home," but the lease is too short to make much of an impression on us. It is, in the sociologist Zygmunt Bauman's (2000) terms, a residential epitome of "liquid modernity," and emblematic of an experience of modern society formed loosely in the temporary, the isolated, and the immersion in the fluid "now." The traveler's residence in a hotel expresses just how far they are disconnected from the place they are in. There are no friends to visit, no family with whom to stay, or if there are, the traveler nonetheless prefers the semi-detached independence that a hotel provides. There they enjoy the status of the stranger, and any acquaintances they strike up, any holiday romance they chance upon will prove to be passing. These stories of haunted hotels are tales of a space unwittingly shared—our self-possession disturbed by the other bed in the room, the other unaccounted-for lodger. The hotel offers a parody of home, combining in one space a functional domesticity with anonymity. It gives us a world without kinship, where the only relations are hierarchical, monetary, or accidental. The fact that the hotel is given over to the casual is one way in which it figures as an erotic space, inextricably linked with the dirty weekend and the affair.

Lodgers, new occupants in the district, travelers, and hotel guests—all make the ideal haunted, for their newness or their ephemerality opens them to an encounter with a ghost or spirit that persists, the true long-term resident of the place. The short story and the novella are ideal literary sites to explore this temporary occupation. As John Bowen (2006) has remarked, short fiction is already in itself "disjunctive, inconclusive and oblique" (37), and just right therefore for a story confined to the parameters of a hotel visit. Wilkie Collins imagined the short story as bound up with gothic sensation and detection. Within its brevity, we find characters who are trapped or confined, and "so, too, their narration is a form of constraint, a controlled space within which the persistent, unaccountable strangeness of their witnessing can appear" (Bowen 2006, 40–41).

Such stories as these are travelers' tales, yet seem often preoccupied with the question as to whether or not they are stories at all. In their encounter with a European elsewhere, the very possibility that such an experience can be contained within the conventions of narrative breaks down. The narrator in Amelia B. Edwards's "A Night on the Borders of the Black Forest" (1874) begins: "My story (if story it can be called, being an episode in my own early life)" (9); here the anecdotal, even the autobiographical origin of the event somehow precludes its gaining the honorary title of "story." This questioning of the possibilities of storytelling to order the world becomes entangled within the British response to the continental – itself imagined at last as a site of stories.

The Hostile Hostel and the Killer inside the Inn

One dark locale to be found in the subgenre of the uncanny hotel is the murder inn. There is a strand of stories in which the protagonists enter as a guest a space controlled by strangers—whether an inn, a hotel, a lodging house, or merely a room for the night—and find out (too late) that the proffered hospitality is homicidal. Above all, the new guest discovers that hospitality has always been murderous there: the protagonist is simply the latest in a sequence of victims. The telos of such a story is finding a way to escape from the snare, the hero rescuing themselves from their plight among malevolent strangers.

When it comes to gothic literature, peril begins once you have crossed the English Channel. The trope is there, most famously in Wilkie Collins's tale of Parisian gambling, "A Terribly Strange Bed" ([1852] 1875), in the farmhouse-inn of Amelia B. Edwards's story, "A Night on the Borders of the Black Forest" ([1874] 1890) and in Sheridan Le Fanu's

"The Room in the Dragon Volant" ([1872] 1993). Such tales persist—most obviously in Eli Roth's Slovakian-set *Hostel* films (2005 and 2007). Here abroad as such is dangerous, and to place yourself in the care of foreigners proves a foolhardy action. The passing possession of a room may become permanent, when the corpse, the ghost, is confined to the hotel, the inn, forever.

"A Terribly Strange Bed" stands as a classic early example of such paranoid examinations of the perils of European travel. Originally published in April 1852, this was Collins's first tale for Charles Dickens's *Household Words*. It is a story that occurs "on foreign ground" (8), in the streets of Paris. Collins had visited France and Italy from 1836 to 1838 (when he was twelve to fourteen) and returned to Paris in 1844. In a prologue written some years after the original publication, Collins presents the far-fetched events as a true story with "all the excitement of the most exciting romance" (28). Collins gives us a tale of "the corroding passion for play" experienced by the gambler (30); as in Pushkin's "The Queen of Spades," the ferocity of the gambler's passion becomes somehow sinister, an example of being given over to a state of mind that takes possession of the rational self. This strange state of intoxication, this gambling fever, will find its parallel later in the mysterious psychological passivity, the "trance" that has the protagonist submissively awaiting his death.

Collins's Parisian gambling den doubles as a lodging house. The hero ascends to a bedroom weirdly presented as a void space; in the absence of visual stimuli, he tries to read it in the spirit of Xavier de Maistre's room-bound fantasy travel book, *Voyage autour de ma chambre* (1794). But there is nothing to read, except the painting of a Spanish ruffian. The room appears unfamiliar and sinister, but also uncannily reminiscent: "The moonlight shining into the room reminded me of a certain moonlight night in England—the night after a picnic party in a Welsh valley" (36). As he lies in bed, the canopy descending so as to suffocate him, he finds himself instead in a Europe that signals a history of iniquity and violence:

> Amidst a dead and awful silence I beheld before me—in the nineteenth century, and in the civilised capital of France—such a machine for secret murder by suffocation as might have existed in the worst days of the Iniquisition, in the lonely inns among the Hartz Mountains, in the mysterious tribunals of Westphalia!
>
> (38)

The story confines its hero to a space, locked up with the ongoing evidence of long-standing European horrors. As later happens in Collins's *The Haunted Hotel* ([1878] 1975), the would-be victim's experiences precisely turn into a story, a commodity of a tale, and is dramatized by three "illustrious play-makers" (42), though the censorship keeps these plays from being performed.

Amelia B. Edwards's story likewise provides a classic example of the conventions of such tales. The "old legendary Schwarzwald" in Edwards's story is dwindling yearly, a space of enchanted stories that seems to be perishing under nineteenth-century progress. In fact, the brutal possibilities of the old tales are just as much alive here as ever.

The murder inn motif depends upon a sense of the vulnerability of sleep. The hotel stands as that place where privacy occurs among the presence of others, surrounding it, perhaps invading it. Claustrophobia frames these tales, bound as they are by the fear of being locked in, of being confined to the width of a room within the vastness of modern Europe. Concepts of perverted hospitality linger in such tales too, the barbaric violence of the Cyclops is there, the giving and sharing of food and drink and shelter turned transgressively into a murderous attack.

Sheridan Le Fanu's "The Room in the Dragon Volant" shows us another threatening lodging, and its out-of-Paris hotel room offers a route into the even starker confinement of premature burial. Le Fanu gives us a story of "English excursionists" (120) improving their minds by foreign travel to a newly unlocked continent, where the British may roam again following the fall of Napoleon. The central character, plain Richard Beckett, is fluent in French, and also happens to be a vain and conceited youth; before going out to meet the woman he loves, in his looking-glass he checks out how well he looks in the moonlight (192). He addresses his lover in the "bombast" of French lovemaking (224) and is given to remark upon the "rose-coloured light, *coleur de rose*, emblem of sanguine hope" (219). However, the romance into which he has been conscripted is in fact of altogether a darker fabric. As so often in gothic stories about the continent, the tale turns on an infatuation with a European woman, in this case the elusive bride, the Countess de St. Alyre. She first appears to him in a mirror, so still as to seem a portrait, or even a "tinted statue" (122). Death and love intertwine, and assignations designed to further an affair may turn out to seal the protagonist into a living grave. As W. J. McCormack (1980) argued, the death that the British traveler almost finds here is one that answers to his own masochistic quest for self-destruction (189).

In this tale, the continent acts as the home-territory for coney-catchers and confidence-tricksters, those skilled in cheating at "play," taking the arts of deception to a level of skill way beyond "our London rogues" (136). The deceptive Countess is something of a "tragedy-queen" and a deceiver (241). The conspirators lure Beckett away from Paris to the "antique and sequestered" (165) out-of-town inn, "Le Dragon Volant." The place has a reputation as a house where foreigners vanish, those who stay in one corner room especially being apt to be lost forever. Le Fanu raises the possible of "revenants" in his tale, only to replace those specters with the image of men "who have *never* returned" (168), about whom there was "nothing supernatural; but a great deal inexplicable" (186).

Yet an atmosphere of the supernatural nonetheless lingers around the tale. An old lady who warns our hero of the danger he is in appears to be "the *genius loci*, the malignant fairy" of a fairy tale written by "the delightful Countess d'Aulnois" (212). Not quite a fairyland, mainland Europe nonetheless seems a place of mystery and possibility to this romantic traveler. The "spirit of romance" (216) guides our hero, leading him to plan that he and the Countess should fly to "one of the most beautiful and sequestered nooks in Switzerland" (216). Indeed the notion of the "sequestered" frames the tale, with its out of the way inn, its corpse of a magician concealed in public inside a tent, its hopes of flight to a land-locked and hidden country, and, finally, its fears of being nailed in and buried alive in the confined space of a coffin. Our traveler escapes but, like the hero of "A Terribly Strange Bed," only to figure as a public figure of ridicule, reduced to the butt of a joke and a text, "figured even in caricatures" (240), his private and once so secret story turning him into a storied person, "a public character." In these stories, the great fate of these almost-victims is to become people contained in stories, pinned down to the small fame of narrative.

The Other Lodger

As we have seen, there is little explicitly supernatural in these tales of the "murder inn." However, one other form of gothic short story, those of the haunted hotel, wished to render the impermanent space of the continental hotel as a ghostly one, a zone to encounter strange spirits of place. The first such stories are crude in their effect, compared to later examples, though nonetheless interesting for all their robust coarseness. Washington Irving's "The Bold Dragoon" ([1824] 1987) is just such a vulgar trifle, its Irish narrator serving up the haunted hotel story as Shandyean farce, a "rigmarole Irish romance" (31) with a "burlesque tendency" (32). The Holland that the Dragoon travels through is "queer, old-fashioned," the buildings themselves "queer" (26). Without any Dutch, he communicates without language, making risqué jokes about "laying" the ghost, while romping (as was traditional with the randy lodgers of boarding-house tales) with the landlord's daughter (28). The inn he stays in is haunted, but without resonance or any trace of the uncanny, the spirits rather boisterously possessing the material furniture of a room.

The story of "The Bride's Chamber" in Charles Dickens's portion of *The Lazy Tour of Two Idle Apprentices* ([1857] 1896) is a darker and more threatening haunting, though the old inn where the ghost lingers is a north country English one, and not the home to a continental spirit. Following a visit by Francis Goodchild (Dickens's alter-ego) to an asylum, we are left with an image from there of the human being rendered asocial, confined. The ghost too finds himself cramped within one house forever, stuck within the constraints of his first-person story. The ghost tells the tale himself, and therefore delivers a vivid first-person account of what it feels like to be hanged before recounting his reminiscences of guilty deeds done in his past. (Drawing on ancestral memories of public corpses, the centrality of the figure of the public hanged to the ghost story is as potent as that of the beheaded to Gothic.)

Writers on Dickens such as Harry Stone (1994), Rosemary Bodenheimer (2007), and Michael Slater (2009) have seen the figure of the ghost doomed forever to tell the tale of how he had murdered his wife as a stand-in for the novelist himself, troubled by his infidelity and the coming end of his marriage to Catherine Dickens. In this sense, the ghostly stranger encountered in the random environment of a hotel acts as a double to the guest, the bearer of private and semi-concealed anxieties. This doubling will turn out to be central to the haunted hotel theme, its energies busy with imagining a shadow other, one that—in the majority of such stories—is also a continental other, a mainland mirror to a British self.In these subtler versions of the haunted lodgings story, we find not a murder inn, gruesome and horrific, but rather a disturbed hotel, where the room—your space, given over for these nights to you—turns out not only to be your own. Other rooms encroach on yours and what you possess grows uncertain. You may stumble into and grasp hold of another person's story. For these more sophisticated tales are particularly interested in the sharing of stories—and how the story itself becomes a way of claiming a territory—and letting others share those claims with us. Both the story and the absence of the ability to form a story are what we share—perhaps also what makes the imaginative territory of Europe.

Again imagining the European place as eerily pre-possessed, Wilkie Collins's *The Haunted Hotel*, serialized in *Belgravia* from June to November 1878, stands as a classic of the genre. A kind of sickness about things pervades this tale, a bafflement at life's perversities and cruelty; its heroine, Agnes Lockwood reflects, "'How much happier we should be...if we never grew up!'" (18). In this tale of Britons abroad in Venice, the "'hotel is under a curse'," as "'crimes carry their own curse with them'" (119). Here, Collins unites the detective mystery and the ghost story in his account of Lord Montbarry, who rejects his home-spun sweetheart Agnes in order to marry the strange and suspect Countess Narona. With the courier, Ferrari, and the Countess's disreputable brother, the Baron Rivar, and a lady's maid, the newly-weds honeymoon in an old palazzo in Venice. There, in mysterious circumstances Ferrari vanishes, and the English Lord appears to die of a chest infection, leaving his vast fortune to the Countess—and her brother. The palazzo becomes a hotel, invested in by Lord Montbarry's younger brother, Henry Sedgwick. Henry loves Agnes, and hopes to make her his bride. The Sedgwick family and Agnes visit the Venetian hotel, and are haunted there by the apparition of the dead lord's severed head. Eventually, a body is found, the Countess dies, perhaps having confessed her misdeeds in a play she is writing for her brother-in-law, Francis Sedgwick, and Henry and Agnes marry.

At the novella's end, the Westwicks quit Italy and honeymoon prudently by the Thames. The home counties ambience by then appears far preferable to "the hidden and sinister life in the palace at Venice" (46). The courier, Ferrari's temper is improved by the prospect of going abroad, an enthusiasm that will come to appear a black mark against him (22). English servants, however, tend to disapprove of continental doings: the lady's maid "disliked the Continent, and wished to get back to her own country. This is not an uncommon result of taking English servants to foreign parts" (36). The continent casts a shade of suspiciousness over a person; the physician in Venice comes "with the additional recommendation of having resided in England, and having made himself acquainted with English forms of medical practice" (38). Good old English decencies seem impertinence to European eyes. The Countess Narona takes Mrs Ferrari's exercise of her righteous indignation to be "insolence": "The ignorant English mind (I have observed) is apt to be insolent in the exercise of unrestrained English liberty. This is very noticeable to us foreigners among you people in the streets" (44). On the other hand, European complexity looks potently suspicious to plain English sight. When she is tracked down, the Countess's English lady's maid turns out to be a woman who is all but a man (57)—a gruff, sexless individual, whom Ferrari nonetheless (in his Italian way) has attempted to sexualize and seduce. This masculine maid considers the Baron and Ferrari to be "birds of a feather," as corrupt as each other. Through her prudish British eyes, she in her turn suspects the probity of the relationship between the Baron and the Countess (though they may be, perhaps, genuinely merely brother and sister).

Despite this inner enmity, the hotel, this Venetian property, stands in strong relation to the English-speaking world. The Palace Hotel Company is after all a good speculation for English servants (53–54), and the hotel itself is designed to appeal "mainly to English and American travellers" (69). The Countess herself embodies a curious amalgam of Britain and the continent, a medley of identities expressed for instance in her penchant for drinking maraschino and tea—a concoction, we are told, that derives from the English Queen Caroline's time on the continent; the Countess's mother shared her English mistress' tastes—"And I, in my turn, learnt from my mother" (80). On her return to Venice, the Countess adopts an English name ("Mrs James"), though she struggles to remember it (85).

Nonetheless, the Countess Narona embodies European dubiety. She enters the tale trailing rumors of her conduct from "Paris, Vienna, and London" (9). She appears both repellent and attractive—beautiful, but scarred, her complexion having been wrecked by some undefined poison she has taken in the past. In fact, she definitively possesses a past; her continental life is a level of depth and complexity, a realm of experience that Agnes, the home-grown heroine, cannot access, and can only perceive as a horror to shrink from, or that men will (against her will, perhaps) shield her against.

Once again, a self-consciousness about the fact of the story they are in being a story begins to direct matters. A still younger brother of the late Lord Montbarry, Francis Westwick comes up with idea of a play to be called "The Haunted Hotel," the tragic circumstances into which his family has fallen striking him as ripe material for cheap art:

> The circumstances related to him contained invaluable hints for a ghost-drama. The title occurred to him in the railway: 'The Haunted Hotel.' Post that in letters six feet high, on a black ground, all over London - and trust the excitable public to crowd into the theatre!
> (74)

Scenting the prospect of success, Francis Westwick considers himself "on the trace of another 'Corsican Brothers'" (83). However, he comments on the action as "sad stuff" while praising the conceit of the various relatives being haunted in turn, as each passingly occupies the room where their brother was murdered: "'Material for a play, Countess—first-rate material for a play!'" (83). The Countess comes to realize her own dramatic instincts, her own talent, perhaps, for writing "The Haunted Hotel." She elects herself to be the play's writer, working for Francis Westwick, for money. She enters "the lists with Shakespeare" and tries "a drama with a ghost in it" (82). Considering her own credentials as the story's writer, the Countess depicts the Mediterranean type as typically "unimaginative": "'To anything fanciful, to anything spiritual, their minds are deaf and blind by nature'." Concerning this fault, she is an "exception," gifted with "that imagination which is so common among the English and the Germans—so rare among the Italians, the Spaniards, and the rest of them!" (81–82) This advantage has its drawbacks, as that imagination has become what she considers "a disease in me" (82).

Yet the tale resists its own bias toward the open disclosures of melodrama. The Countess warns us that her "affairs are my own secret" (81), and that remains true to the end of the tale. The novella falters upon the essential secrecy of others, but especially her secrecy, the Countess being a woman who is exposed by the story's discoveries, and yet is never truly revealed. As with the presence here of the supernatural, the tale asks if we are ready to listen to what is told us, to give it credit. The Countess Narona grows increasingly absent in mind, becoming entranced, remote, dreamy. In her hotel room, Agnes wakes to two shocks: first that of the unconscious, but very physically present form of the Countess; and then the equally mysterious specter of a severed head. Each of these mysteries literally confronts the other, each unreadable in its turn by the sensible English woman who regards them.

In this text, two kinds of detritus linger after a crime—and both stink: the ghosts (who are strongly physical spooks) and the putrid remains. Collins more usually avoided this "emphasis on physical horrors" (Peters 1991, 384). In this continental setting, Lord Montbarry's severed head brings back cultural memory of the excesses of the revolution; it is "like a head struck from the body by the guillotine" (96). It has become "Egyptian" too, mummified but above all disgusting—half-flesh, half-bone, with "bluish" lips, and traces of the hair—above all, it reeks, its "fetid exhalations" filling the confined room (97). Revolted, fearful of what his fingers might close upon, the hotel manager puts on his gloves when he reaches his hand into the hollow space secreted behind the mantelpiece (104). The head itself provokes disgust; it is no longer possible to recognize as a person and is unreadable as a face. Until they find tell-tale dentures, no one can tell if it belongs to Ferrari or the deceased Lord. The tale disrupts traditional hierarchies, with foreign couriers standing in for English lords. Collins flirts with the possibility of other such substitutions: is the Baron, absent for now in America, in fact Lord Montbarry? (99). This turns out to be a possibility not fully realized, but operates in the tale as the kind of guess a good detective-story reader might think up.

The tale's solution instead comes inside the Countess's written drama. As in Collins's *The Moonstone* (1868), the detective figure here becomes the criminal herself, just as she also becomes a figure for the writer of the tale. Detective, criminal, writer, all collapse inward into the person of the Countess Narona, the pseudo-Mrs James, the one-time Lady Montbarry, a person doubled and tripled into so many roles that she becomes an entranced figure of strange emptiness, comatose, catatonic, though her hand moves on desperately writing, always writing. Her story, her play-text, both solves the crime, and leaves its solution hanging. Its provenance as a confession is weak, and the readers cannot be certain if it is to be taken as delusion or fact:

> Was this monstrous plot, revealed in the lines which she had just read, the offspring of the Countess's morbid imagination? or had she, in this case also, deluded herself with the idea that she was inventing when she was really writing under the influence of her own guilty remembrances of the past?
>
> (118)

Further to cast doubt on matters, just before her fatal hemorrhage, the Countess begins her play over from scratch, a second draft of the story commenced, but never completed (119). The presence of the supernatural mirrors the instability that gathers around the person of this scarred, intense, demonic European woman. The ghosts both point to the fact of a crime, but present the thought that any solution will not account for everything in the case; something remains over, like the head that is too difficult to dissolve or destroy.

One key question set up by the text is whether the Countess and the Baron were truly brother and sister, or lovers, or both at once? We never discover the answer to this mystery of incest, of a disrupted and dark European brood, so unlike the extended family, all loving and interconnected—all haunted—of the British Westwick clan. The Countess marries Lord Montbarry in order to spare her brother the taint, the indignity, of marrying a wealthy Jewish widow. The Jewish woman stands for a level of corruption and compromise that is seen to legitimate (or perhaps merely initiate) the much greater compromises opened up by the unfortunate marriage.

The explanation that the Countess offers in her play-text explains little unequivocally. Henry himself can hardly stomach to read the first draft to its conclusion, and indeed never fully completes it (123). He shares the knowledge he has and indeed the text itself with his older brother, the new Lord Montbarry. But his brother doubts the tale: "Because some of the crazy creature's writing accidentally tells us what we know to be the truth, does it follow that all the rest is to be relied on to the end?" (123) Henry reads the remaining pages for the two of them, out loud; though at the very end, the Countess's text breaks slowly into the incomprehensible, first with a double scene to be played simultaneously, and then with lines that break into frenzy and illegibility—"The last page looks like sheer delirium. She may well have told you that her invention had failed her!" (125) It becomes a matter of faith, with the second Lord Montbarry choosing to believe in "nothing, nothing, nothing!" (125). Earlier in the Countess's drama, Ferrari tells her, on receiving her offer of substituting with his employer, "'I have not hitherto been a religious man; but I feel myself on the way to it. Since your ladyship has spoken to me, I believe in the Devil.' It is the Countess's interest" (she writes) "to see the humorous side of this confession of faith" (121). So, we are told, as the manuscript burns, that this is how "Lord Montbarry disposed of the mystery of The Haunted Hotel" (125). The manuscript is consumed by fire, its secrets staying with the two brothers, neither of whom intends to pass them on. In the end, the only solid clue is the false teeth that fall from the rotten head when it is discovered. These revolting physical remains tell a story that seems more solid and substantial than that offered by the apparitions and nightmares, by the weaving of a theatrical plot.

For in the end, Henry Westwick considers Agnes too frail to receive the full knowledge of the narrative; the story, in all its horror and its unrelieved mystery, is something she must be spared. The continental darkness suggests a gloom from which the upright British woman should be protected. There's a fear of the past, of the pagan at work in the tale. The "'merciless marble face'" of the caryatid on the mantelpiece terrifies Agnes; though to Henry, it appears merely a "'conventionally classical figure'" (102). Agnes here intuits horrors to which Henry seems oblivious. Yet Henry concludes that the knowledge of the beheading, this inconclusive discovery, must not be shared with Agnes; the thought of her discovering it too is "a terror to him now" (105). The knowledge that Agnes cannot know, the Countess already possesses. The British woman must be kept ignorant, while the continental female turns into a writer, either inventing horrors, or recalling them; in either case, she has access—by experience, or by her "exceptional" imagination to truths and possibilities that Agnes may not share. Indeed Agnes can hardly bear to see the Countess. In being European, in being corrupt, a woman of the world, the Countess becomes both the subject of and the bearer of a story. It is the possession of stories that counts here, the facility of the writer to mold experience, or otherwise to be overwhelmed by it. For the story, the history indeed, to which the Countess has access also destroys her. Its horrors, its uncertainties, are more than her brain can take. The Countess finds herself inside a story that she cannot conclude. She comes to Henry looking for help with her fourth and fifth acts, requiring a "hint" (110). However, Henry cannot help her either: "The words were suspended on his lips" (110–11). Her brain taxed, the monomania of her desire to find conclusions and to make a denouement exhausts and ultimately kills her. Her predicament matches Collins's. Her play offers a critique of his own magazine detective tale, both deconstructing its pretensions to order and meaning, and being the only way that the hidden narrative of the crime can be revealed. The Countess imagines herself in precisely the same ambivalent way that others do. She turns her own persona in the light and questions it, as though she were another: "It is at once a dangerous and attractive character," she writes of herself; "Immense capacities for good are implanted in her nature, side by side with equally remarkable capacities for evil. It rests with circumstances to develop either the one or the other" (113).

In dying, the Countess enters a liminal place, a zombie-realm, where her mind has gone (the head destroyed by what has been imagined in it), while the body, as a reflex, automatically persists for a while: "'Dead of the rupture of a blood-vessel on the brain. Those sounds that you hear are purely mechanical—they may go on for hours'" (119). The sounds in question are her "heavy stertorous breath, like a person oppressed in sleeping" (119). On the other hand, Agnes will be the happier, the sooner she can escape from Venice, "this horrible place" (109).

Agnes never hears the story's solution, and is therefore "not quite satisfied. The subject troubled her" (127). The destiny set up by the book, that Agnes will be the means to the Countess's destruction, remains uncertain; was it fulfilled, or not? Leaving mystery behind on the continent, Agnes lets her husband keep his secrets, content to be the dutiful wife. And the greater mystery, just as, the story tells us, "the explanation of the mystery of your own life and death" remains an incompletable tale and an open question.

Alienated Rooms

For the remainder of this essay, I shall compare two stories about alienated hotel rooms, lodgings where British identity finds its continental double, its "secret sharer." The first is M. R. James's "Number 13" ([1904] 2011), first published in *Ghost Stories of an Antiquary*, though likely written in 1899, as James claimed, or in 1900, just after a visit to Viborg, Denmark, where the tale is set. The second story is perhaps aptly an interloper here, as it may or may not be a gothic tale at all. I wish to consider Isak Dinesen's/Karen Blixen's "The Young Man With the Carnation" ([1942] 2001) the second tale in her collection, *Winter's Tales*—"the most Danish of Karen Blixen's books" (Thurman 1982, 294). Both tales further the complexities of storytelling as imagined by Edwards, Le Fanu, and Collins, in the context of imagined British excursions into a haunted Europe. "Number 13" is a tale written by an Englishman set in a hotel in Denmark, and "The Young Man with the Carnation" is a story by a Dane, writing in English, about an Englishman in a hotel in Antwerp.

As Scott Brewster explores elsewhere in this book, the inquisitive or acquisitive tourist fairly often seems a suitable victim to James. "'Oh, Whistle, and I'll Come to You, My Lad'" ([1904] 2011) and "A Warning to the Curious" ([1925] 2011) two of M. R. James's most celebrated stories, both take place in East Anglian hotels. These stories have become icons of Englishness. "A Warning to the Curious" has a tourist unwittingly purloin an ancient, pagan protection against continental invasion. It appears that the passing people who stay in hotels may disrupt the loyalties and pieties of others who are rooted permanently in place. "A Warning to the Curious" is a very British tale, one of defenses against continental invasion from Danes, or French, or Germans (the buried crown that magically protects the coast recast in the Martello Tower out at sea, the recent crisis of the Great War lying behind the tale). Yet Paxton, the young man cursed to unearth the ancient crown, is about to migrate to the continent, a rootless fellow without connections ready to make a new life in Sweden (354). In "Oh, Whistle," we find the erotic fluidity of the hotel—the fear, or the desire that is a fear, that your room—the private space around you—may be taken possession of by another.

In "Number 13," Anderson, an historical researcher puts up at a Danish hotel. He has number 14 to stay in; next door is number 12. He speculates that superstition prevents there being a number 13 in a hotel. One evening, after working hard in the archives by day, Anderson goes downstairs to fetch a book, on his return he finds himself trying the door of the wrong room. Where there was no room, Number 13, when he went downstairs, now there must certainly is. And, it would seem, the room is occupied. The occupant is heard, its shadow cast against the wall of the building opposite —that of a man, perhaps a woman (53); though his boots mark him out certainly as a "gentleman," these turn out to belong to the guest in Number 14 (54). By means of the same shadows on the opposing wall, Anderson spies the person in the next-door room dancing and later singing (57–58). We manage a glimpse here into what happens behind closed doors on quiet corridors.

James's male protagonist echoes his neighbor's indeterminate gender, figuring himself as Emily in *The Mysteries of Udolpho* (57), thereby taking possession of a classic locus for the oppressive, labyrinthine property, a place with more rooms than by rights it should have. The ghost's room similarly annexes part of the neighboring rooms. "Number 13" imagines a space that should not be there; the building has been converted into a hotel, and the modernizing process has obliterated the room where historical evil happened. However, that wickedness, that Dionysiac, gender-fluid, dancing refusal cannot be shoved away, but barges back in, reasserting presence within the new architecture of the place.

As in Margaret Oliphant's "A Beleaguered City" (1879), James alludes in this to the expansionist policies of Bismarck's Germany. Much as Oliphant recalls in her occupation of Semur by the dead, the Prussian invasion of France in 1870, there's a faint memory of the shameful defeat of Denmark in the Danish-Prussian wars: "'Is this,' he said, 'the Danish courage I have heard so much of. It isn't a German in there, and if it was, we are five to one'" (60). Both Oliphant and James imply that continental Europe's borders are not intact, but may be pierced and penetrated by wars and occupations. Moreover, Anderson's name—recalling inevitably Europe's most famous literary Dane—itself suggests ways in which identity may be permeable, as this British man bears a name whose provenance suggests Scandinavian inheritance. The British, true-born or not, are hardly able to seal themselves off from their own continental connections. We likewise see this conundrum of dual-identity, nominally British, ancestrally European, in the characters of Despard in "The Young Man with the Carnation" and Lamont in "The Heroine" (another tale of a British writer's hotel adventure) in Dinesen's *Winter's Tales*.

As Scott Brewster quotes elsewhere in this book, there's a cancelled manuscript opening to M. R. James's "Number 13," in which he worries about the effects of tourism. Will recommending Jutland as a place lead to its being spoiled by trippers? It seems that travelers destroy the places to which they travel. The story therefore presents itself in part as something likely to discourage tourists. The tale refers to some genuine Jutland hotels—Preisler's (where M. R. James once stayed) and the Phoenix, though the hotel where the story takes place is a fictitious one. Yet James closes the tale's first paragraph properly by informing us, "But I am not writing a guidebook" (48). The question arises what kind of story is he then writing?

Time in a hotel is a discrete experience, a parenthesis apart from the main tenor of our lives. Similarly, I would argue, what these haunted hotel stories of continental Europe show is that the ghost story acts as a moment complete to itself, something that stands starkly apart from our lives as social beings, our kin, our relations. The moment of the ghost story, its being entirely an incident, means that it does not really reach beyond itself, but is a kind of addendum—though it may intimate just how much our earthly lives are all anyway parenthesis, setting them in the context of a space or zone either side of the brackets. This additional quality of the ghost story does not, of course, exhaust its meanings. For the beyond signaled in its passage finds itself in specific worldly locales. In being located here the ghost story enters contingency and context, and in particular I would argue (following other writers on the genre) the social context of property relations, relationships, and the various ways we frame our lives.

The ghost story—particularly, I think as written by Le Fanu and M. R. James—frequently recounts an event, a persecution, that stands somehow outside the main course of life; eccentricity and extremity separate it from the onward tenor of biography; if it exposes social realities, it does so only by providing a weird mirror for them—in itself, it is other than the real—an event with no before or after, a collision with contradictions that do not connect up with the main flow of experience.

Anderson visits Viborg to work in an archive, constructing his own historical narrative in the daytime, as he lives his own, inconsequential reprise of that history, by night. Religious history imbues the story—it forms after all the motive for the protagonist, Mr. Anderson's visit to Viborg—and the town stands as a place connected back to the peninsula's pagan past and to the strife of the Reformation. What is striking is how night-time experience, purposelessly weird, is to be accounted for by recourse to the library. Though the texts there prove as unproductive as the encounters with the ghost himself—suggesting connections, without their being sealed, sketching frameworks that do not find conclusion.

More even than most James stories, "Number 13" goes nowhere and has no proper end; it proves enough to make implications. No ghost is fully seen, the room is never entered; a manuscript is found under the floorboards, but it cannot be properly deciphered, let alone read. Anderson tells the tale to the story's narrator, but "refuses to draw any inferences from it, and to assent to any that I drew for him" (62). In the story's insistence on its own lack of consequence, its refusal of denouement or explication, it is typical in this respect of the form as M. R. James imagined it.

Blixen's tale is, if anything, even more skeptical about the nature of the story, found as it is in the collision between the British and the European. However, it might be doubted if Blixen, as a continental writer herself, belongs to the discussion. To me, her position feels a productive one in relation to the themes of this book. She is a Danish writer who is also an English writer, famous for tales written in the Germanic vein of Hoffmann that are uniquely both a part of a Danish literary tradition and a British one, though outside her native Denmark, her greatest impact was on America. Her biographer, Judith Thurman (1983), wrote of her that her life "was three lives" (in Welles et al. 1983, 7). Other than her tales written under the pseudonym, Isak Dinesen, her most significant achievement are her memoirs about her time as a

Danish settler in what was then the British colony of Kenya. Her writing exists between cultures, migrating from Europe to Africa, from the English-speaking world to the Danish homeland. As an English-language writer, she emphatically chose Europe as her subject-matter, her tales moving from Italy to Denmark, from France to Belgium, from the Baltic to the Mediterranean.

If storytelling appears to break down in "Number 13," even as the story nonetheless gets written, in "The Young Man With the Carnation," Blixen creates a world that is itself endlessly creating stories, whether those of the novelist, the traveler, or of God himself. "The Young Man With the Carnation" is another tale occupied with the fact of occupation, written and published at a time when the Nazis controlled Denmark. In part, it offers a work of covert resistance to that conquest, as here occupation becomes a kind of joke. It's a bedroom farce that metamorphoses into a mystical fable.

Despite its nineteenth-century setting, one way in which Blixen's tale is not gothic is that (unlike M. R. James's story) the preoccupations and usurpations of space outlined in it are not about the past. It is a present event, an assignation that looks to a future. The "murder inn" tales are similarly insistent on the present—they are not historically distant, but geographically so. There are few if any "murder inns" in the island of Britain; they are imagined to be a continental phenomenon. The only past allowed into those stories are intimations of previous victims. The resisting victim in the tale endeavors not to be the latest in an ongoing series. Their escape posits them as the last to be in this situation—thereafter, law will reassert itself, perpetrators are punished, and safety is established.

"The Young Man with the Carnation" is a tale of an English writer, Charles Despard, the author of a best-selling and much-praised novel of social criticism, heading to Italy to honeymoon with his beautiful wife. Despard believes that he has reached the end of his talent, and, although he is engaged on a second novel, has nothing more to say. He has discovered that he is essentially superficial. He believes that those who love him love him purely because he is a great writer. His wife adores not him, he believes, but a "phantom of her own imagination" (19); only as a story-teller does he deserve response. In Antwerp, having started early on his journey, his wife has arranged to meet him in the Queen's Hotel. He goes up to the room, finds the doors unlocked, lets himself in, discovering her asleep in bed. He gets in beside her, but finds he cannot sleep. As he lies there, there is a knock at the door and a young man with a pink carnation in his button-hole stands before the room. A look of radiant happiness on the young man's face strikes Despard. Each gazes at the other, mutually shocked. Despard asks the young man with the carnation what he's doing there, and the youth declares that he must have made a mistake and retreats. Despard's wife awakes, and he tells her that the young man was probably drunk, and she sinks back to sleep. But again, Despard cannot sleep; the young man's happiness haunts him, presenting all the joy he too once had and has now lost. He has allowed himself to be turned from a human being into "printed matter," a purveyor of literature and good only in so far he transforms himself into books. He realizes that he has turned the good things of the world into words. He decides to leave the room, his wife, the compromise of his writing career, and go out into the real world to find the happiness, the reality, enjoyed by the mysterious young man. He writes a curt farewell note and leaves it on the dressing-table, and goes down to the harbor in search of a ship to board, wandering an Antwerp that is markedly French and not Flemish.

He meets a group of sailors, and sitting in a bar with them starts to weave a series of far-fetched tales about himself, making up stories; the sailors regale him too with tales, yarns of life at sea. He returns to his wife, and finds that the room he had gone to the previous night was not his room, that the young man was the rightful visitor, that the woman he had lain beside was not his wife, and that the note he had left for her must have been read by this other woman. The perfect surprise and symmetry of the event strikes him:

> As Charlie now looked back on the happenings of the night, with the experienced eye of an author of fiction, they moved him as mightily as if they had been out of a book of his own. He drew in his breath deeply. "Almighty God," he said from the bottom of his heart, "as the Heavens are higher than the Earth, so are Thy short stories higher than our short stories."
>
> (32)

Of course, the reader retains the knowledge that the author of this particular story is not God, as Karen Blixen winks at us from behind this passage.

As with the ghostly neighbor in "Number 13," Blixen's hero similarly experiences a moment in which his gender becomes uncertain, as he realizes, too late, the terror likely felt by the young woman with whom he inadvertently shares a bed: "As if he himself had possessed a pair of firm young breasts he was conscious of his heart stopping beneath them" (32). In his perception, by the close of the sentence the breasts he merely imagines have become certainly a physical part of him. This is only one of the ways in which Blixen shows him to be on both sides of the question at once. Despard is a suspiciously French name for an Englishman; so it is also that his mother "had a drop of gypsy blood in her" (27). Our native hero is fluent in French, "for he had in his time been apprenticed to a French hairdresser" (21). Moreover, he is a living man who feels himself to be already dead. Death is to have become, as does the Countess Narona, as do the protagonists of "A Terribly Strange Bed" and "The Room in the Dragon Volant," a person of words, contained in a narrative; the artist becomes as dead and finished as their works of art. In a dazzling revision of the haunted hotel story's tropes, the living man himself takes the place normally possessed by the ghost in the room: "In his agony, for he was really in the grip of death" (21), Despard occupies the position of the corpse in the tale. He figures the ghost in himself, greeted by a revenant, the young man, who is more fully alive than he. Despard becomes the other in the room, and when he confronts the young man at the door, he does so having taken his place, wanting to be him. Donald Hannah's (1960) disappointed reading of the story as a "palimpsest" (95) is truer than perhaps the critic acknowledged. Despard's wife too is substituted, confused with another woman; to the writer's absentmindedness all cats are gray. In this tale, Despard puts himself in the mind of the other; he wonders, in French, what this Belgian must have thought of him—"*Ah, le pauvre petit bonhomme à la robe-de-chambre-verte*" (22)—thinking the thought that he imagines was in the mind of the other. Suddenly he sees himself as an other inside the tale: "it seemed that he was to see himself in it, as God saw him" (33). This Englishman on the continent sees himself in the European other, caught in the illumination offered by a tale, just as he has seen himself in the other in the room. The Briton is the haunter in this Belgian hotel room, the fugitive presence forever caught in the story, the experiences given to him. His final thought is "Oh, the young man... *Ah, le pauvre jeune homme à l'œillet*" ("the poor young man with the carnation") (35), this phrase occurring to him in the same French tongue in which he had previously imagined the other young man thinking of him. These last words of the tale combine condescension, sympathy, and a beautiful merging, the Englishman becoming the European he encounters and imagines.

Hearing early of Despard's Sunday School mind, and witnessing his taste for Biblical references, Blixen prepares us for his final dialogue with his divinity ("a rather obtrusive colloquy," according to Donald Hannah [94]), where he accepts God as an author, akin to but superior to himself: "so are Thy short stories higher than our short stories" (32). Despard wants to be on friendly terms with his creator, in losing his ability to invent stories, "He had become estranged from God, and how was he now to live?" (18). Despard's mind is replete too with classical myth; Theseus also abides there (22). Yet stories become suspect to him; if God is an author, He is, Despard feels for a time, a bad one: "It all goes to prove that the greatest of authors makes mistakes and that one should never become an author" (24). Yet talking with the sailors, Despard rediscovers the storyteller in himself. He tells lies about himself to those men, aware that—or falsely believing that—they will prove more amusing and hence more acceptable (25). The tale praises superficiality—and we may wonder if it too is contentedly superficial, a play of surfaces and coincidences. Through the tales Despard finds that he can feel pity for his wife—not named as "Laura" until close to the tale's completion (27).

Blixen favored an aesthetic of restitutions. As in her masterpiece, "Babette's Feast," the romance of life, its grace, is that the world grants us also what we lose, and more than we deserve. Despard's restitution marks a return to childhood too for, as he returns to his wife's room, he's put in mind of childhood thoughts and reminiscences (31). As Blixen expresses in "The Dreaming Child" ([1942] 2001) another of her *Winter's Tales*:

> 'There is a grace in the world, such as none of us have known about. The world is not a hard or severe place, as people tell us. It is not even just. You are forgiven everything. The fine things of the world you cannot wrong or harm, they are much too strong for that.'
>
> (104–5)

Here, as elsewhere, in Blixen's tales, a superabundance of stories overwhelms us—the plenitude a strange alternative to the apparent absence of story in Edwards or M. R. James. In this tale, Despard finds himself liberated from isolation to conviviality—a conviviality framed around the recounting, the sharing of tales. Accepting his place as a writer means accepting the duty of giving a response, of owing both God and one's fellow citizens an answer.

In his tale, experiencing his own separation from earthly happiness, by being accidentally in the place where another man's joy was supposed to be found, Despard picks up the thread of experience contained in the old, shared European box of tales:

> 'I am thinking, he said very slowly, of the garden of Eden, and the cherubim with the flaming sword…I am thinking of Hero and Leander. Or Romeo and Juliet. Of Theseus and Ariadne, and the Minotaur as well. Have you ever tried, my dear, to guess how, on that occasion the Minotaur was feeling?'
>
> (32–33)

Taking possession of the common European storehouse of shared tales, he wonders over empathy, the writer's uncanny task of putting herself in the place of another.

His nineteenth-century realism meets its challenging riposte in the tall tale, the fable, the parable, the purposeless anecdote, the gratuitous invention. In this way, Despard's tale acts as a mirror to all the narratives outlined in this essay, his falling into the web of narrative symptomatic of the processes that happen to the protagonists of Collins's, Le Fanu's, Edwards's, and M. R. James's fictions of the murder inn and the haunted hotel. If stories are what we tell each other to create, one by one, on the level of private exchange in a public place, a shared image of the world we inhabit together, then we might say that it is truly out of the fabric of stories that the concept of Europe has been constructed. Such stories may play out

anxieties, be acts of unease or aggression, designed to frame our disconnection. Or they may build up a common sense of the world, a continent
of narratives, open in the exchange between text and reader, giving, as
in Karen Blixen's/Isak Dinesen's story, an image of the tale as knit up in
sociability, the individual experience refabricated as a gift, the other self
mirrored in the hotel's passing encounter.

References

Bauman, Zygmunt. 2000. *Liquid Modernity*. London: Polity Press.

Bodenheimer, Ruth. 2007. *Knowing Dickens*. Ithaca, NY: Cornell University
Press.

Bowen, John. 2006. "Collins's Shorter Fiction." In *The Cambridge Companion to Wilkie Collins*, edited by Jenny Bourne Taylor, 37–49. Cambridge:
Cambridge University Press.

Collins, Wilkie. 1975. "The Haunted Hotel." In *Three Supernatural Novels of
the Victorian Period*, edited by E. F. Bleiler, 1–127. New York: Dover.

Collins, Wilkie. 1875. "A Terribly Strange Bed." In *After Dark, and Other
Stories*, 28–43. New York: Harper & Brothers.

Dickens, Charles. [1857] 1896. *The Lazy Tour of Two Idle Apprentices*. New
York and London: Macmillan and Co.

Dinesen, Isak/Karen Blixen. (1942) 2001. *Winter's Tales*. London: Penguin
Books.

Edwards, Amelia B. [1974] 1890. "A Night on the Borders of the Black Forest."
In *A Night on the Borders of the Black Forest*, 7–43. New York: Frederick
A. Stokes.

Hannah, Donald. 1960. *"Isak Dinesen" and Karen Blixen: The Mask and the
Reality*. London: Putman and Company.

Irving, Washington. 1987. Tales of a Traveller, by Geoffrey Crayon, Gent. In
The Complete Works of Washington Irving, Vol. X, edited by Judith Giblin
Haig. Boston: Twayne.

James, M. R. 2011. *Collected Ghost Stories*. Edited by Darryl Jones. Oxford:
Oxford University Press.

Le Fanu, Sheridan. [1872] 1993. *In a Glass Darkly*. Edited by Robert Tracy.
Oxford: Oxford University Press.

McCormack, William John. 1980. *Sheridan Le Fanu and Victorian Ireland*.
Oxford: Clarendon Press.

Peters, Catherine. 1991. *The King of Inventors: A Life of Wilkie Collins*.
London: Secker & Warburg.

Slater, Michael. 2009. *Charles Dickens*. New Haven and London: Yale University Press.

Stone, Harry. 1994. *The Night Side of Dickens: Cannibalism, Passion, Neces-
sity*. Columbus: Ohio State University Press.

Thurman, Judith. 1982. *Isak Dinesen: The Life of a Storyteller*. New York:
St. Martin's Press.

Welles, Orson, et al. 1983. "Isak Dinesen/Karen Blixen: A Homage." *Munger
Africana Library Notes* 70 (October): 1–20.

7   Daphne du Maurier

Sex and Death the Italian Way

Avril Horner and Sue Zlosnik

Daphne du Maurier's reputation as merely a "Cornish novelist" is misleading. She certainly felt an enduring affinity with Cornwall; her rebellious, artistic nature found its peripheral geography and dark history appealing and she saw her writing life there as liberating her from the metropolitan codes of feminine dress and behavior she had left behind in London. Moreover, her powerful sense of place meant that some of her best-known work is set in the county (most notably *Jamaica Inn* [1936] and *Rebecca* [1938]). However, many of her tales find their place elsewhere in Europe. France provides the milieu for explorations of the past, particularly the family history of the du Mauriers, but it is her Italian settings that offer the opportunity to explore an often destructive sexual ambivalence. In her Italian fiction she tapped into a tradition of gothic fiction from the eighteenth and nineteenth centuries that appealed to her dark imagination, using the location to represent a haunted self. Italy has been a looming presence in the gothic novel since its inception. In his introduction to an issue of the journal *Gothic Studies* devoted to Italy and the Gothic, Massimiliano Demata (2006) identifies Italy as "a major source of inspiration for the late eighteenth-century British Gothic novelists," going on to state that "Gothic Italy" was viewed as "a nest of enormous narrative potentialities...represented as a place of violence and passion" (1).

For du Maurier, Italy serves—as it did in gothic fiction from the eighteenth and nineteenth centuries—to signify a malign "otherness." A striking early example is Ann Radcliffe's *The Mysteries of Udolpho* (1794), an English gothic novel set in France but featuring an Italian villain, Signor Montoni, a brigand who has married the French heroine's aunt. Another is her novel *The Italian* (1797), with its wicked but fascinating character Schedoni, who threatens the life of the young heroine. Such antipathy to Catholic European countries, particularly Spain and Italy, is evident in many gothic novels of the late eighteenth century and had its roots in the Reformation and the subsequent evolution of Protestantism in Britain.[1] Catholicism came to stand for a specifically continental form of idolatry, tyranny, and corruption, all vividly represented by the Spanish priest who falls from grace in Matthew Lewis's

The Monk (1796), and the Vatican's presence in Rome meant that Italy in particular was the focus of much opprobrium. This animosity rumbled on throughout England during the nineteenth century, despite the Roman Catholic Relief Act of 1829 and subsequent changes to the law, and continued to be reflected in literature. The equation of Spain and Italy with villainy and/or Catholicism held an important place in Victorian civilization and in its literature. The sinister Count Fosco and his wife, from Sicily, in Wilkie Collins's *The Woman in White* (1860), for example, threaten both the life and the mental health of the two half-sisters, Laura Fairlie and Marian Halcombe. Nor was suspicion of Catholicism confined to England. Only nine years before that novel appeared, the *Reformation Journal,* published in Edinburgh, included an article in its first issue for 1851 entitled "The Blight of Popery." In this essay, Catholicism was castigated in no uncertain terms as a dire threat to human integrity that degrades both the spirit and the body. The author took pains to link the religion not only with "a retrograde movement in virtue and civilization" but also with sexual decadence and the effete:

> The arts of painting and sculpture may flourish, for these do not require a proficiency in mental culture; and the poesy of love and of nature's beauties may be warbled in the melting paths of a melodious voice, or be set to the strings of the light guitar; but manly emotions are checked, and sensual desires occupy the place of virtuous affections.
>
> (Begg 184)

The British construction of masculinity is here seen as threatened by continental deviancy which, when combined with the Catholic faith, is particularly virulent. Du Maurier's choice of Italian settings thus draws upon a centuries-long cultural tradition that associates Italy with corruption and deviance.

Throughout her life Daphne du Maurier felt a sense of unease regarding the norms of sexual identity imposed by the culture of her time. She would have been more comfortable with today's acknowledgment of gender fluidity. In correspondence with Ellen Doubleday (the wife of her publisher in the post-war years) she referred to herself as a "half-breed" and "disembodied spirit" (Forster 1993, 221, 228). This spirit, she claimed, was associated with the boy her younger self had metaphorically shut up in a box so that she might conform to accepted notions of femininity. While this may not have made for the happiest of lives, it provided a powerful creative impulse for her writing, which she associated with that masculine side of herself. Later in life, she read the work of Carl Jung, which enabled her to see her writing identity as a male second self and helped her to understand better her own resistance to contemporary configurations of gender.[2] In her work, both femininity and masculinity are represented as being fissured and contested. Male characters (often narrators) who experience a conflicted sense of masculinity appear frequently in her fiction. Not surprisingly, therefore, these anxieties about subjectivity attracted du Maurier to the gothic tradition with its dark history of giving shape to the unspeakable. Its enduring fascination with Italy provided her with the setting for her darkest imaginings about herself and society. Unconsciously or not, she was profoundly influenced by both a specific cultural legacy and the gothic tradition, which resulted in a distinctive reworking of Italy as "Other" and the dramatic exploration of a haunted self.

Her four works set wholly or partly in Italy are focused through male characters who embody a masculinity that is morally flawed and perceptually limited. Three of these characters are Englishmen; the fourth, an Italian. For the English characters, contact with Italy provokes crises of identity and, for one of them, results in death. The city of Venice with its labyrinthine structure and history of masquerade provides a fitting location for two sinister tales of corruption and death. "Ganymede" ([1958] 1970) has echoes of Thomas Mann's *Death in Venice* with its elusive beautiful youth. "Don't Look Now" (1971) portrays a man who, struggling to come to terms with the tragic loss of his daughter, is no match for the sinister duplicities of the city and ultimately perishes as a result. In the novel *My Cousin Rachel* ([1951] 1992), set largely in Cornwall but partly in Italy, English suspicion of Italian foreignness is exploited to create an ambiguous narrative of sexual desire and cultural dissonance. In *The Flight of the Falcon* ([1965] 1992), inspired by a visit to Urbino, the barbarism of the medieval past and the pressures of modernity collide with dramatic results.

In *My Cousin Rachel*, Philip Ashley, inheritor of a thinly disguised Menabilly,[3] is a conflicted and insecure male narrator. Philip becomes besotted by Rachel, who is his dead cousin's widow, and willingly hands over his patrimony to her, retrieving it only by knowingly allowing her to go to her death. Half-Cornish and half-Italian, Rachel remains an ambiguous figure who is culturally more akin to her Italian mother than her Cornish father. Her Italian identity comes to signify the exotic, alluring, strange, and threatening. Initially, Rachel's foreignness both fascinates and repels Philip. Before he meets her, he is obsessed with her image, and his infatuation is compounded by his visit to Italy in response to anguished letters sent by Ambrose. There he is confronted by a landscape he finds alien: the "otherness" of Italy. He notes that "the valleys were baked brown, and the little villages hung parched and yellow on the hills with the haze of heat upon them" (29) and sees the Arno as "a slow moving turgid stream" in comparison with the "blue estuary" of home (30). He has expected Rachel to be old and is shocked to find a woman in her thirties; yet he also associates her with the ancient knowledge of Italy. In Philip's mind such knowledge seems sinister, a perception which is reinforced by repeated reference to poison in the novel. Called to Italy by Ambrose's fear that Rachel is trying to kill him, he describes the Arno as, "something to be tasted, swallowed, poured down the throat as one might pour a draught of poison" (30). Much later, after a nearly fatal illness and fearing himself poisoned, he remembers Rachel's explanation of her knowledge of herbs: "I learnt them from my mother...We are very old and wise, who come from Florence" (262).

There are powerful echoes of earlier gothic novels in *My Cousin Rachel*. The opening chapters create a sense of gothic mystery in contrast with the descriptions of domestic life in early nineteenth-century Cornwall. When Philip reaches the Villa Sangaletti, the description of its interior offers an inventory of gothic features:

> The rooms all led into each other, large and sparse, with frescoed ceilings and stone floors, and the air was heavy with a medieval musty smell. In some of the rooms the walls were plain, in others tapestried, and in one darker and more oppressive than the rest, there was a long refectory table flanked with carved monastic chairs, and great wrought iron candlesticks stood at either end.
>
> (34)

The typical gothic setting of a religious house is evoked here, even though there is no further evidence that the Villa Sangaletti has been one. The same effect is created by the room where Ambrose died which is described as being "bare like a monk's cell" (36).

Furthermore, Philip's encounter with Rachel's friend and lawyer, Rainaldi, gives us a portrait of a classic gothic villain. He has "a pale, almost colourless face, and lean aquiline features" and "something proud and disdainful about his cast of countenance like that of someone who would have small mercy for fools, or for his enemies." Philip most notices his eyes "dark and deep-set" (42); "Was it my fancy, or did a veiled look come over those dark eyes?" (43) but in the event, Rainaldi proves to be merely an innocuous and peripheral figure, for the psychological dynamic of the novel lies in the triangulated relationship between Philip, Rachel, and the dead Ambrose. Philip's reading of this dynamic is the real plot of the novel and he is not a reliable reader. Gothic conventions are used at this stage in the novel rather as they are in Jane Austen's *Northanger Abbey*, as a means of signaling unreliable understanding. Although Philip is no Catherine Morland, in some ways he re-enacts the role of the vulnerable heroine in classic gothic fiction. Like Ellena in Radcliffe's *The Italian*, for example, he is embroiled in something he does not understand and believes to be sinister, resulting in feelings of confusion and powerlessness. His ambiguous relationship with Rachel is not unlike that of Ellena's with Schedoni, whom she finds both repulsive and strangely attractive. Thus, Philip's vulnerability effectively feminizes him in the world of the gothic novel. The ambiguous figures of Rachel and Rainaldi appear equivalent to the gothic "villains" who plot and control, thereby inverting the usual gender dynamic of the classic gothic novel. Even the novel's dénouement shows Philip reasserting his rights in a passive manner, not by killing Rachel but by failing to prevent her falling to her death.

Having succumbed to Rachel's charm once she has arrived in Cornwall, Philip then becomes plagued again by doubts and suspicions that the reader shares even beyond the very end of the novel, which closes on a note of uncertainty. Is she a Borgia-like monster who demonstrates the worst of "feminine" evil that patriarchy can imagine: a wanton profligate who has poisoned her husband? Or is she an innocent and maligned widow, a victim, albeit one who is trying to protect her own interests? Philip's ambivalence about Rachel is summed up in these terms at the end:

> I looked on her in profile. She was always a stranger, thus. Those neat clipped features on a coin. Dark and withdrawn, a foreign woman standing in a doorway, a shawl about her head, her hand outstretched. But full-face, when she smiled a stranger never. The Rachel that I knew, that I had loved.
>
> (295)

His ambivalence is thus never resolved and it is left to readers to make their own judgment.

In contrast with *My Cousin Rachel*, *The Flight of the Falcon* (1965), written over ten years later, is set entirely in contemporary Italy, featuring a cast of Italian characters. Although one of du Maurier's lesser known novels it is one of her most ambitious. It places the dynamics of fraught familial relationships within the long patriarchal history of a Europe haunted by the traumatizing effects of World War II. As du Maurier's biographer Margaret Forster (1993) notes:

> The germ for *The Flight of the Falcon* was sown on a visit to Urbino with Kits, and on another holiday with Tessa [her daughter] during which she had seen an old woman asleep in a doorway of a church and she had put some money into her hand.
>
> (336)

In the novel, Urbino becomes Ruffano. Writing to her friend Oriel Malet, du Maurier commented:

> I have to study the plans and postcards of Urbino, and the books about the University there, day after day, so that I could, in a way, find my way blindfold about the place!...then when I come to outline

the story I find the first suspense idea, and the *son et lumière*, all become involved with deeper levels - I mean, there has to be an explanation of *why* the person directing the acting in the *son et lumière* (a professor at the University), begins to make it all come real to himself, and to the students etc, etc, what is his deep unconscious motive in wanting to re-enact history, and the wicked Duke.

(Malet 1993, 167)

In *The Flight of the Falcon*, du Maurier's abiding interest in the relationship between the past and the present reaches its most complex expression and her exploration of masculine identity in relation to history achieves a new sophistication. As in *My Cousin Rachel*, she again adopts an undeveloped inadequate male narrator, this time in the figure of Armino Fabbio. Armino is a tour guide in his early thirties, the younger son of the deceased Aldo Donati, pre-war Superintendent of the Ducal Palace at Ruffano. Because of a tragic and disturbing event in Rome, Armino returns to his home city for the first time since the war, where he finds his older brother, Aldo (whom he had presumed dead) very much alive and Director of the Arts Council.

Exploiting the links between past and present, du Maurier uses gothic motifs in order to evoke a medieval world in the midst of Italy in the 1960s, complete with fashionable Vespa scooters. The ancient university of Ruffano has established a new faculty of Commerce and Economics and the city is now a busy place where the new clashes with the old. There is rivalry in the university between this new faculty and the old-established Arts Faculty, the former perceiving itself as the epitome of the modern world in comparison with what it sees as outmoded Arts. Ruffano's other famous feature is the Ducal Palace, symbolic of the old Italy and redolent of the darkness and mystery that characterize the gothic tradition. The Palace remains unchanged in the heart of the modern city, representing a barbaric past which has never gone away. Its dark spaces with their secret passages and stairways and its dynastic portraits are an ever-present reminder of the sinister Renaissance world of Duke Claudio ("The Falcon"), a tyrannical and capricious ruler who committed many atrocities. Within the walls of the Ducal Palace, Aldo meets in secret with his band of acolytes who, dressed in period costume, appear to bring the past to life. Orphaned children of war, now young men, they act out the part of "lost boys" in this sinister never-never land. Twelve in number, they provide a disturbing and parodic echo of the apostles. In mentoring these young men, Aldo sees them as surrogates for a young brother he presumed dead. As Armino arrives in Ruffano, preparations are under way for the annual festival, in which Aldo is planning to re-enact certain feats of The Falcon, including his Icarus-like leap from the palace tower, thus echoing his own experiences as a wartime pilot.

Barbarism and horror are not confined to medieval history, however; only two decades before, Europe had suffered the atrocities of fascism on a scale undreamt of by the Old Duke. In a sense, Armino and Aldo are both casualties of war. There are frequent references to what they see as their mother's betrayal of them and their dead father: taking Armino with her, she had left Ruffano in the later stages of the War in the company of its German commandant. The figure of the mother is threaded through the story. The tragic and disturbing event in Rome at the beginning of the novel involves a chance encounter with a woman vagrant that stirs memories of Armino's past. She reminds him of his childhood nurse, Marta; this, in turn, evokes memories of the altar-piece in San Cipriano, a church in Ruffano, which to his young eyes had seemed to represent Marta looking on at the raising of Lazarus. This image inextricably links with memories of Aldo, whom he still believes to be dead at this point. After the vagrant is found murdered, Armino becomes convinced that she was indeed Marta. He believes himself to be partly responsible for her death because on impulse he had placed a 10,000 Lire note in her hand, which had presumably supplied the motive for her killing. It soon becomes apparent to Armino that Aldo is over zealous in his preparations for the festival, to the extent of rousing the students to engage in genuine street fighting, and he begins to doubt his sanity. He believes himself to be wanted by the Roman police for Marta's murder and, fearing arrest, allows Aldo to have him smuggled out to the coast. There, a series of clues culminate in the discovery that Aldo is not his true brother but had been adopted at birth. He deduces, wrongly, that Aldo has murdered Marta to silence her, and returns to Ruffano. There, he tells Aldo that he knows the truth about his birth and that he understands why he killed Marta. After a reckless chariot ride through the streets of Ruffano, they have a last encounter before Aldo attempts his re-enactment of the Falcon's climactic "flight." After admitting that he knows that Marta had been his real mother but denying her murder, he leaps to his death. The novel closes with his obituary, which refers to Armino's staying on in Ruffano to continue his older brother's work with orphaned students.

Armino's recognition of Marta in Rome thus starts a process whereby a family history of secrets and guilt (the characteristic subject matter of the gothic novel) is uncovered. While Aldo had returned to Ruffano after the war to reinstate the Donati family as custodians of the city's history, Armino, on the other hand, has remained a dispossessed figure, choosing a profession that required him to be always on the move. He makes frequent reference throughout the novel to his nomadic childhood, trailed about Europe by his mother to live in various hotels, first with her German and then an American lover. An adolescence spent in close proximity to what he perceives as his mother's sexual promiscuity (he refers to her as a "beautiful slut" [*FF* 33]) has given him a mistrust of women. This mistrust, verging on misogyny, at times manifests itself as physical revulsion. He finds aspects of femininity abject: on one notable occasion, while waiting in the flat of a woman he has met in Ruffano (Carla Raspa), he goes into the bathroom and, seeing some stockings soaking in the bidet, is overcome by nausea (222).

Carla's attempt to seduce Armino meets with a slap in the face. Indeed, Armino perceives her active and assertive sexuality as monstrous, comparing her with both a "praying mantis" (88) and a vampire (161–62). His memories of his nurse, Marta, are rather different. If he has come to see his mother as a whore, he associates Marta in his memory with a more pure maternal femininity. Marta had been, like her biblical namesake, Martha, dedicated to a life of domestic service: "she who had been clean, fastidious, forever washing, pressing, folding clothes and fresh linen and laying them away in closets" (86). Thus, he has constructed these two mother figures, the real and the surrogate, as patriarchy's two polarities of femininity. This is disrupted for him by the "huddled, drunken figure" with "the sour, stale smell" that Marta had become (86). Aldo is as misogynistic as Armino: he lives alone with a male servant (a former wartime subordinate) and he excludes women from active participation in the festival. His contempt for women is matched by his respect, even reverence, for what he believes to be his paternal lineage. Thus Aldo's assertion of patriarchal values takes a different turn. Unable to live in the old family home, he has tried to recreate it in a house in the same street, the Via dei Sogni (literally, "street of dreams"). Armino's first visit to this house has an uncanny effect on him as he finds all the furniture and belongings from his old home arranged there.

Having recently discovered the secret of his parentage, Aldo becomes haunted by it, believing himself to be an impostor; he knows Armino to be the only rightful heir to the Donati name. His revelation to Armino, just before the chariot ride, that he has known this since the previous November helps to make sense of his behavior in relation to the Falcon and the festival. He may be seen as attempting to compensate for his own sense of dispossession at the familial level through his apparent affinity with Duke Claudio. The relationship between the two brothers proves to be of key importance. Armino, the younger, grew up in the shadow of his dominating brother. His initial encounter with Marta in Rome has prompted bad dreams in which he is transported back to "that nightmare world where Aldo was my king" (17). Recalling the altar-piece in San Cipriano, he dreams of being locked in a linen cupboard for a tomb and being forced to play Lazarus to Aldo's Christ or Satan, depending on his whim. Just before Aldo's death both brothers acknowledge their complicity in the deaths of their mothers. Aldo's denial of the literal murder of Marta is all the more convincing because of his admission that he was nonetheless responsible for her death: "Yes, I killed her...but not with a knife—the knife was merciful. I killed her by despising her, by being too proud to admit the fact that I was her son. Wouldn't you say that counts as murder?" (279). Armino, in turn, recognizes that he too is guilty in the same way of murdering his mother, having refused contact with her when she was dying of cancer.[4] Both admissions echo the reflection of Armino upon the statuette of the Virgin Mary in San Cipriano: "It seemed to me then that the Mother played a sorry part in her Son's story" (266). Thus Marta's central significance in the text becomes clear. What *The Flight of the Falcon* demonstrates is the cost at which patriarchal lines are preserved.

As in *My Cousin Rachel*, the cultural matricide identified by French theorist Luce Irigaray is played out. For Irigaray (1974), Western culture has been predicated upon a masculine subjectivity which relegates the feminine maternal to the status of inchoate matter out of which the male must, through a painful and complex process, rise; in Plato's terms this is his journey out of the cave and into the light (243–364). The Western iconography of flight is a cultural expression of this masculine subjectivity. If Aldo's flight into air may be seen in these symbolic terms, his deliberate plunge to earth can be viewed as a final acknowledgment of the maternal. The polyvalence of Marta's name becomes fully apparent: Marta/Martha/mater/matter/martyr (Williams 1995, 77). From a figure of cultural abjection, the despised "refuse" in Rome, she is reconstructed in Armino's memory as a Martha figure but then comes to represent what, in Irigaray's terms, is martyred in the process of establishing and sustaining patriarchy. Thus Marta, as martyr, is absorbed within the discourse of Christianity which recurs so frequently and so powerfully in the text, but in such a way as to question the very foundations of that patriarchal culture of which Christianity is a cornerstone. What is so significant is that both brothers recognize the martyrdom of Marta; thus the binaries which separated her and the other mother figure, Aldo's adoptive mother and Armino's natural one, break down.

While du Maurier was clearly not influenced by Irigaray (whose work appeared later), the novel provides a powerful fictional representation of what the theorist was to identify as forming the foundation of Western gendered culture. The influence of du Maurier's reading of Jung in the mid-50s is apparent in the novel; this may also be seen at work in *The Scapegoat* (1957), a novel in which the doubles John and Jean function as each other's shadow.[5] The brothers Aldo and Armino seem to replicate this psychological dynamic and this, indeed, may have been what du Maurier intended. Each is, in his own way, inadequate but the death of Aldo will, the end of the novel suggests, be the making of Armino. In childhood, Aldo's dominance had been dependent on Armino's submission; in adulthood, the relationship seems to have perpetuated itself as the charismatic Aldo sweeps a reluctant Armino along in his plans. This is brought to an abrupt close by Aldo's fatal emulation of the Falcon's flight. *The Flight of the Falcon* is the culmination of Daphne du

Maurier's mature phase as a novelist and it is the last gothic novel she wrote. It seems that this so-called "agreeable writer of agreeable fiction," as Quentin Bell described her, was able to represent some of the most intractable problems of twentieth-century history in a manner which was accessible to a wide range of readers.[6]

Whereas the two novels we have discussed adopt a carefully judged historical perspective in critiquing the limitations of conventional masculinity, du Maurier's two "Italian" short stories are more personal. Significantly, they are both set in Venice. They reflect her own struggles with gender identity: her coded term for her desire for women was her "Venetian tendencies"—a desire that she needed to keep secret and that she knew could destroy her social identity (Forster 1993, 28, 418). Du Maurier looked to Venice, with its labyrinthine structure and history of masquerade, as a fitting setting for two sinister tales of corruption and death, "Ganymede" and "Don't Look Now." Written during the 1950s, and perhaps inspired by a visit in 1952, "Ganymede" (1958) is clearly a reworking of Thomas Mann's *Death in Venice* in which Aschenbach, a cultured older man, becomes infatuated by a beautiful young boy. The first-person narrator of "Ganymede" (whose name we never learn) is a fastidious and well-traveled classical scholar living in London's "Little Venice," an area of intersecting canals in the city. We learn that he has chosen to live there because it reminds him of Venice, despite the fact that an autumn holiday in the Italian city went disastrously wrong and ruined his professional life. A repressed homosexual, his hidden sexual identity has only come to public notice because of a trip to Venice; once his superior became aware of his "unsavoury practices" (89), he was dismissed from his post. But, for the narrator, traveling to Venice promised to fulfill a dream. He had fantasized that he would find there, "A different secret...the Venice within ourselves" (91) and, indeed, he remembers how, on arrival, he felt "a loosening of restraint" (91) and that he became "at last, myself" (93). He even associates the watery by-ways of the city with "the waters that usher us into this life at birth" (92), as if he anticipates that he will somehow be reborn in the city. But the word "secret," repeated throughout the first two parts of the story, suggests that this transformation will be transgressive and socially unacceptable.

In a sudden *coup de foudre*, the nameless narrator quickly becomes besotted with a fifteen-year-old waiter whom he thinks of as "Ganymede," the name evoking the Greek myth in which Zeus abducts the beautiful young Greek boy to be his cup-bearer and lover. Culturally, the myth served as a model for the Ancient Greek social custom of *paiderastia*, the socially acceptable romantic relationship between an adult male and a young male adolescent. In time, "Ganymede" became a symbol in literature for the beautiful boy who attracts homosexual desire and love although it also had a more debased meaning: as A. D. Cousins points out, "Ganymede was a generic name in early modern England for a boy prostitute" (219). The narrator, who feels as if he has been "jerked into consciousness from a lifetime of sleep" (95), is seized by physical desire for the boy and romanticizes their relationship (in reality one of customer and waiter or potential client and rent-boy) as carrying "the stamp of the immortals" (96). In a moment of prophetic fantasy, he imagines himself as Zeus transformed into an eagle carrying the body of Ganymede, only to find that he has gripped the hand of the young waiter across the restaurant table. Manipulated by the boy's unpleasant uncle (whom the narrator thinks of as Zeus's rival, the god Poseidon),[7] he agrees to pay for a boat-trip to the Lido where he imagines he and Ganymede will spend a quiet and romantic day reading Shakespeare's sonnets. Instead, the young waiter's vulgar uncle arranges for a noisy speed-boat trip to the Lido, where the narrator finds himself paying for the whole family's dinner. On the return journey there is a terrible accident which is partially the narrator's fault: the boy is caught in the boat's propeller and suffers a ghastly death. The narrator agrees to pay the wretched uncle a vast sum of money as compensation and returns to London. Venice provided him with an arena for his repressed desires but it has also destroyed him. Having lost his job, he no longer works and he has dropped his friends. Although his life has changed for the worse, he is still driven by his "secret" longings: as the story closes, he is about to visit a London restaurant where a fifteen-year-old waiter has caught his eye. Nor has the experience provided him with any insights into himself, although the reader is made privy to the fact, near the end of the story, that when he was five years old he suffered the loss of his younger brother: "but I don't remember him at all: I've never given him a thought" (126). Perhaps du Maurier is here suggesting that unresolved grief and loss lie at the heart of the narrator's desires; if so, this pathologizes his sexual identity—but the narrator's behavior is not condoned in the story in any way; indeed sexual activity with a child under the age of consent was and still is a criminal offence. However, du Maurier's ambivalent presentation of the narrator perhaps reflects the conflict she experienced in relation to what she saw as her own problematic sexual identity. Although she was physically drawn to women as well as men, she always vigorously denied that she was a lesbian, preferring to use the term "half-breed," to signal her attraction to both sexes (Forster 1993, 418, 222). Her bisexuality was, though, something she needed to conceal, just as the narrator in "Ganymede" has to keep his desires secret.

"Don't Look Now" (1971) achieved wide fame through its memorable 1973 film adaptation, directed by Nicolas Roeg. Again, du Maurier's Venice represents the precariousness of "normality": a holiday resort, it is nevertheless haunted by death. In "Don't Look Now" the city appears warm and sheltered by day but this "bright facade" (25) gives way to an "altogether different" place at night with the long narrow boats on the dank canals looking "like coffins" (19). The story opens with a conversation between John and his wife, Laura, who have come on a short holiday to Venice, attempting to recover some sense of normality following the loss of their five-year-old daughter, Christine, who has died from meningitis. They are briefly distracted from their grief by the sight of two older women at a restaurant table nearby; it transpires that the women are Scottish twin sisters in their sixties, one a retired doctor, the other blind, who are also tourists in Venice. The blind sister is psychic and claims to have had a vision of the couple's dead daughter, which she communicates to Laura. John dismisses the women as eccentric and interfering, although later—because of their hold over Laura—he begins to demonize them. A well-educated man who has embraced a very conventional gender model (he finds it shameful when he is reduced to tears and sneers at the twin who appears rather masculine), he represses his grief about his daughter's death, encouraging his wife to do the same, at times infantilizing her. He negotiates Venice by map and bows to his male doctor's opinion of what Laura "needs." He is deeply suspicious of anything beyond the rational and the logical. Early in the story, then, du Maurier sets up a tension between sight, insight, and blindness (both physical and metaphorical). In fact, John's confidence in his ability to think clearly and logically leads him to make a number of misjudgments, which include assuming that his wife has been kidnapped by the sisters and which eventually result in his death. A series of events culminates in John becoming lost in the labyrinthine passages of the city and seeing a child-like figure in a pixie-hood whom he has spotted on earlier occasions and now believes to be in trouble. She seems to be running for her life; this time he follows her, assuming she is fleeing from a male killer who has recently committed several murders in the city, since he spots a man in pursuit. Anxious to protect her, he follows the child into a room in a building and locks the door behind him, against the pursuing male. He turns to reassure the "child"; her hood falls away from her head and he is faced with an unveiled, monstrous spectacle:

> It was not a child at all but a little thick-set woman dwarf, about three feet high, with a great square adult head too big for her body, grey locks hanging shoulder-length, and she wasn't sobbing any more, she was grinning at him, nodding her head up and down... The creature fumbled in her sleeve, drawing a knife...
>
> (55)

The story closes with his consciousness fading as the blood runs from his body, the knife having pierced his throat. The veil which obscures the beauty of the eighteenth-century gothic heroine is here grotesquely travestied. In fact, the "pixie-hood" bears more resemblance to the sinister cowl of gothic fiction which often drops to reveal a similarly murderous intent, as in Ann Radcliffe's *The Italian* when Schedoni reveals his "intense and fiery eyes" and draws "a poniard from beneath a fold of his garment" (318).

John's faith in the rational has failed him, with disastrous results. He fled from a male figure, who, it turns out, was probably a policeman, when he should have fled the female dwarf—an interesting variation on the classic gothic "pursuit" scene. The story, like much gothic fiction, offers a powerful critique of Enlightenment rationality and fixed ideas about gender and identity. In defining his own identity in opposition to the superstition and irrationality that the twin sisters seem to represent and to his wife's "emotional" nature, John makes himself vulnerable to what Irigaray (1974) has described as the repression of the feminine in Western culture. "Don't Look Now" can, then, be read as exposing the supposedly neutral discourses of science and medicine as discourses of the *masculine* subject (Whitford 1991, 53). Read in this manner, the dwarf woman's act of plunging a knife into John's throat can be seen as retribution for the old woman's death in *The Flight of the Falcon*, published six years earlier. For in that novel Marta died twice, physically as she was stabbed to death in the streets of Rome but also metaphorically through Aldo's refusal to acknowledge her existence as his mother.

In both "Ganymede" and "Don't Look Now," du Maurier brilliantly uses Venice as a location for not only physical but also psychological disorientation. Writing about the city as an invisible and imaginative space as well as an actual place, Julian Wolfreys (2009) comments, "No map, no diagram or text can save you from becoming lost, fallen" (104), adding:

> The very condition of the uncanny experience, then, is that there is always the inexorable slide, inescapable as well as ineluctable, from the familiar to the unfamiliar, the homely to the unhomely, the "canny" or "known" to the "uncanny." And this equally has to do with one's "self," one's identity or being and one's location, where location or context determines who one thinks one is and how the subject is orientated or disorientated not only in the present but also in relation to the past, to personal, and to cultural memory.... Topography becomes or is already haunted by tropography.
>
> (105)

It is perhaps not surprising, then, that du Maurier's portrayal of Venice in her fiction obliquely communicates her personal fears. As we have seen, "Ganymede" is haunted by du Maurier's concerns about her own "Venetian tendencies." "Don't Look Now," as well as being a gripping tale of the uncanny, also expresses du Maurier's personal anxieties—this time about aging. The story was written almost twenty years after

"Ganymede," when du Maurier was 63 (the same age as the twin sisters in the story) and was depressed about growing old. Writing to Oriel Malet about some photos Kits had taken of her, du Maurier commented:

> they make poor Tray [a family nickname] look just like an old peas-ant woman of ninety...and I nearly cried when I saw them. I know I am lined, but I had not realized how badly! And the awful expres-sion on my face, like a murderess.
>
> (Malet 1993, 194)

Known for her beauty and vitality when young, she now felt herself to be asexual and potentially monstrous. The very grounds of her identity seemed to be shifting beneath her. On the one hand, then, "Don't Look Now" expresses a masculine revulsion from the older woman, but also the feminine fear of *becoming* that grotesque figure. On the other hand, du Maurier's tale offers a warning against a gender-based complacency, vindicating as it does the wisdom of "old women" (the twins) rather than that of the more youthful John through whom all the events are fo-calized. Thus du Maurier's story perfectly captures the precarious status of the aged woman in Western society as one that slides between that of wise seer and death-dealing grotesque.

Throughout du Maurier's life and her fiction, Italy provided settings for her darkest imaginings about herself and society. These works fol-low the conventions of the classic gothic tale in which Italian cities fre-quently appear as sites for sophisticated intrigue, the exotic, the sinister, and the transgressive. In a letter to Maureen Baker-Munton, Daphne du Maurier wrote of herself and her husband, "We are both doubles. So is everyone. Every one of us has his, or her dark side. Which is to overcome the other?" (Forster 1993, 424). Du Maurier was haunted by what she saw as her dark side and for her that internal struggle between the light and the dark was never fully resolved. Its most dramatic expression, however, is to be found in those works she set in Italy.

Notes

1 Victor Sage's *Horror Fiction in the Protestant Tradition* (1988) traces the an-tipathy to Catholicism in Gothic fiction. Maria Purves in *The Gothic and Catholicism* (2009) challenges this critical view that the roots of the Gothic lie in anti-Catholicism, arguing for the influence of Catholic aesthetics and the French Catholic "sentimental" origins of many of Gothic's themes and motifs.
2 Writing to her friend Oriel Malet in 1962, she stated that she had collected all the volumes of Jung's work over the years (Malet 1993, 33, 39, 141). Nearly forty years later, Jung's depth psychology was to be subjected to fem-inist theorization in the work of Susan Rowland and identified as offering potentially fruitful concepts to feminist and gender theory.
3 Menabilly, near Fowey in Cornwall, was the ancestral home of the Rash-leigh family. Du Maurier leased it from them and lived there between

1943 and 1969, leaving only reluctantly when the Rashleighs declined to extend the lease any further. Before securing the tenancy, she was fascinated by the house and it became the inspiration for Manderley in her most famous novel, *Rebecca* (1938).

4 Francesca Donati suffers the same fate that would have befallen Rebecca had Maxim not murdered her: cancer of the womb. This is perhaps a symbolic representation of the opprobrium and punishment visited by society upon "promiscuous" women.

5 Du Maurier advised Oriel Malet to read *Modern Man in Search of a Soul*, but does not make reference to any other title (Malet 141). Margaret Forster notes that in letters to her seventeen-year-old daughter Flavia, du Maurier claimed that she had always been able to "feel within herself two quite separate personalities" which was clarified for her by Jung's theory of duality (Forster 276).

6 Quentin Bell, quoted in *The Times*, 6 August 1996 (commenting on du Maurier's inclusion in the Royal Mail's series of stamps featuring great twentieth-century women).

7 Cousins (2013) notes that "Poseidon does not feature in ancient myth as Jove's rival for Ganymede. He does so, however, in Christopher Marlowe's *Hero and Leander*" (220).

References

Begg, James. [1851] 1968. "The Blight of Popery." *The Reformation Journal* 1: 41–43. Reprinted in *Anti-Catholicism in Victorian England*, edited by E. R. Newman, 183–85. London: Allen & Unwin.

Cousins, A. D. 2013. "Daphne du Maurier's Ganymede." *Explicator* 71, no. 3 (July–September): 218–20.

Demata, Massimiliano. 2006. "Italy and the Gothic." *Gothic Studies* 8, no. 1: 1–8.

Du Maurier, Daphne. 1971. "Don't Look Now." In *"Don't Look Now" and Other Stories*. Harmondsworth: Penguin Books.

Du Maurier, Daphne. [1965] 1992. *The Flight of the Falcon*. London: Arrow Books.

Du Maurier, Daphne. [1958] 1970. "Ganymede." In *The Blue Lenses and Other Stories*. Harmondsworth: Penguin Books.

Du Maurier, Daphne. [1951] 1992. *My Cousin Rachel*. London: Arrow Books.

Forster, Margaret. 1993. *Daphne du Maurier*. London: Chatto and Windus.

Irigaray, Luce. 1974/1985. "Plato's *Hystera*." In *Speculum of the Other Woman*, translated by Gillian C. Gill, 243–364. Ithaca and New York: Cornell University Press.

Malet, Oriel, ed. 1993. *Daphne du Maurier: Letters from Menabilly—Portrait of a Friendship*. London: Weidenfeld and Nicholson.

Purves, Maria. 2009. *The Gothic and Catholicism*. Cardiff: University of Wales Press.

Rowland, Susan. 1999. *C. G. Jung and Literary Theory: The Challenge from Fiction*. Basingstoke: Palgrave Macmillan.

Radcliffe, Ann. [1797] 1991. *The Italian*. Oxford: Oxford University Press.

Sage, Victor. 1988. *Horror Fiction in the Protestant Tradition*. London and Basingstoke: Palgrave Macmillan.

Whitford, Margaret. 1991. *Luce Irigaray: Philosophy in the Feminine*. London and New York: Routledge.

Williams, Anne. 1995. *Art of Darkness: A Poetics of Gothic*. Chicago: University of Chicago Press.

Wolfreys, Julian. 2009. "Venice Imagined: The Invisible & Imaginary City, or, 'Les Lieux de La'." In *The Idea of the City: Early-Modern, Modern and Post-Modern Locations and Communities*, edited by Joan Fitzpatrick, 93–107. Newcastle upon Tyne: Cambridge Scholars Press.

8 Dennis Wheatley's Satanic Continent

Evert Jan van Leeuwen

During a career spanning four decades, Dennis Wheatley (1897–1977) wrote over fifty books and sold "over 40 million copies in Britain" alone (Bloom 2008, 228). Even though his historical novels and spy stories outnumber his Black Magic fictions, Wheatley became a horror celebrity because he not only wrote stories about Satanism and witchcraft, but also lectured and published newspaper articles on these topics (see Wheatley 1963a); on TV he spoke about his childhood encounter with a ghost and flaunted his acquaintance with occultists such as Aleister Crowley, Rollo Ahmed, and Montague Summers (BBC Four 2006). He eventually published the non-fiction compendium, *The Devil and All His Works* (1971),[1] which suggests that the sinister occult events portrayed in his novels are firmly anchored in history. Phil Baker (2009) explains that the ex-wine-merchant had always had "a flair for publicity" (251) and a knack for advertising (241); Wheatley was very good at convincing his audience that Satanism was a real threat to the British way of life. His occult fictions contain topical themes such as the rising political tensions on the continent in the 1930s, British immigration anxieties in the early 1940s, the rise of the welfare state after the war, or the growing Red Menace in the 1950s. Wheatley always included historical details to enhance the verisimilitude of his sensational fictions, from real-life personalities to the British tax laws. His occult novels contain editorial prefaces claiming, amongst other matters, that Black Magic and Satanism are a real and present danger, as the Devil is "a fundamental principle of the Christian faith" (1948, n.p.). As well as emphasizing the author's deep knowledge of the occult, these prefaces also highlight Wheatley's familiarity with their settings. One preface emphasizes that "Mr. Wheatley knows the South of France so well that he almost brings to the chapters set in it a breath of the mimosa-scented air" (1953a, n.p.).

This essay will show that in his occult fictions Wheatley deliberately cast the Satanic threat to British civilization as distinctly continental. With its detailed portraits of Satanists involved in international Communist conspiracies meant to undermine conservative British socio-political traditions, Wheatley's foundational occult thrillers, *The Devil Rides Out* (1934) and *The Haunting of Toby Jugg* (1948), should be understood as products of the "cultural propaganda" (Welch 2013, 23) machine that got into gear in the 1930s and sped up throughout the post-war period. Andrew Defty (2004) explains that after World War II, Britain was "faced with a worsening economy and a declining position as a world and imperial power" (28). In response, "the Labour Government placed considerable faith in the projection of British power and achievements through propaganda" (Defty 2004, 28). Wheatley believed in British power, but while the propaganda of the government was designed, amongst other ends, "to depict Britain as a leading exponent of social democracy and the leading power in the development of progressive welfare legislation" (Defty 2004, 29), Wheatley's propagandistic occult thrillers—including the derivative *To the Devil-A Daughter* (1953a) and *The Satanist* (1960)—cast Britain more and more as an isolated stronghold of reason, order, and progress that needed to be defended against the irrational, chaotic, and destructive continental force of Communism that was threatening to cross the channel and engulf the British Isles.

Gina Wisker (1993) argues that "the titillation of the potential daily presence of true evil" in Wheatley's occult fiction "is comfortingly matched…by an equal certainty that order and the status quo will be resolved; that honour, honesty and the wartime spirit of Britain can overcome anything nasty lurking in the visible or invisible enemy's plans" (99). However, Wheatley's obsession with the Satanic-Communist menace over three decades and the ever-returning threat of Baphomet being raised on British soil suggest rather that he genuinely believed the British way of life to be in serious danger of destruction. While Scott McCracken (1998) describes Wheatley's political views as "laughably dated" (131), the author remains one of the best-selling British thriller writers of his generation. In the age of Brexit, his propagandistic representation of Satanism as a specifically continental Communist threat warrants a closer critical examination.

One of the key features of Wheatley's success was that he developed an "author-persona" (Walker 1991, 114) early on in his career, marking himself out as a true expert in the fields of the occult and international political history. Such a "persona is a mask that may be related simultaneously to the biographical data available about the author and to other cultural and literary voices" (Walker 1991, 114). In his biography of Wheatley, Baker (2009) paints a magisterial portrait of a self-made national hero, and a true British striver and grafter—to borrow Philip Hammond's words—who cares passionately about the welfare of the British nation. Throughout his career as a popular novelist, Wheatley always stressed the significant international political insight he developed as an advisor to Churchill's war-time government, the entrepreneurial savvy he developed when he took over his family's wine business, and his literary talent for telling a good yarn.

In fact, Wheatley's literary and political talents influenced each other. During World War II, Wheatley (1959) explains, he shifted "his natural imagination and storytelling genius to the fields of statecraft and strategy" (9), when he became special advisor to the Joint Planning Staff of the War Cabinet. Wheatley's task, his war papers suggest, was to imagine ways in which Britain could best defend itself from a potential invasion and counter the Nazi menace. The officials who read Wheatley's papers were impressed with the way in which he could imaginatively enter into the minds of the German forces: "'We've been playing this war like cricket...but Wheatley thinks like a Nazi'" (quoted in Baker 2009, 402). Judging by the sales figures of Wheatley's novels, the reading public was equally impressed by his fictional accounts of continental Satanic conspiracy. In fact, for Wheatley the line between fiction and non-fiction was persistently blurred.

Having produced strategic papers in the early 1940s, Wheatley (1963) was pleased "to use such talents as [he had] been blessed with on propaganda" (1) after the war. The British government's Information and Research Department (IRD), in charge of propaganda, decided to produce popular anti-communist fictions for the Middle Eastern market (Defty 2004, 91). Wheatley produced only one official "propaganda romance" (Baker 2009, 469) for the IRD, but his post-war novels, *Jugg*, *Daughter*, and *The Satanist*, are to all intents and purposes anti-communist propaganda aimed at stifling the rise of socialism in Britain. They are the popular-fiction equivalent of the early 1950s Conservative propaganda poster that sported the slogan: "Let the lighthouse of conservatism save 'S.S. Britain' from the rocks of socialism" (Smith 2015).

In 1953, the same year that he produced his propaganda romance for the IRD and *Daughter*, Wheatley gave a Cantor lecture for the Royal Society of Arts, titled "The Novelist's Task." In it, he explains to his audience that

> in Victorian times many novels were written to edify; again, the novel is often used as a vehicle for propaganda. You will recall that several of Dickens's finest works were written with intent to stir the public conscience concerning certain social evils of his day.
>
> (1953b, 761)

Thus, for Wheatley, writing a novel was not merely an artistic endeavor but a social service, or rather, a party-political broadcast, a message to the public about his perception of the state of the nation. Barker is spot on when he argues that Wheatley's "books were an attempt to influence the mass consciousness of Britain" (BBC Four 2006). David Welch (2013) defines propaganda as

> the deliberate attempt to influence the public opinions of an audience, through the transmission of ideas and values, for a specific persuasive purpose that has been consciously thought out and designed to serve the self-interest of the propagandist, either directly or indirectly.
>
> (2)

In his occult novels, Wheatley (1959) deliberately attempted to convince British readers what he had communicated to the Joint Planning Staff in July 1940:

> we are the champions of Light facing the creeping tide of Darkness which threatens to engulf the world. Every man and woman must rise in answer to the call; so that in a thousand years the valour of our generation shall still be told and hearts shall quicken to hear the tale of how Britain stood alone—but triumphant.
>
> (104)

The most remarkable detail in this piece of ideological sublimity is Wheatley's desire to think of Britain as standing alone. Like the propaganda poster in which the Conservative Party is portrayed as the sole guiding light that will bring storm-tossed Britain safely ashore (Smith 2015), Wheatley takes pride in the fact that Britain is like no other nation and no other nation can save the world from the continental menace of Communism.

One propagandistic ploy Wheatley utilized to persuade his readers of the "truths" contained within the sensational world of his first occult thriller was to construct a close-knit international set of protagonists. Their devotion to each other, the novel illustrates, is determined by their devotion to the political principles to which Wheatley subscribed himself, which his novels reveal included a belief in the inherent virtue of traditional British institutions like the Church of England, the monarchy, parliament, a *laissez-faire* economy, and a strictly hierarchical social structure, in which people were grouped along distinct class, race, gender, and, in Wheatley's mind, above all monetary lines. By bringing a seemingly random selection of characters—only one of whom is actually a born Brit—together under the above-mentioned socio-political ideals, Wheatley was able to suggest that the British way of life he admired actually embodied an objective international standard of socio-political values that could save the wider world from communism.

In *Devil*, the leader of Wheatley's "Modern Musketeers" (1963, 113) is the epicurean Frenchman, the Duke de Richleau. Having been involved in a royalist uprising in the French Republic, Richleau has adopted Britain as his new home. In *Forbidden Territory*, published a year before *Devil*, readers were introduced to Wheatley's most beloved hero, and learned how much he had fallen in love with Great Britain, or rather, particularly with its traditional aristocratic culture. He talks enthusiastically

> of Windsor and Balmoral—then Ascot and Goodwood—the yachting week at Cowes, days in the Leicestershire country, hunting

with the Pytchley, summer nights on the gentle river that flows by
Maidenhead—of the spires and courts of Oxford, and the beauty of
the English country lanes in autumn.

(1933, 184–85)

The second musketeer is Rex van Ryn, son of "the President of the Ches-
apeake Banking and Trust Corporation" (1933, 15). Rex is the "great
hulking American with the ugly face and the enormous sense of fun"
(1933, 12). This heir to the throne of American finance provides the
brawn to complement the Duke's brain. The third is Simon Aron, a
"frail narrow-shouldered English Jew" (1934, 7), who, like Rex, works
in finance (1933, 15). Richard Eaton is the only native Brit in the novel,
and is also the least foregrounded of the four musketeers. Yet he proves
to be the backbone of Wheatley's band of heroes. In *Devil*, Eaton's country manor, Cardinal's Folly, functions as a safe-haven for the musketeers
and becomes the site of the climactic supernatural battle between the
forces of divine good—the musketeers—and prime evil: the French/Irish
Ipsissimus Damien Mocata and his band of foreign Satanists.

In *Devil*, London is the center of civilized society to which all the best
products produced in the world are shipped and consumed by the best
men at the finest West End gentlemen's clubs. Trouble starts when Simon
moves from the "one small room at his club" (1933, 23) into "a rambling
old place" (1934, 9) in St. John's Wood. In Wheatley's day "a faint air of
impropriety clung to" (Doniach 1955) NW8. Rex remarks that Simon's
new residence lies beyond Regent's Park and wonders why Simon did not
purchase a place nearer Richleau in the central and more affluent district
of Mayfair (1934, 10). From the outset of the novel, Wheatley builds
up a geo-political map of civilization that consists of a series of concen-
tric circles, with London's W1 standing as the heart of civilization. On
this map, St. John's Wood is already in the circle surrounding the heart
and thus slightly less civilized and prone to degradation. In the course
of *Devil*—and almost all of Wheatley's occult fictions—the further out
from Mayfair his heroes move, the greater their trouble. In *Devil*, the
musketeers find Satanists in St. John's Wood, disturb a Black Mass on
Salisbury Plain, and eventually chase Mocata through Paris and down
to Greece, as he attempts to release the four horsemen of the apocalypse
to start World War II.

That Mocata is half Irish and half French is no coincidence. Both
nations are Britain's direct neighbors; both are Republics in which the
Catholic faith has been predominant for centuries. Both lie in a circle further outside of Wheatley's geo-political center. Politically and religiously
they form a complete contrast to the Anglican and monarchical traditions to which Wheatley and his characters are devoted. Mocata, the ex-
priest who had tried, and failed, to raise the devil in England, is described
by the narrator as "pot-bellied, bald-headed...with large, protuberant,

fishy eyes, limp hands, and a most unattractive lisp," reminiscent of "a large white slug" (1934, 10). In London, Mocata stays with Simon Aron, who explains to his friends that his guest suffers from "irritable fits" (1934, 119) that lead to bouts of "debauchery down in the slums of the East End" (1934, 119) about once a month. Richleau explains to Rex that Mocata has a "queer servant" (1934, 10) from Madagascar, who is "a 'bad black' if ever I saw one" (1934, 10). Other new friends of Simon are "a fat, oily looking Babu in a salmon-pink turban and gown" and "a red-faced Teuton, who suffered the deformity of a hare lip" (1934, 15). In *Devil*, North and East London districts, as well as nearly all European regions East and South of the British Isles—including Paris and Greece—are aligned with the inhuman and evil from the outset.

Welch (2013) explains that

> in terms of propaganda, the use of contrasts has proved one of the most identifiable stylistic devices. Not only do strong contrasts contain a greater emotional intensity than more subtle nuances, but they also guide the audience's sympathies with more certainty.
>
> (152)

Wheatley was clearly aware of this formal aspect of propaganda. Throughout *Devil* he complements his geo-political and moral dichotomy with an elaborate spiritual dichotomy that universalizes the categories of good and evil. Richleau, the personification of "the old civilization of Western Europe" (1933, 44), turns out to be a white magician, capable of battling the Devil on the astral plane, as well in St. John's Wood. He tells Rex about "Ozamund and Ahriman" (1934, 25).[2] According to Richleau, this myth represents "the eternal powers of Light and Darkness," that wage war "without cessation for the good or ill of mankind" (1934, 25). He explains that all religions and mythologies can be reduced to a single overriding spiritual teaching in which "Light typifies Health and Wisdom, Growth and Life; while Darkness mean Disease and Ignorance, Decay and Death" (1934, 25). Wheatley would repeat this notion *ad nauseam* in all his occult novels and his non-fiction writings on the occult. Of course, the island of Great Britain is the home of the Light, and the rest of the world is identified as the birthplace and playfield of the Dark forces. In *Devil*, Britain really does stand alone and is not yet triumphant.

Since Wheatley so unambiguously casts Britain as the stronghold of right reason and proper religion, it may seem strange initially that Richleau identifies the eastern "Yoga of Tibet" as "the preservers of the Way of Light" (1934, 26). Tibetan monks reside far from the center of Wheatley's civilization. But Wheatley, a devout supporter of British Empire, must have been aware that at the end of the nineteenth-century Lord Curzon—viceroy of India—"had declared his intention to protect British India from Russian expansionism" (Van Schaik 2011, 170) and consequently planned an invasion of Tibet, which took place in 1904. Van Schaik (2011) explains that this invasion "would embroil Britain in Tibet for the next seventy-five years" (179). The year before *Devil* was published, James Hilton's depiction of Shangri-La in *Lost Horizon* successfully tapped into "the misty-eyed spiritualism that was popular in England in the early twentieth century" (Van Schaik 2011, 179). Wheatley's spiritual dichotomy of light and dark should be understood in this colonial context. Judging from his depiction of "the East" more generally, Wheatley subscribed to the colonial ideology of the "white man's burden." For him, Eastern spiritual philosophies become charming and enchanting when encountered under a colonial banner; evil lurks in the corners of the globe where Britain has not gained a foothold, like the former Spanish and French colony of Haiti, "the evil island" in Wheatley's *Strange Conflict* (1941), where the Nazi's find a voodoo-priest whose magic they enlist into their service. Richleau explains to Rex that Voodoo typifies the powers of Darkness and points out that this evil force, while now associated mostly with Haiti, originated on the island of Madagascar (1934, 26). Madagascar was a part of the world that the British government had struggled but failed to incorporate into its empire. By the late nineteenth century, the island had become a French colony, which it remained until 1958. Richleau's spiritual philosophy supports Wheatley's geo-political moral dichotomy as the British-influenced Tibetan spiritualty is set off against the Voodoo cult of French-influenced Madagascar or of Haiti (as in *Conflict*).

For Wheatley, not only French-controlled parts of the colonial world were dangerous. The French Third Republic itself was a deeply problematic nation. Not only had it proven to be a rival in the empire building game, but moreover, by 1932 the *Cartel des Gauches* had won the general election. The narrator of *Devil* describes France as a socialist republic that forced Richleau into exile after his part in a Royalist uprising during the 1890s (1934, 213). In Paris Simon Aron does business with Laurent Castelnau, a black magician using his occult powers to manipulate the stock market in his favor, while he converts others to Satanism (1934, 117). It is through Castelnau that Aron befriends Mocata and Mocata comes to England to find an innocent victim to offer up to the Devil during the Black Mass that will release the four horsemen of the apocalypse. It is the French countess D'Ufré, another member of Mocata's Satanic circle, who controls the exotic Eastern-European neophyte Tanith, whose seductive presence almost eliminates Rex from the battle. In *Devil*, all danger to the musketeers, and to the political status quo in Britain, originates directly from the leftist French Third Republic.

The Duke explains that "Europe is ripe now for any trouble and if [the four horsemen] are loosed again, it will be final Armageddon" (1934, 121). For Wheatley, in 1934, the trouble brooding in Europe did not primarily lie with the rise of fascism in Italy and Germany. In fact, in

Mediterranean Nights (1963), Wheatley reveals his admiration for Mussolini's style of government, lamenting only the Italian dictator's decision to become Hitler's ally during World War II (60). From the outset of his writing career, Wheatley was specifically agitated by left-wing political movements that sought to break down the traditional sociopolitical hierarches that had ordered the world in which he had grown up, and which he so much admired. These "left-wing" evils are always continental, and forever threatening to infect the British political and social structure. In *Territory*, Wheatley had set his heroes up against the "blind, monstrous power" (1933, 45) of "the Soviet machine" (1933, 274). When his musketeers are gathered together at a dinner, having rescued Rex from imprisonment in the USSR, their British diplomat friend Gerry Bruce calls on Mother Nature to solve the political problem when he toasts: "May Russia freeze the Bolshies" (1933, 287). In his first adventure, Richleau steals from and kills Soviet Russians without any moral scruples, while bemoaning the slaughter of the old Russian aristocracy during the Revolution. From his first to his last adventure, all characters on the wrong side of Richleau's political allegiance deserve the capital punishment they receive.

In order further to impart a sense of objectivity to his geo-political-moral-spiritual dichotomy Wheatley's heroes frequently discuss world mythology. To convince the down-to-earth and rational Englishman, Richard Eaton of the true existence of the Dark spiritual forces they will have to battle, Richleau turns to the Egyptian myth of Isis and Osiris. According to him, "Osiris was…a fair-haired, light skinned man, alien to the Egyptian race"; he ruled the Egyptians "with great intelligence," and "brought them many blessings" (1934, 163). His brother Set, by contrast, "was a dark man," a "charming but unscrupulous rogue who might have entertained you with lavish hospitality and brilliant conversation yesterday—yet would do you down without the least compunction if he met you in the street to-morrow" (1934, 163). According to Richleau, the dark Set conspired against the divine authority of his light brother out of a sheer will to power. The mind boggles at Richleau's understanding of Egyptian mythology, but it clearly serves Wheatley's propagandistic purpose to develop a Manichean sense of good versus evil along geo-political, class, and color lines. Mocata is just like Set and in the course of the novel Richleau—the embodiment of Wheatley's conservative values—will play the role of Osiris: the initially unwitting, but ultimately triumphant target of Mocata's Satanic conspiracy. During the climax of the novel, Mocata lures Richleau to his Satanic lair on the dilapidated outskirts of Paris. While the musketeers had only recently dined on luxury victuals at a fashionable restaurant in the old heart of Paris, it is here—on the city's grim periphery—that the leftist authorities in France try to arrest the royalist campaigner on the charge of treason against the French Republic.

Readers of *Territory* will know that the musketeers are not afraid to get their hands dirty when it comes to defending themselves and the socio-political values for which they stand. On the point of being arrested, Richleau and Rex hammer the French authorities and escape France as they pursue the evil Mocata to the ruins of an ancient monastery on Mount Peristeri, in Greece, where he intends to recover the Talisman of Set, raise the Goat of Mendes, perform a Black Mass, sacrifice the Eatons' daughter Fleur (whom he abducted from Cardinal's Folly) to the Devil, and release the four horsemen of the apocalypse. Just as all seems lost, Marie Lou Eaton saves her daughter and all of humanity from falling into another age of darkness by voicing an incantation from the mysterious, medieval book of occult lore, the *Red Book of Appin*—a British book—that calls down a Lord of Light from the highest astral plane. In the visage of this immortal spiritual being are amalgamated the best aspects of the "Aryan" and "Mongolian" race (1934, 241). His figure showed "all the health and vigour of a man" in the prime of his life and the "beauty which is only seen in that of a frail, scholarly divine who has devoted a whole lifetime to the search of wisdom" (1934, 241). This Lord of Light embodies Wheatley's fantasy of the perfect hero: he is Osiris reborn, physically Western and spiritually Eastern, which, unsurprisingly, makes him just like the Duke de Richleau, of whom Marie Lou remarks, "somehow I always think of you really as an Englishman" (1934, 213).

In 1945, the British Labour Party's

> general election manifesto *Let Us Face the Future* boldly claimed that 'the Labour Party is a Socialist Party, and proud of it,' and that its ultimate purpose was 'the establishment of a Socialist Commonwealth of Great Britain—free, democratic, efficient, progressive, public-spirited, its material resources organized in the service of the British people'.
>
> (Francis 1995, 223)

By 1949, in *Labour Believes in Britain*, the Party "began its definition of socialism with a commitment to the pursuit of equality: both equality of opportunity and equality of income and property" (Francis 1995, 225). For an arch conservative like Wheatley, such socialist propaganda must have suggested that the continental Communist disease had at last managed to break down Britain's immune system. In his now infamous "Letter to Posterity" (1947), which he buried in his garden for future Britons to discover, Wheatley lamented that

> the coming of the machine age enabled the politicians of the all-men-are-equal school to get into ever closer touch with the masses. Under the banners of liberation they preached against every form of

privilege, thus making the masses discontented with their lot. Later, the socialists, they openly advocated equality in all things; all men are not equal. Some have imagination and abilities far above others. It is their province and their right to take upon themselves the responsibility of leading and protecting the less gifted.

(n.p.)

While Wheatley lived decades beyond this rant, and this one letter should not be understood as his definitive political position, the novel he published the following year, *The Haunting of Toby Jugg*, celebrates the entrepreneurial spirit and patriotism of those Britons with "imagination and abilities above others"—and also concerns the threat their way of life faces from leftist continental immigrants. Wheatley structures the story as a journal/memoir in which Toby Jugg—heir to Albert Abel Jugg's business empire—recounts how he became the subject of an occult attack by a continental Satanist attempting to get hold of the Jugg millions to fund a campaign to paint the British government red. Welch explains that good propaganda "is intrinsically emotional and excludes all alternatives" (2013, 188). By casting Toby's revelations about the satanic plot in the form of a personal memoir, Wheatley was able to heighten the emotional character of his novel and to present, unambiguously and above all passionately, his English hero's perspective on events and his efforts to overcome the red menace. As a war-hero, Toby is not easily defeated, even if he is deeply scared and suspicious to the point of being paranoid at the outset of the novel. In the opening journal entries, Toby takes his reader on a journey from skepticism to faith, making his eventual testimony about the Satanic plot all the more believable. Moreover, the reader learns that Toby is paralyzed from the waist down after getting shot during a dogfight with the Germans. This leaves him ostensibly helpless. But the reader learns that Toby was nicknamed "The Viking" (1948, 5) and had a Herculean torso (1948, 100). Toby is definitely down when the story opens, but far from being out for the count. The novel is a story of stereotypical "British pluck" (Hawes 2017) winning out against the odds.

The reader learns that Toby had spent his earliest childhood in a mansion in Kensington Palace Gardens (1948, 74). This place, like Richleau's Mayfair apartment, becomes the geo-political center of the novel. This stands as the spiritual home of the Jugg family, even though their roots lie up north in Yorkshire (with wealth comes taste and good sense, Wheatley's novels always suggest). Once again, the further away from this center of order and tradition Toby wanders, the more open to continental corruption he becomes. When the novel opens, he finds himself held hostage on his reclusive aunt's Llanferdrack estate in Wales by his one-time mentor, the Czech Satanist Helmut Lisický. Forebodingly, Toby explains that his former home in Kensington Palace Gardens has become part of "the Soviet Embassy" (1948, 182).[3] Toby reveals that as he grew up his happy-go-lucky uncle Paul became his guardian. Paul was the family's prodigal son who had spent time abroad living a debauched life. He had returned to the family fold with his beautiful Italian wife Julia, a member of a noble Roman family, who had been denied the wealth she believed to be rightfully hers. At seventeen Julia had been initiated into the Left-Hand Path at "a Witches' Sabbath in the Alban hills" (1948, 281). She had married Paul because he was a trustee of the Jugg millions and thus could become a means to achieving her financial ambitions. Importantly, in the Wheatley scheme of things, Julia and Paul do not live in central London but out west, in Kew. At this home séances are held and Toby encounters a ghost. It is through Paul and Julia that Toby becomes a pupil of the Czech Satanist Helmut Lisický.

Lisický had come to Britain in 1933 with his servant Konrad "a typical Slav; big, fair and boisterous, with a hearty laugh that deceives people, until they come to know him well and find out how cunning he is below the surface" (1948, 103). Lisický and Konrad know Paul and Julia because they are members of the same continental masonic lodge, which Toby emphasizes is not related to British-style masonry. The aim of continental masonry, Toby explains, is to influence British politics and business (1948, 44) with the ultimate plan "to finance a Communist revolution in Britain" (1948, 248). Unwittingly, Toby's youthful move from Kensington to Kew was also and unwittingly his first step into the secret world of the continental Satanic-Communist conspiracy.

From Kew, Toby moves further afield to Weylands school in Cumberland. Here Lisický becomes his German language instructor and all-round mentor. The school's motto is Aleister Crowley's (and Rabelais's) maxim: "do what thou wilt shall be the whole of the law" (1948, 39). Toby's narrative gains in credence because he confesses that he initially enjoyed the promiscuous life-style encouraged at Weylands. After encountering a strange phantom at the nearby ruined Abbey, and witnessing his aunt's and uncle's strange behavior on a visit to Weylands, Toby smells a rat and runs away. Unfortunately, Weylands turns out to be a prep-school for the Continental Masons and the Satanist Lisický has already been able to exert enough influence over Toby to control him mentally from afar. Significantly, it is the injury Toby sustains in his heroic war effort that allows lazy Paul, beautiful Julia, and demonic Lisický to regain and strengthen their occult influence over him. Trapped at Llanferdrack, and set upon by a demonic force unleashed by Lisický, Toby becomes aware that he is expected to serve the Satanic conspiracy by handing over the family fortune to the "red" cause as soon as he comes of age.

Welch explains that within propagandistic strategies "identifying an object of hate means exploiting stereotypes—conventional figures that come to be regarded as representative of particular classes, races, nations and so on" (2013, 154). In *Devil*, Wheatley had done his best to stereotype the French Third Republic. In *Jugg*, Wheatley stereotypes continental immigrants. His nurse, Deborah Kain, is a German-Jewish refugee of Russian descent. Like Lisický, she came to Britain in 1933, "when hundreds of refugees from Nazi Germany, most of them Jews, arrived in the United Kingdom" (London 2000, 16). In 1933, "Britain was struggling to shake off [economic] depression. Unemployment was high" and "severe restrictions on aliens entering for work or settlement remained in force" (London 2000, 19). Judging from his attitude toward Deborah, Toby clearly imbibed British worries about the consequences of mass immigration from the continent in the 1930s, when the Nazis "singled out socialists, communists, trade unionists, and Jews for persecution" (London 2000, 25). Individuals belonging to the first three of these four groups, even the most casual perusal of Wheatley's oeuvre reveals, form the wrong kind of people in most of his novels. While Wheatley made the English Jew Simon Aron one of his musketeers, he certainly held an ambiguous attitude toward the influx of Jewish immigrants. In the character of Deborah Kain Wheatley conflates all the groups that Louise London identifies as the Nazi's key ideological enemies. According to Toby, Deborah "holds most advanced views on political reform" (1948, 36) and turns out to be a devoted Communist who has been sent to Britain from the continent to infiltrate British life and spread the red gospel. He emphasizes that Deborah's case is not uncommon in Britain and that many British coastal towns are "packed with Jews" (1948, 119). While Toby believes that "British Jews"—like Wheatley's Simon Aron— "are pulling their weight" (1948, 120), he has doubts about "the Jewish refugees to whom we have given asylum" (1948, 120). He wonders: "how is it that there is always such a high proportion of Jews in the 'safe' places where there is still good food and soft living to be had?" (1948, 119). The novel suggests that there is a Satanic conspiracy of continental Jewish Communists operating in Britain to take over power from the national government. Toby also suspects Lisický of "hav[ing] a dash of Jewish blood acquired two or three generations back" because "his ears are low on his skull" (1948, 48). London (2000) explains that during the 1930s, when many European Jews emigrated from Continental Europe, the British government "opted for caution and pragmatism, subordinating humanitarianism to Britain's national interest"; this policy, London emphasizes, was not peculiarly British but adopted by various countries at that time (1). Though set during the war, and detailing the paranoid speculations of its British hero, Wheatley's post-war occult thriller does not just re-invoke the British government's pre-war policy of self-interest over altruism but disturbingly creates a British war-hero protagonist who overtly displays his xenophobia. Having revolved the arguments in his mind for and against Lisický being a Satanic-Communist, Toby concludes that his one-time mentor "is the nigger in the wood-pile" (1948, 79). He puts on a great front as a naturalized Brit and a devoted guardian of the Jugg millions, but as soon as Toby resists his preternatural machinations,

Lisický gets angry and authoritarian, and his "Czech accent" becomes "perceptible" (1948, 106). Since Deborah is a Communist "under orders of the Party" (1948, 120), and a naturalized British citizen with ambitions to enter into politics, she must be in league with Lisický. The notion that a woman like Deborah Kain can become an MP "positively horrifies" Toby as "a monstrous perversion" (1948, 126) of British democracy.

Despite being hounded by a giant spider from the astral plane, Toby has much room in his journal for political speculation. For instance, he proposes banning every "man or woman whose parents were not British *born*" from becoming members of parliament (1948, 127). Toby's right-wing, xenophobic, political ideals are given credence because of the way he develops them whilst in a state of utter terror at the evil powers that are being let loose in Britain, and against himself, as the heir to an honestly earned fortune. His ideas are born out of direct experience and suffering under the very forces he is determined to oppose at the cost of his own life if necessary. What gives Toby's immigration policy even more clout is that his mother is American. Should his vision be realized, Toby would be barred from British politics. Such a self-sacrificial attitude enhances Toby's patriotism, and he emphasizes that he would gladly forfeit his right to represent the people "if it helped to ensure that Britain should continue to be ruled by the British" (1948, 127).

From the moment Toby acknowledges his belief that the socialists are winning over many people and are transforming them into "human robots" (1948, 73), his personal struggle against the Satanic-Communist conspiracy becomes a deeply ideological one in which hymns like "Onward Christian Soldiers" (1948, 146) turn out to be weapons against Lisický's supernatural evils. And just as in *Devil*, a force of Light is called up by a true believer to spoil the Satanists' Black Mass on Walpurgis Night. Toby manages to defeat the Satanists by tapping into the most powerful white magic of all: Divine Love. His weapon, like Marie Lou's in the earlier novel, is not a physical but a spiritual one: "I called on God and the Virgin Mary; on all the Powers of Good and Light and Love that there had ever been in the world....I cried aloud my defiance of Satan and all his works" and "God had heard my prayer" (1948, 288). Welch explains that "the propaganda image of the enemy must...remain of stylized simplicity. The message must be expressed in a way that does not invite discussion" (2013, 188). At the climax of *Jugg* no doubt remains about the status and allegiance of the hero. He is a born-and-bred Englishman, descendent from, and heir to the fortunes of a hard-working Victorian Yorkshireman who had settled at Kensington Palace Gardens, the exemplar of the new working rich—with which Wheatley aligned himself—that had built, governed, and were now fighting to retain the Great British Empire. Evil, as in all Wheatley's occult novels, is embodied in the continental Satanic-Communist conspiracy, seeking to raise the Goat of Mendes in order to contaminate Britain's green and pleasant lands with a deadly red toxin.

In the 1950s Wheatley's occult propaganda machine showed no signs of slowing down. In his two major occult fictions of the period, *To the Devil-A Daughter* and *The Satanist*, he repeated the formula of his first two supernatural successes, but also introduced a more modern defender of his own High Tory ideals: Colonel William "Conky Bill" Verney, of Special Branch, who shares with the earlier musketeers the habit of dining at his club in central London (1960, 22) and joining the Pytchley hunt in his free time (1960, 11). In the Verney novels, Wheatley lashes out at what he believed to be Clement Attlee's poor management of the country after the war and how it had stifled the British economy (1953a, 51). The characters caught up in Satan's snare belong to the hard-working and ambitious upper-middle class: the thriller-author Molly Fountain (lover of Conky Bill); her son, the young interior decorator Johnny; Henry Beddows, director of Beddows Agricultural Tractors, and his daughter Christine; as well as special branch officer Teddy Morden and his wife Mary—and not to forget the lovable Irish rogue turned special agent, and heir to the estate of Larne, Barney Sullivan. Johnny Fountain speaks for all these characters when he tells a young French aristocrat that "since in both our countries the Government has become only another name for the People, it really amounts to the idle and stupid stealing from those who work hard and show initiative" (1953a, 93). The Verney novels present a Britain victorious in war, but defeated by the rise of a welfare state that leaves Conky Bill— a "hearty species of British manhood" (1953a, 238–39)—with "too much desk work" (1960, 11) properly to defend the nation against the red menace. Unlike Richleau, who was very much a free agent, Verney is a committed government servant: he "supervise[s] the watch that is maintained in every port in the kingdom against undesirables entering it; [is] responsible for security in all secret Scientific Establishments; [has] at least fifty potential spies or saboteurs either hunted or kept under observation" (1960, 275). Verney knows from experience that Satanists are not just hedonists, but are out "to foment wars, class-hatred, strikes and famine; and to foster perversions, moral laxity and the taking of drugs" (1953a, 81–82). He knows for a fact that "one of Russia's prime objects is to disrupt our industry, in order to create the unemployment and discontent which always results in the spread of Communism" (1960, 16) and is "help[ing] the T.U.C. in its big campaign to purge the British Labour movement of Russian influence" (1960, 15) because all those "wildcat stoppages eat into profits like rats into corn" (1960, 14). Because Wheatley's new hero works at the center of government, the Verney novels become more explicitly propagandistic than *Devil* or *Jugg*, containing frequent instances in which the protagonists engage in the kind of overt political sloganeering quoted above.

While Wheatley's new hero was no longer an aristocratic white magician, but patriotic government employee, his villains were cast of exactly the same mold as Mocata and Lisický. In *Daughter*, the chief Satanist is played by an Englishman, Canon Copley-Syle, who not only resembles but actually knew Mocata. He also knows the Satanic temple at St. John's Wood and that Mocata was defeated by a superior White Magician (1953a, 216–17). Such intertextual referencing creates the kind of fictional continuity that gives apparent substance to Wheatley's stories. His characters do not live in an isolated fictional universe, but in realistically rendered British and continental landscapes and they have a recognizable and shared history. The fact that Copley-Syle is an Englishman working his Black Magic on orders from the Kremlin suggests that the Satanic-Communist conspiracy really has struck roots in home soil. Of course, Copley-Syle's Black Magic is authentically continental. He is a student of Count von Küffstein, of Tyrol, and the Italian Abbé Geloni, whose pioneering work in creating homunculi was later picked up by Count Max Lemberg and Count Franz-Joseph von Thun, and continued by the great Paracelsus (1953a, 221). Copley-Syle is creating a supernatural army for the Soviets that can march "under the hypnotic direction of their masters" and can live off "the blood from the bodies of their enemies" (1953a, 225). Apparently, "the minds of nearly half the population of the world" are now "attuned in opposition to the so-called Light" (1953a, 226).

If Copley-Syle is the new Mocata, Lothar Khune, in *The Satanist*, is the new Lisický. Lothar is one of a set of American identical twins of German descent. Both are the seventh son of a seventh daughter, and therefore unusually susceptible to psychic powers (1960, 35). While Otto Khune married a British girl and became a patriotic British citizen, Lothar was a power-hungry Nazi sympathizer in the 1930s, and joined the German Research Works at Peenemünde (1960, 37). Of course, Lothar is not merely a German-American mad-scientist Nazi, but a Satanist who aims: "to disrupt all stable forms of government; to create a state of world anarchy, so that...the Devil will come into his own again" (1960, 382). Lothar's Satanic coven consists of mostly foreign and grotesque figures (1960, 82). The caretakers of the temple are Haitian zombies. His right-hand man in London is a "slimy Babu" (1960, 106) called Krishna Ratnadatta, "a fat, squat Indian wearing thick-lensed glasses, and with protruding teeth" (1960, 49) and breath like "bad lobster" (1960, 70).

In both Verney stories, central London remains the heart of civilization, while its off-center districts are shown to be open to infiltration. Lothar establishes his Satanic temple, The Brotherhood of the Ram, in "a house off the far end of the King's Road, Chelsea," and Barney explains to Verney that this part of town "is now made up of big blocks of post-war Council flats, mostly built on sites that were left derelict by bombs, and streets of slums that escaped them" (1960, 160). St. John's Wood, the site of the Satanic temple in *Devil*, and the Cremorne Estate in SW10 are almost equal distance from Curzon Street in Mayfair, where Richleau lived. In *Daughter*, the Satanic temple is situated in Little Bentford, near Colchester, a similar distance from London as Salisbury Plain, where Mocata attempted to raise the devil in 1934. When

Molly Fountain—living in the south of France for tax reasons—suspects her neighbor Christina of being in the power of Satanists, she immediately decides to telephone the British capital (1953a, 79), which means calling Conky Bill at Special Branch. Both Verney novels uphold the geo-political, moral, and spiritual dichotomy of *Devil* and *Jugg*. The presence of foreigners in the capital signals something is amiss. When Verney's right-hand man Barney Sullivan infiltrates a spiritualist circle in SW5, "only the Indian" (1960, 60), who turns out to be Ratnadatta, strikes him as a potential threat. In *Daughter*, Copley-Syle is in league with a French nobleman-turned-businessman, Marquis de Grasse, who runs a shipping company that "covers a multitude of sins," including drugs smuggling, white slavery, and "smuggling Jews out to Palestine, and arms to anyone in the Near East who wants to make trouble for us" (1953a, 57). In *Devil* and *Conflict*, chaos thrived where British influence was weakest, and, in *Daughter*, Molly Fountain laments that the government's failure to manage its post-war economy has limited British presence on the Riviera (1953a, 51), allowing figures like De Grasse to build their criminal empire.

Unsurprisingly, the climactic confrontation between Wheatley's heroes and the Satanists in the Verney novels takes place on the continent. Failing to bring Christina to Little Bentford, Copley-Syle takes his homunculus to the Riviera, where Christina had been hidden away by her father. The British Ipsissimus knows that Satanic altars can be found "in every big city in the world. All over Europe they are scattered in the country parts too; mostly in ruined abbeys, old castles and such" (1953a, 323), and the Cave of Bats near Nice will serve his purpose just as well as Mount Peristeri, in Greece had served Mocata. Lothar Khune escapes to the Swiss Alps where he hides in a cave with his Chinese henchmen, whilst he constructs a nuclear rocket from materials stolen from British and American military bases in Britain. When Mary Morden learns that Lothar is "aiming to put it on Moscow" she says: "I can't help feeling sorry for the Russians; but thank God it's not London" (1960, 395).

P. M. Taylor (1999) explains that

> most people in the twentieth century have perceived the wider world around them not through personal experience but via the mass media....This would suggest that a tremendous responsibility has been placed on the media to represent events accurately and without prejudice to the 'truth'.
>
> (ix)

Wheatley was well aware of the power of the mass media as a vehicle for disseminating visions of "the truth" and Baker's biography suggests that he believed firmly in what he published. Looking back on his career, Wheatley explained in an interview that he always aimed "to make it plain to the reader what is going on...I couldn't care less if it's grammatical or not grammatical" (BBC Four 2006). What Wheatley believed was going on in Europe between 1933 and 1971 was highly colored by the conservative ideology to which he subscribed. Paradoxically, in Wheatley's eyes, Britain was a bastion of freedom, on a political, social, and economic level, exactly because the nation was built on traditional hierarchies of class, race, and gender. The freedoms British citizens enjoy, Wheatley's occult novels suggest, can be safeguarded only by perpetuating the British monarchy, the British Empire, the British parliamentary structure, British *laissez-faire* entrepreneurialism, and by retaining a social, intellectual, masculine elite that through its sense of national pride and Christian duty looked after the masses. As Richleau concludes at the end of *Conflict*:

> as long as Britain stands the Powers of Darkness cannot prevail. On Earth the Anglo-Saxon race is the last Guardian of the Light, and I have an unshakable conviction that, come what may, our island will prove the Bulwark of the World.
>
> (1942, 291)

Notes

1 I have quoted from early unexpurgated editions. The latest Bloomsbury editions are edited (modernized/censored) editions. In order not to overcrowd the text block with dates, I refer to the original date of publication only in the parenthetical source references. The date of the edition quoted from is stated in the reference list.
2 Wheatley refers here to Ahura Mazdā, or Ohrmazd, and Angra Manyu, or Pahlavi Ahriman. In *The Spirit of Zoroastrianism* (Yale UP, 2011), Prods Oktor Skjærvø explains that "Ahura Mazdā ordered the cosmos and upholds the cosmic Order, and he is the benevolent ruler of the ordered cosmos" (13). By contrast "the ruler of the world of darkness is the Dark Spirit...Angra Manyu (Pahlavi Ahriman)" (20).
3 This is one of Wheatley's typical historical details. The Russian Embassy in London really does stand on the edge of Kensington Gardens, on the border with Notting Hill.

References

Baker, Phil. 2009. *The Devil Is a Gentleman: The Life and Times of Dennis Wheatley.* Sawtry: Dedalus.

BBC Four. 2006. *Dennis Wheatley: A Letter to Posterity.* www.youtube.com/watch?v=qeXEj2_v6i4. Accessed on 26 July 2018.

Bloom, Clive. 2008. *Bestsellers: Popular Fiction Since 1900.* 2nd ed. Basingstoke: Palgrave.

Defty, Andrew. 2004. *Britain, America and Anti-Communist Propaganda, 1945–1953.* Abingdon: Routledge.

Doniach, Thea. 1955. "The Story of St John's Wood." www.stjohnswoodmemories.org.uk/content/new-contributions/__trashed-4. Accessed on 19 October 2018.

Francis, Martin. 1995. "Economics and Ethics: The Nature of Labour's Social-ism, 1945–1951." *Twentieth Century British History* 6, no. 2: 220–43.

Hawes, James. 2017. "The Great Myth of British Pluck (and why it's a sym-bol of decline)." *The New European*, 21 August. www.theneweuropean.co.uk/top-stories/the-great-myth-of-british-pluck-and-why-it-s-a-symbol-of-decline-1-5157183. Accessed on 21 January 2019.

London, Louise. 2000. *Whitehall and the Jews, 1933–1948: British Immi-gration Policy, Jewish Refugees and the Holocaust.* Cambridge: Cambridge University Press.

McCracken, Scott. 1998. *Pulp: Reading Popular Fiction.* Manchester: Manchester University Press.

Skjærvø, Prods Oktor. 2011. *The Spirit of Zoroastrianism.* New Haven, CT: Yale University Press.

Smith, Evan. 2015. "Tory Anti-Communism in the Early 1950s." https://hatfulofhistory.wordpress.com/2015/07/02/tory-anti-communism-in-the-early-1950s/. Accessed on 2 November 2018.

Taylor, Philip M. 1999. *British Propaganda in the 20th Century: Selling Democracy.* Edinburgh: Edinburgh University Press.

Van Schaik, Sam. 2011. *Tibet.* New Haven: Yale University Press.

Walker, Cheryl. 1991. "Persona Criticism and the Death of the Author." In *Contesting the Subject: Essays in Postmodern Theory and Practice of Biogra-phy and Biographical Criticism*, edited by William H. Epstein, 109–21. West Lafayette, IN: Purdue University Press.

Welch, David. 2013. *Propaganda: Power and Persuasion.* London: British Library.

Wheatley, Dennis. [1971] 1973. *The Devil and All His Works.* London: Arrow.

Wheatley, Dennis. [1963] 1973. *Mediterranean Nights.* London: Heron Books.

Wheatley, Dennis. [1963a] 1979. *Gunmen, Gallants and Ghosts.* London: Arrow.

Wheatley, Dennis. 1960. *The Satanist.* London: Hutchinson.

Wheatley, Dennis. [1959] 1976. *Stranger than Fiction.* London: Arrow.

Wheatley, Dennis. 1953a. *To the Devil a Daughter.* London: Hutchinson.

Wheatley, Dennis. 1953b. "The Novelist's Task." *Journal of the Royal Society of Arts* 150, no. 4908 (September): 761–70.

Wheatley, Dennis. [1948] 1951. *The Haunting of Toby Jugg.* London: Hutchinson.

Wheatley, Dennis. 1947. "A Letter to Posterity." http://www.denniswheatley.info/sams_books/ lettertoposterity2.htm. Accessed on 26 July 2018.

Wheatley, Dennis. [1941] 1942. *Strange Conflict.* London: The Book Club.

Wheatley, Dennis. [1934] n.d. *The Devil Rides Out.* 147th Thousand. London: Hutchinson.

Wheatley, Dennis. [1933] 1951. *Forbidden Territory.* 77th Thousand. London: Hutchinson.

Wisker, Gina. 1993. "Horrors and Menaces to Everything Decent in Life: The Horror Fiction of Dennis Wheatley." In *Creepers: British Horror & Fantasy in the Twentieth Century*, edited by Clive Bloom, 99–110. London: Pluto Press.

9   Robert Aickman and the English Abroad

Nick Freeman

"Neither Logic Nor Moral": Strange Aesthetics

The novelist Elizabeth Jane Howard, Robert Aickman's sometime lover and collaborator, described him as "unusual and intriguing" (Cooper 2016, 70). Her biographer, Artemis Cooper (2016), is less forgiving, depicting Aickman as "'a strange man' notable for his 'high-minded intensity'," his hatred of technology, his rosy vision of the past, and his disregard for marital fidelity (69, 70). Another recent commentator, Darryl Jones (2010), remarks that he was "very odd" in many ways (61), a point reinforced by the many reminiscences of Aickman's friends in *Robert Aickman: Author of Strange Tales*, a documentary by Ray Russell and Rosalie Parker (2015) of Tartarus Press, the firm which has done much to restore his work to print. As the film's participants make clear, Aickman's personal idiosyncrasies frequently crossed over into his fiction, leading him to reject the conventional definitions of gothic and the ghost story when characterizing his work. To Gothic's fascination with what Robert Miles (2002) terms "rupture, disjunction [and] fragmentation" (3), Aickman added elements of surrealism, and at times comic theatricality, and an often sardonic sense of Englishness. As Glen Cavaliero (1986) observes, his "haunting and poetic" stories depict man "trapped in a vortex of subtle, symbolic terror, a victim of forces over which he himself has no control" (2). With his habitual precision, Aickman characterized his fiction as "strange," for his stories are strange, not simply because they feature peculiar and inexplicable happenings but because they dwell obsessively on questions of subjectivity, selfhood, and estrangement.

As that last word suggests, the roots of the word "strange" lie in Old French, and its connotations of foreignness, alterity, and difference entangled with "native" English run through Aickman's oeuvre, from the three stories he contributed to his collaboration with Elizabeth Jane Howard, *We Are for the Dark* (1951) to *Intrusions* (1980). An influential and provocative anthologist, Aickman (2015a) used his editorship of the Fontana *Great Ghost Stories* series (1964–72) to advance his belief that such tales draw "upon the unconscious mind in the manner of poetry" and, defying rational explanation, need "neither logic nor moral" (279). A great ghost story—and Aickman (2015a) felt that there were "only about thirty or forty first-class ghost stories in the whole of western literature" (274)—concerns itself "not with appearance and consistency, but with the spirit behind appearance, the void behind the face of order" (295–96) and "giving satisfying form to the unanswerable" (292). Conventional understandings of time and chronology are suspended or disrupted, while events themselves defy understanding and articulation. Aickman's protagonists repeatedly find themselves unable to comprehend or communicate the impossibility of their situation; often, they end the story lost, bereft, isolated, or silent, changed forever in ways which refuse rational explanation or the comforts of Providence.

This sense of estrangement is especially prevalent in two settings. One is the ritualized world of English middle-class suburbia, which fascinated Aickman throughout his life and which he explored in stories such as "A Roman Question" (included in *Powers of Darkness* [1966]), "Marriage" (*Tales of Love and Death* [1977]) and "The Same Dog" (*Cold Hand in Mine* [1975]). The other is continental Europe, and it is on some of Aickman's tales of the English abroad that this essay will focus. In doing so, it will be informed by a set of conventions that William Hughes (2003) identifies as "Tourist Gothic" (127) but will show too how Aickman breaks with these in stories such as "The Houses of the Russians" and "Into the Wood" from *Sub Rosa* (1968), and "The Clock Watcher" from *Cold Hand in Mine*.

Aickman was born in June 1914; he spent World War II as a conscientious objector, one of very few excused any form of war work. Like many others of his generation, his conception and experience of Europe were shaped by military and political rivalry and violence—his mother was killed in an air raid, the explosion heard by Aickman and his wife who were walking nearby—and he did not visit the continent with any regularity until the 1960s. By the time he did so, the age of the package holiday had begun, and the conservative, hyper-refined aesthete recoiled in horror from busy airports and the coach tours memorably satirized in Mel Stuart's film, *If It's Tuesday, This Must Be Belgium* (1969). Relationships between Britain and Europe entered a new era, with competitive events such as the Eurovision Song Contest (beginning in 1956), and sports tournaments (notably football's European Cup, inaugurated in 1955, and what is now the European Championship, founded in 1960), fostering largely friendly Anglo-European rivalries alongside the more complicated diplomatic and financial collaborations of the European Economic Community formed by the Treaty of Rome in 1957 but which the United Kingdom did not join until 1973. Aickman detested popular music, most sport, and a great many politicians, his imagination being drawn instead to a Europe he could never experience, the late nineteenth-century world which was the setting for his posthumously published novella, *The Model* (1987), and which he regarded as a last flowering of art and beauty before the triumph of the machine in the age of industrial warfare, "the strange debacle of 1914, when man ceased to run his own world" (Aickman 1966, 27). Already separated from this Europe by the inconveniences of temporality, he was further removed from what remained of it by the democratization (or, as he saw it, vulgarization) of the experience of travel. He forcefully expresses his disgust with these retrograde developments in "The Wine-Dark Sea" (*Powers of Darkness*), where Greek islands are despoiled by sun-tan lotion and transistor radios, "Never Visit Venice" (*Sub Rosa*), which depicts a mean-spirited world dominated by "currency" in which men sit "looking foolish, fretful, bored, insufficiently occupied, and, above all, out of place" (Aickman 1999a, 301), and "The Cicerones," another story from *Sub Rosa* in which Belgian cathedrals are treated not as shrines but as places of "dingy bustle" and "neck-craning," filled with Americans and tourists who hold "a guide book like a breviary" (363). Many of his other stories evince a growing despair with the mechanized and soulless culture of "the Motor Moloch" (301), the tyrannical ruler of the Western world (Aickman never learned to drive). Echoing Matthew Arnold's horror of the "strange disease of modern life,/With its sick hurry, its divided aims" (146) in "The Scholar-Gipsy" (1853) and Max Weber's notion of *Entzauberung*, the disenchantment which is an (inevitable) consequence of secularization and bureaucracy, Aickman's stories show culture growing irresistibly coarser with each supposed technological "advance." Telephones ring ever more insistently (notably in "Your Tiny Hand is Frozen" from *Powers of Darkness*), while television is a vexatious and stupid distraction from the higher culture of art, literature, theater, and classical music. "Every time you take a television into your house...you bring *1984* nearer," he remarked in 1956 (Aickman 2015b, 222). When Aickman's characters visit Europe, they do so in part to escape such horrors, though as Fern finds in "Never Visit Venice," they may also embody them.

It has often been suggested that British fiction of the 1950s and 1960s was parochial and inward-looking, dominated by a realism obsessively preoccupied with questions of social class. This may have been the case in certain areas of "literary" and indeed, middlebrow fiction, but experimentation thrived in the margins, where writers looked to Europe, the United States, and Latin America for technical invigoration. Aickman's marginality was however of a different kind. He had little interest in the break-up of the Empire or the activities of the Commonwealth, and in the course of wide and eclectic reading paid scant attention to William Burroughs or Alain Robbe-Grillet, the potent influences on the chroniclers of "inner space" appearing in Michael Moorcock's *New Worlds* magazine. He preferred subtler distortions of familiar settings and storytelling, a less overt derangement. What might be termed his "weird realism" bent the quotidian into idiosyncratic and often unresolved incidents and experiences whose strangeness crept up on the reader without self-advertisement (Freeman 2017).

European settings were crucial to this endeavor. Of the fifty-six stories published in Aickman's lifetime, almost a quarter are set on the continent and a number of others feature European characters living in or visiting Great Britain. Settings include France, Belgium, Finland, Slovenia, Sweden, what was then West Germany, Italy, and, in "Just a Song at Twilight" from James Turner's *The Fourth Ghost Book* (1965), what seems to be a Balearic island. The range of locations recalls the similarly peripatetic Algernon Blackwood whose work Aickman admired—he chose "The Wendigo" (1910) for his first Fontana anthology. However, where Blackwood's European travelers often move through a wild landscape imbued with pantheistic and mystical significance, Aickman's usually tend to find themselves in unremarkable urban areas, testimony to the shrinking of the world identified in "Never Visit Venice." Nature can appear as a source of mystery and empowerment, but Aickman tends to be more concerned with interactions between human beings than with the sort of encounters Blackwood stages in "The Willows" (1906), *The Centaur* (1911) and elsewhere.

William Hughes's (2003) notion of "Tourist Gothic" (and the imperial variant which preceded it) succinctly outlines a recurrent narrative in which:

> A traveller encounters strange practices in an alien environment, discovers that these customs and the landscape itself are an effective preface to some inner voyage of discovery, and departs from the scene chastened, changed, though not necessarily incorporated.
>
> (127)

This outline fits well with some of Aickman's stories, notably "The Wine-Dark Sea," in which an English tourist travels to the Greek island home of women who may be goddesses (Freeman 2008), but his expanded definition, encompassing elements of what has become known as "folk horror," seems more useful still:

> The classic geographical locations of tourist Gothic lie at the margins of familiar countries...The traveller characteristically arrives there by rail or motor coach, and is frequently engaged upon a walking or cycling holiday rather than a business trip. The tourist is frequently disorientated within the environment—ambivalent signage, deliberate misdirection by a local person or sheer bad luck will divert him or her into an even more obscure place within the unknown: a house, village or other communal space that is uncanny in its slight resemblance to the known, but alien with regard to its customs, worship, or inhabitants.
>
> (Hughes 2018, 150)

Some of these elements are present in Aickman's work where they are deployed with knowingness or irony, but his Europe is rather more than a set of gothic conventions, a foreign place in which nasty things happen to English visitors. Even an apparently familiar narrative opening, such as the visit to a gothic Belgian cathedral in "The Cicerones," can slide swiftly into a wholly different order of delirious menace. More oblique and reticent than many of his gothic forebears, Aickman instead uses European locations to question prevailing notions of the self that exist "back home," and in this sense, he might be seen as having certain similarities with Joseph Conrad, Graham Greene, or, more particularly, E. M. Forster, whose fiction asks such questions of the English in *A Passage to India* (1924) and the Italy of *A Room with a View* (1908). An encounter with otherness tends to leave Aickman's characters again recalling those of Arnold, notably the speaker in "Stanzas from the Grande Chartreuse" (1855), who is caught "wandering between two worlds...with nowhere yet to rest my head" (113); removed from his country of origin but unable to fully assimilate the European. At the same time, Aickman resists the temptation to use Belgium or Slovenia as simply the backdrop to an English trauma or dissolution, though as can be seen from "Into the Wood" for example, the move to Europe can trigger fresh insights and perspectives unavailable in domestic settings. While gothic narratives tend to kill their protagonists, leave them the Coleridgean "sadder and wiser man," or, in Ann Radcliffe, for example, to forge a stronger, more integrated personality in the crucible of terror and trial, Aickman's offer alternative possibilities. Rather than "The Ancient Mariner" (1798), his guiding influence seems to be Robert Graves's poem "In Broken Images" (1929), where the two disputants end with "a new confusion of my understanding...a new understanding of my confusion" (Graves 89). Characters and readers alike are disquieted, bewildered, and inexplicably enlightened.

"Never Quite Dark": "The Houses of the Russians"

Sub Rosa is Aickman's most international collection. Although it is at times stridently dismissive of tourists and their despoliation of cathedrals and canals (as a founder of the English Waterways Association, Aickman was especially protective toward the latter), the collection did not maintain this attitude throughout. In "Ravissante" ([1968] 1999a), for example, an English painter meets the widow of a symbolist artist, only to be subjected to a terrifying ordeal in her Brussels flat which destroys his creative talent. Prior to meeting her, the painter encounters kindness from almost everyone he meets, and though he speaks only "very little French" is able to be "absolutely happy" (265). After his encounter with Madame A., however, he is left with a series of troubling and unanswerable questions: "What is to become of me? What will happen to me next?

What can I do? Who am I?" (276). As Philip Challinor (2010) remarks in the course of an incisive reading of the story, "Ravissante" "piles an artistic humiliation on the top of a sexual one" (75), with the result that the painter is rendered creatively impotent ever afterward, but the story also distinguishes between his experience in Brussels and his ability to recollect it, at least partially, once he is back in England. In Belgium, he felt "under a spell" but "[t]he English Channel proves to have loosened this spell considerably" (265) and the "fascination" has begun to wear off. It seems that the Continent, rather than safer, duller England, stimulates epiphanic moments of heightened consciousness but such experience comes at a terrible cost. Aickman may not have approved of The Beatles, but had he managed to lend a sympathetic ear to "The Inner Light," a song from the same year as *Sub Rosa*, he may have agreed with George Harrison's adaptation of Lao-Tse: "The farther one travels/The less one knows/The less one really knows" (Macdonald 2005, 274).

"Ravissante" then has clear affinities with the notion of "tourist gothic," but another story from the collection, "The Houses of the Russians" ([1968] 1999a), breaks with it from the outset, featuring as it does a pair of surveyors visiting Finland on a business trip in the summer of 1923. Mr. Purvis and the unnamed young underling who narrates the story are in the small lakeside town of Unilinna on behalf of a client who has an interest in a nearby timber plantation. Purvis is "quite the Englishman abroad" (339) and spends his time ogling women and partaking of the Finns' generous hospitality, but his assistant is more inquisitive, and keen to explore his surroundings. As so often in "strange" fiction, those that H. G. Wells terms in "The Door in the Wall" (1906) "men of vision and the imagination" (161) are attuned to the world in ways that "normal" people are not, but their heightened sensitivity is as much a burden as it is a blessing. When the assistant finally gets some time to himself, he crosses the bridge to the wooded island in the lake where he finds a number of attractive dwellings, each different from the others, and observes that so far north, it is "never quite dark" (342). In Finland, he observes, "houses are much more alike" than they are in England (344), but those on the island recall the Italianate flourishes of "gentlemen's villas" in Sydenham and Stoke Newington. Seeking, as many travelers do, to comprehend the foreign through reference to the familiar, the young surveyor unwittingly offers a subtly disorienting amalgam of London, Italy, and Finland. He is professionally impressed by the houses' design and construction, but the misty island seems deserted, the summer residences apparently empty.

Increasingly perturbed—all the more so for not quite knowing why—the surveyor finds some of the islanders enjoying "a jolly party," perhaps "some kind of national celebration" (346). He sees a woman with very bright blue eyes and a Russian Orthodox priest, whose black vestments present an alarming spectacle in the misty woods and mislead the reader about the type of ghost story he is telling. He also meets a small boy who presents him with a medal which seems to be a protective charm. He makes his way back to the mainland without further anxieties, perhaps because of his gift's talismanic properties. The narrator has never been abroad, having been too young to fight in the Great War, and like most Englishmen then and now, his knowledge of Finnish history is hazy. When a local estate agent (of sorts) called Kirkontorni hears he has been to the island, he explains that:

> Finland used to be a kind of Russian colony...and we didn't like that, though most of us had nothing against the Russians personally. And since then we've had our civil war, when we starved, and they tried to enforce Bolshevism here and would have done if we hadn't had assistance form the Germans. Today most people want to hear no more of the Russians than they can help. In fact, their houses are supposed to be unlucky, and no one goes near them. If anyone did, he wouldn't be very popular....No one's ever bought them from the Russians: first because it wouldn't be thought right; second because there've been no Russians to buy from.
>
> (349)

Kirkontorni's explanation refers to Finland having been a Grand Duchy of Russia until July 1917, when, taking advantage of the political turmoil there, the Finns proclaimed their independence. Civil war followed, before Finland became a democratic republic in the summer of 1919. Having a border only nineteen miles from Leningrad heightened Russo-Finnish tensions for decades afterward. The houses on the island belonged to Russians, serving in some cases as holiday homes. Armed with his new understanding of local politics, the young man crosses the bridge again, only to discover a scene of utter carnage in one of Hughes's (2018) "communal space[s] that is uncanny in its slight resemblance to the known, but alien with regard to its customs, worship, or inhabitants" (150). "There was nothing but blood," the narrator recalls. "Blood everywhere...I could see the shapes of bodies as they had lain there; many bodies" (352). It initially appears that the Russians were murdered by the Finns during the nationalist uprising, but Aickman's story has a subtler conclusion. The houses somehow record the deaths of their former occupants once they have returned to the violent chaos of the Bolshevik revolution and the civil war which followed it; what the narrator sees on the island echoes perhaps the slaughter of the Romanovs amid the sanguinary chaos of the cellar at Ekaterinburg. All of this is related decades later, during which time the twentieth century has endured still greater horrors.

When the tale begins, the now elderly surveyor has narrowly avoided injury in some sort of road accident and is enjoying a restorative whisky in a pub nearby. Here he falls into conversation with students in the bar who note how he crosses himself before drinking in an unusual way (the Orthodox rather than Roman style). A reluctant raconteur, he nevertheless tells them of his trip to Finland, and of the medal, which is inscribed in Russian, "The Feast of the Sleep of the Theotokes." This was the festival that he observed on the island, but "the details you'll have to discover for yourself," he says, not revealing that the feast commemorates the passing of the Blessed Virgin (353). The medal offers a mother's powers of protection to her child, something underscored by the old man's avoidance of the accident, and indeed, any significant harm during his long life. "Crossing" therefore assumes a double significance in the story, alluding to both Christian symbolism and to the act of walking to and from the island of the Russian houses, the passing between past and present, life and death. It echoes too the Channel crossing in "Ravissante" in its movement between stimulating (if terrifying) alterity and the convivial havens of English life.

Aickman's story blends the familiar and unfamiliar, and indeed, the notion of "tourist gothic," to masterful effect. Its opening—the old man who looks as if he has seen a ghost and recounts a strange tale to an audience of fellow tipplers—is steeped in the traditions of the clubland tale beloved of so many writers in the later nineteenth and early twentieth centuries, but his account unfolds in unexpected ways. The notion that a haunting is a result of the building's somehow recording events, the chilling hypothesis behind Nigel Kneale's much-praised teleplay, *The Stone Tape* (1972), which offers an intriguing explanation of the "haunted house," is made still more powerful, with the houses acting not simply as site-specific repositories of violent death but as psychic satellites which replay the fates of their distant owners to those sensitive enough to receive them. Aickman offers no such technological parallels, but the houses clearly possess an intimate connection with their former occupants, one which allows him to stir in a suggestion of his beloved Freud. *Heimlich* and *unheimlich* simultaneously, the houses become quintessentially uncanny.

In playing out such ideas, many writers would have been unable to resist making the blood-soaked houses a site of horror which actively imperils the narrator. In Aickman's story however, the surveyor feels less fear than "a great sadness" (351), realizing that he seems to be "the only person who cared" about the Russians (351). Aickman's fascination with pre-revolutionary Russia was evident in *The Model*, but in 1968, the temperature of the Cold War was falling fast, with the Soviet invasion of Czechoslovakia that August prompting widespread outrage. In such a climate, "The Houses of the Russians" asked its readers to examine international tensions from a fresh perspective, with Russians driven out of their territories and then killed by their own countrymen. It was not a plea for sympathy. Rather, it showed the ruthless progress of historical cycles and the horrible ironies which accompanied them at the same time as it intimated the centrality of Christian belief in what would become the officially atheistic Soviet Union.

The story teased its readers where the supernatural was concerned, but it did not confine its hauntings to the sights the young man sees in the Finnish village. "The Houses of the Russians" also implicitly invited its readers to consider a Europe haunted by violent nationalism and savage political reprisal. As the narrator remarks, Russians "are so often something else; Ukrainians, Georgians, Asiatics, and, since 1939, Lithuanians, Latvians, and Estonians, so far as any have survived" (340). 1968 was a remarkably turbulent year across the globe, and while political turmoil in mainland Britain was nowhere near as serious as it was elsewhere, the country saw demonstrators battling with mounted police in Grosvenor Square (17 March) and Enoch Powell's notorious warning of "rivers of blood" (20 April). A quietly told tale of an incident in Finland over forty years earlier would not seem to be at the forefront of Cold War fictions; it is hardly Len Deighton's *Funeral in Berlin* (1964), John Le Carré's *A Small Town in Germany* (1968), or one of Moorcock's "Jerry Cornelius" satires (1965–). Nevertheless, while it does not foreground its political content, "The Houses of the Russians" remains imbued with unsettling resonance, its images of violence and bloodshed refusing to be safely corralled within the expectations of the gothic genre.

Cuckoo (Clock) in the Nest: "The Clock Watcher"

If "The Houses of the Russians" can be read as an ingenious set of variations on the "classic" ghost story, "The Clock Watcher" ([1975] 1999b) is one of Aickman's most bizarre conceptions, though it begins quietly enough. Joe Richardson, a young draughtsman, is married to Ursula, a German woman he met when serving in the army at the end of World War II. Ursula's father was a clock manufacturer in Freudenstadt in the Black Forest who was killed, along with her mother, when French and American forces attacked the city in April 1945. It is possibly in memory of him, Joe thinks, that his wife begins to fill their home with "cuckoo clocks, painted clocks and huge clocks in dark spiky wood or in polished spiky metal that chimed and struck and kept tabs on the phases of the moon" (119). Joe asks: "What normal, ordinary person—English person, anyway—could like those particular clocks?" (123). When he learns that Ursula is visited by a mysterious clock-repairer when he is at work, their relationship begins to deteriorate. At the end of the story, the man seems to have carried off Ursula and her various timepieces, but the latter did not go willingly, Joe's neighbors observing that "It was as if Mrs Richardson had to fight with the clocks" (136) when getting them into the large black van that stole them away. Only three are left behind, one of which is the traveling clock which Ursula took with her on their honeymoon and which "purred like a slinky pussy" (121). Joe gathers them and smashes them to pieces, for "There are no beautiful clocks. Everything to do with time is hideous" (138).

Ursula's background is significantly different from her husband's. She is socially privileged, attending "a costlier school" and emerging "better educated" (118). She is also Roman Catholic, taking her name from the martyred Saint Ursula, supposedly killed by the Huns along with her 11,000 virginal followers at the siege of Cologne in 383AD. Saint Ursula's story is poorly documented, and by the time Aickman published "The Clock Watcher" she had been removed from the Roman Martyrology. However, Ursula Richardson does "[look] like a saint," with "a gentle, trusting gaze" and "a mouth like a soft flower" (119). When she comes to England, she is unable to secure paid work without British citizenship meaning that she and Joe marry in a Catholic ceremony which Joe, as a non-Catholic, finds "one of the most unnerving experiences I had by then been through, war or no war" (120), a significant admission when he had been involved in what he (ironically?) terms, "the pleasant job of routing out the local concentration camp" during his military service (118). Joe is intimidated by the "bitterly antagonistic" young priest who conducts the ceremony and wills his conversion, but Ursula is far more secure; "This was territory that was hers, and not mine," Joe remarks, "and more, of course, than just territory" (121).

Folktales frequently emphasize the dangers of marrying those from outside one's own culture or region. The "foreign" partner is maybe monstrous or animalistic—a wolf, a fox, a seal, a snake—reverting to type following the marriage. Aickman's story plays off this reactionary narrative archetype to suggest that Ursula's otherness (her name does, after all, mean "little she-bear") is unwitting and as much a danger to herself as it is to her husband. Three decades after the end of the war, British popular culture continued to replay the conflict—it is a measure of "The Clock Watcher's" topicality that it was published the same year as John Cleese's demented hotelier barked, "Don't mention the war!" in *Fawlty Towers*. Aickman was rather more progressive in his attitudes than Basil Fawlty, of course, not simply in his repeated distinguishing between Germans and Nazis but in sympathetic portrayals of German characters in stories such as "The Inner Room," another tale from *Sub Rosa*, and "Niemandswasser" (*Tales of Love and Death*), a Ruritanian extravaganza in which Prince Elmo, an amalgam of Ludwig II of Bavaria (on whom Aickman had written an article in 1956) and the Austrian Crown Prince Rudolf (of Mayerling fame), encounters something monstrous in an Alpine lake. Ursula is a troubled young woman, orphaned and attempting to exist in an alien culture which regards her with suspicion. Joe does not always grasp the complexities of her predicament though he is impressed by her rapid mastery of English and her effortless command of "swimming, sailing and fell-walking" (121), skills probably acquired through the summer camps and physical training offered by the *Bund Deutscher Mädel*, the League of German Maidens which was the female counterpart to the Hitler Youth organization.

Ursula and Joe both reject the markers of unions; he refuses to wear a wedding ring (deeming this a continental habit), while she will not wear a watch (though Joe is unsure whether she "can't wear a watch" or "can't bear" one (122)). Joe's reluctance to wear a ring perhaps hints at his insecurities regarding the marital union, but Ursula's is less clear-cut. On their honeymoon, Joe notices that "for all her obvious interest in clocks, Ursula never had the least idea of the time" (121); she is at once obsessed by the temporal and desperate to deny its existence. Her dislike of watches implies she wishes to live life in her own time rather than the "clock time" which, as Stephen Kern (1983) has shown in *The Culture of Time and Space 1880–1918*, increasingly regulated life following the adoption of the Greenwich Meridian in 1884 and the division of the world into "time zones." In dramatizing this distinction, Aickman revisits the ideas of Henri Bergson that underpin Woolf's *Mrs Dalloway* (1925), playing a personal or subjective version of time against that signaled by the cavalcade of chiming clocks. Yet he does not seem to be proffering an overtly feminist interpretation of the temporal; though Ursula's clocks chart the phases of the moon, "The Clock Watcher" is not Julia Kristeva's *Women's Time* (1979), and neither does it seem to be explicitly concerned with the chiming of biological clocks, even though the marriage at its center is a childless one.

Like many of Aickman's strange tales, "The Clock Watcher" invites allegorical interpretations but refuses to confirm them. Joe's observations seem ambiguous and unreliable. His first-person narration denies access to Ursula's thoughts, and the story leaves a great deal unanswered, stacking up circumstantial details which may (or may not) possess greater significance, another familiar Aickman tactic which at once enhances yet undermines the story's realist credentials. Its symbol of the cuckoo clock suggests a concern with time and sexual infidelity, with Joe increasingly willing to see the clock-repairer's visits as sexually motivated, the more so as the marriage dwindles into companionship, and his violent assault on the remaining clocks in the story's final pages may suggest a sublimated revenge on the lovers.

It would nevertheless be reductive to see "The Clock Watcher" as no more than a parable about infidelity; the clock that purrs like a slinky pussy does not necessarily have sexual connotations. Instead, the clocks bind Ursula to German origins which, despite her marriage and her move to England, she cannot evade or transcend. Here however Aickman refuses to provide the story with a unitary meaning. What is the link, if any, between Ursula and the unverifiable history of her saintly namesake? Once filled with shrieking clocks, the Richardsons' house seems much like "a dark glade in which some unfortunate traveller had been deserted—or had merely lost his way" (124). Is this an allusion to the opening of the *Divine Comedy*? Does it suggest a parallel between their home and the Black Forest, a place which, from the early days of eighteenth-century gothic to the Nuremburg Trials, has been seen as a source of evil emanations? "There was a great deal to be said in favour of the Nazis," Joe says, "The Germans wouldn't have fought so hard and long, if it hadn't been so" (117). He also draws a comparison between the industrious reconstruction of post-war Germany and England's decline, with the election of "little Attlee" and the beginning of the "long soft greyness" which followed (119). Yet Ursula seems distinct from the vigorous new Germany, valorizing the craftsmanship and aesthetic appeal of her clocks while denying their symbolic meaning or, in her rejection of a wrist-watch, their hold over her. Like "The Houses of the Russians," the story plays out a richly ambivalent relationship between the past and the present, the historical cycles whose movement is echoed by the hands on the circular clockfaces and the individuals who attempt to escape them.

"I Want to Be Alone": "Into the Wood"

"The Clock Watcher" does not fit with Hughes's (2018) notions of "tourist gothic," though its core structure sometimes suggests the raw material of imperial gothic, notably the trope of disruptive intrusion whereby something brought back (or pillaged) from a subject culture wreaks vengeance in (and on) previously safe English domestic space (92). "Into the Wood" ([1968] 1999b), the concluding story in *Sub Rosa*, seems closer to the touristic archetype in some respects, notably in the conceit of being a *voyage à l'intérieur*, though that convenient taxonomy robs it of ambiguity and strangeness.

When the story opens, Henry and Margaret Sawyer are in Sovastad in eastern Sweden, where Henry's construction company is involved in building a road through the mountains into Norway. The hospitable Swedes invite Margaret (or "Molly" as she appears on the couple's Christmas cards) to accompany her husband, but Sovastad's charms are soon exhausted and she is glad of the chance to go for a Sunday drive with her hosts. In the hills above the town, she sees "a sizeable, wooden edifice, painted white, and with a slate roof": the Kurhus (372). This is a sanatorium of sorts, though the "rest cure" which it offers has "fallen out of fashion" (373). The place appeals to Margaret, not least because its location allows her to see the sunset, and when Henry is called away to Stockholm, she resists the offer of lodging with some of his business contacts and books into the Kurhus instead. It is a lightly taken decision which will change her life forever.

The Sawyers' home is a Cheshire town that has become "a sprawling and sleeping area for Manchester" (370). Margaret lives surrounded by the types of gadget Aickman so deplored, glumly aware that although they are designed to allow her to spend less time on housework and more time with her three children, "it seldom worked that way" (370). As the story unfolds, it becomes increasingly clear that, to borrow a phrase of from Philip Larkin's "Afternoons" (1964), something is pushing Margaret "to the side of her own life" (71)—she distinguishes between her various identities as Molly, Mrs Sawyer, and Margaret (her true self) but little suspects that her husband's aside that she will become "a completely new girl" (373) while he is Stockholm is in fact a prophecy.

Margaret attracts the attention of another Englishwoman, the overbearing Sandy Slater ("No one has ever called me Alexandra" 375), who informs her that the Kurhus is, properly speaking, the *Jamblichus* Kurhus, taking its name from one of the sleepers in the ancient Christian legend of the seven sleepers of Ephesus. It is designed as a refuge for insomniacs—it is "not a place for a holiday...still less for a rest," Sandy announces (376). As Margaret has just woken from a sleep in the sunshine, she initially underestimates the significance of these words and sees the name as suggestive of Lewis Carroll or Edward Lear, but she slowly begins to recognize a fundamental change in herself.

Lear's "Jumblies" famously denied conventional opinion and "went to sea in a Sieve," embarking on a twenty-year voyage from which they returned changed but inspirational (264, 268). The semi-comic allusions to Alice and Lear hint at Margaret's own voyage of discovery; she may not have a green head and blue hands or have gone through the lookingglass, but she begins to recognize herself as fundamentally different from the other Cheshire wives she knows in her dormitory town, and the Kurhus may yet serve a purpose analogous to the Jumblies' journey to "the Lakes, and the Terrible Zone,/And the hills of the Chankly Bore" (268). The insomniacs who live there are not simply people who have trouble sleeping, for in this story, insomnia is a more profound condition, one which Aickman invests with powerful symbolic meaning. The sleepless are regarded as unnatural, even monstrous, and those who can sleep banish them to the margins of their society. As Sandy explains:

> Even the most normal people teeter all their lives along a narrow line between good and evil; between impulse and judgement, as we may say. Sleep does two things for the normal person. It gives him constant, long periods of respite from the conflict. It also enables his impulses in dreams, especially his most lawless impulses.
>
> (377)

Insomniacs come to the Kurhus from all over Europe. They are cared for by two doctors (the most common crises are "frequent mania and sudden death" (387)), and while nothing is actively forbidden, tend to shun alcohol, cigarettes, and caffeine. The establishment lends itself to quiet reflection, especially at night when a number of the residents wander the woods outside. Margaret's first woodland walk "had perceptibly shifted the four points of her inner compass" (387), for "The rustling, sunny forest, empty but labyrinthine, hinted at some other answer" to the mystery of her existence, "an answer beyond logic, beyond words, above all beyond connection with what Margaret and her Cheshire neighbors had come to regard as normal life" (385).

In a later story, "The Next Glade" from *Intrusions*, another English housewife bewails the fact that the woods near her house are not big enough to get lost in. In both tales, the wood (or forest) suggests the blindly meandering pathways of the unconscious mind in the same ways as the Bruges canals do in the symbolist art of painters and poets such as Georges Rodenbach and Fernand Khnopf echoed in "Ravissante". Aickman's Freudian sympathies are especially apparent in this story, not simply in the use of the wood, a dark, unknown place in which those of heightened consciousness lose (and find) themselves. The significance of the buried, repressed, and secret is evident from the outset of the story. Sovastad runs alongside a "vast black lake" which legend insists is home to "a creature of enormous bulk" and "origin unknown to all" (371). In the lake, the forest, the Kurhus but above all, within the self, lurk things which trouble and disturb the surface of life. Margaret's awakening, literalized by her increasing fear of what the Kurhus means and her growing sleeplessness, means that she is slowly removed from her former routine, one to which she is only feebly connected through telephone calls and postcards home. When she is reunited with her husband at Sovastad railway station, he tells her, "These Swedes just aren't like us English" (396), but while Margaret feels little affection for her hosts, she has passed beyond national identification. "As a woman I want no country" (129), writes Woolf ([1938] 2006) in *Three Guineas*, and Margaret's behavior echoes this as she moves from her erstwhile role as suburban housewife to a resident of the Kurhus, a place where national concerns are irrelevant besides the search for the true self. At the end of the story, she and Henry argue over her wish to remain in Sweden, Margaret discovering she is "developing new resources now, even though she had little idea of what they were." The story finishes with her final comment to her husband, "I'll let you know immediately as soon as I get out of the wood...It's one of those things you have to live through until you emerge the other side" (398). "We're not out of the woods yet," one might say, and Margaret clearly has a great deal of self-examination and solitary thinking ahead of her. Even in the early stages of her time in the Kurhus, she knows that it has "recharged the battery of her life, rewound the spring" (387), and while at the story's beginning, she was "insufficiently grown for happiness or unhappiness" (370), she changes quickly. Before long, she is separating herself from the social rituals which surround and define her. "Like a famous Swede," she tells Sandy, "I want to be alone" (389).

"Into the Wood" uses various aspects of the "tourist gothic" template, notably the alienating effects of language differences, a mislaid passport, unhelpful taxis, and the "strange practices" which "preface an inner voyage of discovery." Nevertheless, the story's subtleties and allegorical intimations make it fit uneasily within the confines of the definition. Introducing a collection of Aickman's work, the novelist Peter Straub (1988) singled out "Into the Wood" for particular comment, seeing it initially as "an extended metaphor for the separation, even estrangement, between the artist and the conventional world" but then deciding that it was in truth universal in its insight. "[T]here is a great wild forest within you," he wrote, and reading the story entails:

> understanding that you must go into that forest in search of your own limits; and doing so with the knowledge that many other people have felt that a world of unsentimental grandeur lies within and that to deny or ignore it is to choose an uneasy half-life.
>
> (10)

Setting "Into the Wood" in a famously neutral country allows Aickman to give Margaret the distance necessary for her to reflect on the unsatisfactory nature of her life in England, but tellingly, he does not make an encounter with a Swede the agent of this revelation. Instead, the Kurhus itself becomes the point from which Margaret can realize that she is not who the world thinks she is or would like her to be: the sunshine and woodland combine to offer her an alternative to the world of business, industry, and domestic routine. Wandering the woods amounts to "a melancholy liberation but it is liberation nonetheless" (172), concludes Timothy Jones (2018).

(in)Conclusion

As these stories demonstrate, Aickman did not have a monolithic conception of Europe. Neither did he attach to it a consistent meaning or make it a convenient "other" against which he could assess the behavior and attitudes of his English protagonists. Rather, it was a place of enigmatic invention where strangeness and estrangement could intertwine, leaving characters by turns frightened, bewildered, and even, at times, ecstatic: one thinks of Grigg's blissful, if transitory, encounter with the women of the island in "The Wine-Dark Sea." Aickman's admirable willingness to grant complex subjectivities to his European characters was distinctive, even unusual when compared with the dominant strands of Gothic (and horror) during the 1960s and 1970s, but the bizarre content of his stories often distanced him from similar trends in more mainstream fiction. Europe is haunted in these tales, but the specter is what T. S. Eliot called in "Little Gidding" ([1942] 1963) a "compound ghost" (217) rather than anything more easily defined or taxonomized.

References

Aickman, Robert. 2015a. *Night Voices*. Leyburn: Tartarus Press.

Aickman, Robert. 2015b. *The Strangers and Other Writings*. Leyburn: Tartarus Press.

Aickman, Robert. 1999a. *The Collected Short Stories I*. Horam: Tartarus Press.

Aickman, Robert. 1999b. *The Collected Short Stories II*. Horam: Tartarus Press.

Aickman, Robert. 1966. *The Attempted Rescue*. London: Victor Gollancz.

Arnold, Matthew. 1994. "The Scholar-Gipsy" and "Stanza from the Grande Chartreuse." In *Selected Poems*, edited by Timothy Peltason, 142–6, 108–14. London: Penguin.

Cavaliero, Glen. 1986. "Aickman, Robert [Fordyce] (1914–1981)." In *The Penguin Encyclopaedia of Horror and the Supernatural*, edited by Jack Sullivan, 1–2. Harmondsworth: Penguin.

Challinor, Philip. 2010. *Akin to Poetry: Observations on some Strange Tales of Robert Aickman*. Baton Rouge: Gothic Press.

Cooper, Artemis. 2016. *Elizabeth Jane Howard: A Dangerous Innocence*. London: John Murray.

Eliot, T. S. 1963. *Collected Poems 1909–1962*. London: Faber.

Freeman, Nick. 2017. "Weird Realism in Robert Aickman and M. John Harrison." *Textual Practice* 31, no. 6: 1117–32.

Freeman, Nick. 2008. "A Country for the Savant: Paganism, Popular Fiction and the Invention of Greece, 1914–1966." *The Pomegranate: The International Journal of Pagan Studies* 10, no. 1: 21–41.

Graves, Robert. 1988. "In Broken Images." In *Selected Poems*, edited by Paul O'Prey, 89. London: Penguin.

Hughes, William. 2018. *Key Concepts in the Gothic*. Edinburgh: Edinburgh University Press.

Hughes, William. 2003. "'An Angel Satyr Walks These Hills': Imperial Fantasies for a Post-Colonial World." *Gothic Studies* 5, no. 1: 121–28.

Jones, Darryl. 2010. "Robert Aickman, the Ghost Story and the Idea of Englishness." In *The Ghost Story from the Middle Ages to the Twentieth Century*, edited by Helen Conrad O'Briain and Julie Anne Stevens, 61–80. Dublin: Four Courts.

Jones, Timothy. 2018. "'German has a Word for the Total Effect': Robert Aickman's Strange Stories." In *The Routledge Handbook to the Ghost Story*, edited by Scott Brewster and Luke Thurston, 168–76. London: Routledge.

Larkin, Philip. 2012. "Afternoons." In *The Complete Poems of Philip Larkin*, edited by Archie Burnett, 71. London: Faber.

Lear, Edward. 1943. *Nonsense Omnibus*. London: Frederick Warne.

Macdonald, Ian. 2005. *Revolution in the Head: The Beatles' Records and the Sixties*. London: Pimlico.

Miles, Robert. 2002. *Gothic Writing 1750–1820: A Genealogy*. 2nd ed. Manchester: Manchester University Press.

Straub, Peter. 1988. "Introduction" to Aickman's *The Wine-Dark Sea: A Collection*, 7–10. New York: Arbor House/William Morrow.

Wells, H. G. [1906] 1927. "The Door in the Wall." In *Complete Short Stories of H.G. Wells*, 144–61. London: Ernest Benn.

Woolf, Virginia. [1938] 2006. *Three Guineas*. New York: Houghton Mifflin Harcourt.

10 "Look into the Dark"

A Ghost Story for Christmas on the Continent: An Interview with Leslie Megahey, Director of *Schalcken the Painter*

Michael Newton

Through the 1970s, the BBC produced a series of subtle, unnerving period ghost films for Christmas. For the most part, these confined themselves to a darkly nostalgic view of the English past. However, the last—and perhaps the best—of them, Leslie Megahey's *Schalcken the Painter* (1979) frames a refracted vision of Holland, a world of the interior, fabricated from Dutch art, a relation to money, and a sinister image of exchange. Megahey's film proves to be a masterly evocation of a specifically Dutch spirit, a troubled vision of a continental elsewhere, broadcast into the home on that most domestic and inward-looking of occasions, the British family Christmas.

Though *Hamlet* is, among other things, a Christmas ghost story, it is Charles Dickens's *A Christmas Carol* (1843) that sealed the bond between Christmas and the spooky. From then on, the link was a matter of course, one of the nation's ongoing pieties, deeply linked to the preservation of traditions and the sense of place. The Christmas ghost story contrasts jollity with terror, invites a specter to the feast, and traces the anxiety within the festivity. There's the strong disparity too between the darkened world without and the brightened home within; but, above all, there's the suspicion that there's something restless inside that home, something unappeased. The image of the nation here was also a haunted one. Moreover, there lingers around such tales the fact that Christmas celebrates incarnation as such, even as the stories themselves draw our attention to the dis-incarnated, the lingering remnants of the dead, or the never-embodied presences beyond the veil.

Inspired by Jonathan Miller's Freudian-tinged short film, *Whistle and I'll Come To You* (1968), for a number of years each Christmas the BBC embodied these unembodied spirits in a series of marvelous short ghost films, brought together under the title, *A Ghost Story for Christmas*. Largely directed by Lawrence Gordon Clark, the best of these were adaptations of works by three masters of the Victorian and Edwardian ghost story: Dickens's "The Signalman," Sheridan Le Fanu's "Schalcken the Painter" (both written and directed by Leslie Megahey), and, above all, a series of versions of M. R. James's well-mannered ghost stories, those inconsequential masterpieces of agitation and doom. (M. R. James's ghost stories themselves found their origin in a ritual festive reading at King's College, Cambridge, an all-male, annual immersion in sophisticated fear.) The first of Clark's films, *The Stalls of Barchester* (1971), was well-reviewed, and its success led to the production of the next Christmas film, *A Warning to the Curious* (1972). At this point, the BBC's drama department took official control of Clark's original enterprise, with Rosemary Hill acting as producer. As well as giving up his role as producer, from now on, though he continued to direct, the writing credits were also no longer Clark's. *Lost Hearts* appeared in 1973, then the following year came *The Treasure of Abbot Thomas*, and then in 1975, *The Ash Tree*. Breaking with M. R. James, when initial plans to do a version of "Number 13" began to look prohibitive—as it would have meant filming abroad—, Clark instead turned to Dickens in 1976 for *The Signalman* (scripted by Andrew Davies), and then to the present-day for *Stigma*, in 1977. With a different director, Derek Lister, another contemporary story, John Bowen's *The Ice House* appeared for Christmas 1978.

A yearning homesickness for the past permeates these brief films, first of all for the Victorian and Edwardian worlds they resurrect, but now also for the seventies when they were screened. One of the pleasures of these films is seeing such fine work by an especially gifted generation of actors: Denholm Elliott, so irritably unsure in *The Signalman*; bluffly apprehensive Robert Hardy in *The Stalls of Barchester Cathedral*; in *A Warning to the Curious*, the usually threatening Peter Vaughan at his most vulnerable.

With their enchanted and poetic engagement with the English landscape—the cathedral closes, the railway junctions, the bare fens—these films are close to "heritage TV," though it's an inheritance marked out as troubled and uneasy. Englishness captivates them, not the continental. It is noteworthy that David Rudkin, famous for his marvelous TV play, *Penda's Fen* (1974), a work enraptured by the English countryside and committed to the fertility that imbues the parish, also scripted the last of Clark's M. R. James adaptations for the BBC, *The Ash Tree*. Here in these films, characters who disinter objects from the island's past quickly find themselves beleaguered, oppressed. The nostalgic viewer should perhaps take care; old times were perhaps a dark place. When we engage with ghosts, we are also inevitably engaging with history. In *The Stalls of Barchester*, a pagan Britain infects the life of the modern, rational Anglican cathedral, as oak-wood from a sacred grove of sacrifices is put to use in carving a church pew. There are other yesterdays summoned up in these films, both the national past and the self's, the dread conjured up evoking the barely suppressed fears found in childhood and the childhood home. These tales are home-grown, imbued with the land, set against Europe. In *A Warning to the Curious*, the ghost specifically persists in order to guard against continental invasion, a bulwark against the foreign.

Toward the end of Gordon Clark's run, the attention turned to the present; these last two films (*Stigma* and *The Ice House*) are arguably the weakest in the sequence, the ones unredeemed by the charm of the middle-distance. The ghost film of the period that most successfully takes the contemporary for its subject is instead Nigel Kneale's wonderfully disconcerting *The Stone Tape* (broadcast on Christmas Day, 1972), a film that happily combines elements of science-fiction with the Victorian-style tale, as well as intimations of the horrors of a persisting evil abiding from antiquity.

After *The Ash Tree*, Lawrence Gordon Clark bowed out, though he went on to make an updated version of James's *Casting the Runes* for ITV (1979). However, on the BBC, the strand would find a magnificent coda in Leslie Megahey's *Schalcken the Painter*. It was only now, some four years after the referendum that gave the nation's blessing to the UK's membership of the European Economic Community, that one of these films turned its attention to the shared cultural inheritance of mainland Europe. The film was broadcast during the first Christmas of the new Conservative government headed by Margaret Thatcher. In the period of monetarism, Megahey was to make a ghost film ominously preoccupied by money transactions, and the distortions brought about by financial exchange.

Both Lawrence Gordon Clark and Leslie Megahey had made a prior reputation in documentary, especially in Clark's case for his 1966 series on one Islington locale, *Six Sides of a Square*. Indeed *Schalcken* and Jonathan Miller's seminal first film in the sequence found a place on screen as part of that excellent arts documentary series, *Omnibus*. The relation to documentary is not fortuitous; the classic ghost stories vivified in these films all depend on a sequence of the slight disturbances in the everyday world, a crescendo of unease.

Born in Belfast in 1944, Leslie Megahey began a distinguished career with the BBC in the late 1960s. In 1968, he made a rare film with J. R. R. Tolkien at Oxford, a process about which Tolkien himself was skeptical, though he was also ready to praise the "very young" director as equipped with intelligence and insight. Megahey worked as both a producer and director at the BBC for a number of years, before making his writing debut with *The Savage* (1977), a TV film about Gauguin. He was the editor of the BBC arts documentary program *Arena* from 1977–79 and again from 1982 to 1983, and in 1980, he won a BAFTA for his editorship of *Omnibus*; over his career, he has written, directed or produced a number of films about painters, including documentaries on Rodin, Stubbs, Landseer, and Rouault, among others. As producer, among many others, he put together a documentary on Orson Welles

(*Arena*, 1982) and a docudrama on Leonardo da Vinci, starring Mark Rylance as the painter, *Leonardo* (2004). He wrote and directed the TV play, *Cariani and the Courtesans* (1987), with Paul McGann playing the painter, Giovanni Cariani, and also the wonderful absurd comedy film, *The Hour of the Pig* (in the United States named *The Advocate*) (1993), starring Colin Firth, Ian Holm, and Donald Pleasance. (Earlier Megahey had written a script for a version of Le Fanu's "The Room in the Dragon Volant" that would have starred Firth as the naïve young hero of the tale, though very sadly, this project never reached the screen.) In 1998, he collaborated with Jana Boková (Megahey's wife) in writing the award-winning *Diario para un cuento* ("Diary for a Tale"). In 2007, he was one of the writers for the documentary nature film, *Earth*. He continues to be active as a filmmaker and writer.

Sheridan Le Fanu's "Strange Event in the Life of Schalcken the Painter" (May 1839 in the *Dublin University Magazine*) reappeared in the collection, *The Purcell Papers* (1880), and in-between in slightly revised form in *Ghost Stories and Tales of Mystery* (1851). In this short story, Le Fanu traces an imagined tale about the real-life Dutch painter, the Leiden-based Godfried Schalcken (1643–1706), the pupil of Gerrit Dou (1613–75). It was some quality of mystery in Schalcken's works that first seems to have engaged Le Fanu; the artist's portraits are notable for their sitters' air of challenge, of mischievous confrontation; they engage with us, flirting, all but cajoling. Later in his life, Schalcken came to London to paint, a continental artist in one of Europe's great capital cities, working at a time when Britain had a Dutch king. In Le Fanu's history, Schalcken falls in love with Dou's niece, Rose Velderkaust, though his own poverty as an apprentice mean that the two of them cannot marry. Before Schalcken can propose to Rose, a mysterious elderly and uncanny stranger, one Vanderhausen of Rotterdam, visits the house and asks to marry Rose, in return for a casket of perfect gold ingots. Dou greedily accepts the bargain, and, much against her will, Rose is taken off to be married to the dismal stranger. Schalcken devotes himself to the dreary task of amassing money through his painting. Some time later, Rose suddenly returns to the house, alone and in a wild state, attempting to flee her dreadful husband, and declaring that "the dead and the living can never be one." However, Rose vanishes again, and is only seen once more by Schalcken, in the great church of St. Lawrence (the "Laurenskerk") at Rotterdam, where a muffled female figure leads him toward the vaults; he follows her down there, when she turns and from the shadows a lamp illuminates her arch smile, as she pulls back the curtains around a bed, where her aged, dead lover sits bolt upright. Schalcken passes out, and is found the next morning lying by a large coffin. Ever after in his paintings, the artist returns to an image of a woman, illumined by candle-light, beckoning the viewer into the darkness.

Le Fanu engaged with continental subjects in several of his tales. *In A Glass Darkly* (1872) has its Germanic physician, Dr. Hesselius, as its presiding spirit, as well as the Styrian vampire tale, "Carmilla" (considered elsewhere in this book by Rahel Schmitz) and a long story of conspiracy and living-burial set in post-Napoleonic France, "The Room in The Dragon Volant." In "The Haunted Baronet" from *Chronicles of Golden Friars* (1871) (a very much adapted version of the earlier "The Fortunes of Sir Robert Ardagh" [1838]), the fated Sir Bale Mardykes hankers for the European freedom he has given up for the sinister roots that his family have put down on his Northumbrian estate. However, for the most part, Le Fanu's tales take his native Ireland as their source or are set firmly in England (particularly in the north). Ever since 1947 and Elizabeth Bowen's ground-breaking introduction to Le Fanu's novel, *Uncle Silas* (1864), it has been common critical practice to see all Le Fanu's settings as so many masks for the Ireland that was in fact his primary concern. For "Schalcken" and for "The Dragon Volant," such identifications feel spurious; in particular, the Leiden of Le Fanu's tale is certainly an attempt to engage with a mainland nation.

Megahey's adaptation actually improves on Le Fanu's already excellent original tale, deepening and expanding the story into a pregnant meditation on love, money, and art. In spirit, it's more of a folk-tale than a ghost story, a fable of patriarchy and power. In Robert Muller's portmanteau series, *Supernatural* (1977), both Jeremy Clyde (who plays Schalcken) and John Justin (who takes the part of Vanderhausen, the spirit) had already appeared together in another (very loose) adaptation of a Le Fanu story, "Dorabella," an echo of his vampire tale, "Carmilla." A comparison between the two programs brings out the particular excellence of Leslie Megahey's film. *Supernatural* confidently leaps over-the-top; there's an intense amount of cackling, quothing, and scenery-chewing; it's all very unlike the understated disquiet of the Christmas ghost story films.

After the entranced landscapes of Gordon Clark's films, *Schalcken* turns to the interior. It is hardly surprising that a film that depicts two great Dutch masters, the elderly Gerrit Dou (played by the ever-testy Maurice Denham) and his pupil, Godfried Schalcken, should be so painterly in style. Visually, it's an affair of shadows and luminescence, of perspectives and doorways, replete with tributes to the still realism of Dutch art, evoking the becalmed domesticities captured by Vermeer or Pieter de Hooch. The film self-consciously enacts what Schalcken himself would do, transforming living people into the immobility of art. Women here are "property," purchasable commodities, like the paintings—and perhaps the films—that frame and preserve them.

Here again, the tale's aged ghost offers his casket packed with unalloyed gold in exchange for Dou's young niece, Schalcken's unattainable beloved. Megahey's version brings into touch the deadness of money with the living human being, stagnant gold with a woman's animated presence. There's something truly perplexing about Vanderhausen, the weary, mahogany-colored, unbreathing ghost, his hang-dog hideousness both disgusting and curiously fascinating. Vanderhausen visits the house from another interior, a space hidden within the great church in Rotterdam. It's to this unlocated, placeless place that he drags Rose.

Asked to pose with a pair of scales that weighs a dead bird against a string of pearls, one of Schalcken's models inquires, "What's it mean?" "It's only a story," the artist stolidly informs her. Sometimes it's best to remind yourself that the worlds imagined in these ghost films are also only stories, for who would want to reside in such entrapment and strangeness?

The Interview [9 June 2016, at Leiden University in The Netherlands]

LESLIE MEGAHEY (INTRODUCING THE FILM): There's something rather nice, which is nothing to do with the film, and it's that this whole idea came about through a collaborator I worked with for many years, called Paul Humfress, who's the film editor on *Schalcken*, and who actually found the story [Humfress was also the co-writer, editor and co-director of Derek Jarman's movie, *Sebastiane* (1976)]. He sent it to me in the early 1970s, having typed it out, while he was living in Holland. Paul sent it to me to London, showing me the story, and so I wrote a script of it. Before I came here to Leiden, I told Paul, who now lives in Australia, and is in his eighties and runs a smallholding, and chops down trees, and drives tractors, and breeds horses. I told him that I was coming to Leiden, and he said, "well, go to number 3, Sterrenwachtlaan, and just tap the wall—because that's the house where I typed out 'Schalcken'." And I now found out that that's just a block or two from here. Well, if you know Edgar Allan Poe, "The Mystery of Marie Rogêt," he begins that story by speaking of "scarcely intelligible *coincidences*," and nothing more. I hope you enjoy the film!

[After the screening]:

MICHAEL NEWTON: The last thing we see when watching *Schalcken the Painter* is the word "*Omnibus*" – the name of a very resonant program for people of my generation, but much more so for you, of course, who worked for the BBC making programs for *Omnibus*. It's extraordinary to me that *Schalcken* was produced under the aegis of such a documentary series. How did that come about?

MEGAHEY: The BBC had done their Christmas ghost story films. The first of these was Jonathan Miller's fully-dramatized version of the

M. R. James story, "'Oh, Whistle, and I'll Come to You, My Lad'." That was eleven years before *Schalcken*, and that was also done for *Omnibus*, which was indeed an arts and music documentary strand, always of one-off films, made by directors who were trying to push the boundaries of documentary making. *Whistle and I'll Come to You* is certainly one of the great ghost stories on film. They remade it, a few years ago, with John Hurt, and they updated it, and jazzed it up. But the Jonathan Miller version is such a fantastic and simple story, with such a simple ghost. When you see the ghost, you know how it's done, and yet it's utterly, utterly chilling. So Jonathan started something off with that. I was there at the time, because I was making arts documentaries, biographies of artists like Goya and Rodin. But then ten or so years later, Paul Humfress and I had been talking (Paul had edited all my early films) about doing for an arts strand like *Omnibus* an arts documentary that goes wrong, a program that "goes bad," as it were, and doesn't fulfill the expectations of a biography but goes off into some weird world of its own, and keeps trying to pull you back into the biography, but then keeps subverting the rules of that form. We didn't know how to do this, but we thought that it would be a wonderful thing to do.

Then it was Paul who found the Le Fanu story. He sat and typed it out, and sent it to me in London as a typescript. After that, I tried to get the BBC to do it in an arts slot, because I was working for the arts department. The first thing that happened was that my head of department liked the idea, and was quite open to the odd, experimental aspects of it. But he assumed that I had written it for a drama director to direct, because the script clearly looked like a drama. And so he suggested that the man who had done all the BBC Christmas ghost stories up to that point, who had just stopped the year before *Schalcken*, Lawrence Gordon Clark might be a good director for it. Whereas I had written it—although I didn't say so to my head of department—for me to direct. So for a while it slightly fell by the wayside. And then, as luck would have it, I just happened to be appointed the series editor for *Omnibus*, a couple of years later. And so *Schalcken* was my present to myself, and I could now direct it, because now I was in charge!

So that's how it came about and how it got done outside the aegis of a television drama department. The arts department was an incredibly adventurous department that had included people like Ken Russell and John Schlesinger—at one stage, John Boorman did films for it. Lawrence Gordon Clark had started doing his ghost stories entirely on his own, as director and often as writer and editor as well. Later on, when the BBC drama department realized that they had something good going here, they insisted on taking over the Christmas ghost stories. And I believe that Lawrence himself has publicly said that as soon as he had a drama producer foisted upon him, some of the life, some of the pleasure, went out of the films. I had the great joy of being the producer on *Schalcken* as well as director and writer.

NEWTON: Were you a fan of Lawrence Gordon Clark's ghost-story films before you came to write *Schalcken*?

MEGAHEY: I was aware of them; I didn't watch them, so to speak, religiously, but I was a fan of them. I have DVDs of several of them and still look at them with pleasure. I didn't have quite the same concern with the Victorian or Edwardian aspect of the ghost story. A lot of *Schalcken* is shot by candlelight and so forth, but because it's imitating Dutch seventeenth-century painting, there's deliberately an incredible clarity in it. When it comes to films of Victorian ghost stories, I'm always expecting something to happen, because it's so dark, and there's a bit of red there, and it's shaky and flickery. So in a sense I'm not so surprised by whatever it is that turns up. My view was always that perhaps the most frightening ghost would be the one who appeared by daylight. That doesn't really happen in *Schalcken*, but I feel it has a touch of that with the domestic setting, and the ghost as someone that just dropped in and comes to dinner, someone with whom you can make an appointment.

NEWTON: Watching it again, I wondered is it a ghost story?

MEGAHEY: I don't know. I always assumed that he's Death personified, or the devil, or whatever. Someone wrote something about it that's very interesting. They said it could be death, or a ghost, but he could also simply be a very nasty husband. In a way when Rose comes back, she looks to me like a wife who's been badly abused, as opposed to someone who's been living with the undead. Directors do this thing when they say, "I didn't know what the film was about until I just saw that review." I think such a director is lucky, and the wonderful thing is when people find things in your work, because I don't think a director should be that conscious of what things actually mean, of what things "equal."

NEWTON: Clearly one thing that's present in *Schalcken*, as throughout your career, is your passion for painting. As a filmmaker, what is it about painting that attracts you?

MEGAHEY: I think what attracts me to painting in its potential for a ghost story is something rather different to what interests me in it as a documentary maker. In the latter case, apart from simply loving paintings, it's finding the visual source materials for it, finding the ways an artist discovers their subject. One of the things you get when you see great paintings is the traces of that discovery. Picasso said of Van Gogh, that when he saw how Van Gogh painted a group of potato-eaters, he remarked how absolutely wonderful it was to find a new subject: Van Gogh had found a subject in such an everyday thing as peasants eating potatoes. I love the idea of putting together a film with images and words that engage with the kinds of sources that push a painter in a certain direction. I sometimes employ a narrative voice that gives plain facts, but I try to avoid having one that makes judgements or connections for you. Those are for you to make yourself.

With *Schalcken*, because it's such a cold story, I was fascinated by our voyeurism, by how we look at a painting, and how there's no way we can enter into that two-dimensional space. I was very intrigued by the fact of shooting a drama where if I were filming two of you here in the audience, I'd have a wide shot of you with the people behind, but if you start to engage in a conversation, automatically the filmmaker will construct shots from first your perspective, and then from yours, cross-cutting. And I thought since this is about a painting, and it's such a cold eye, so baleful an eye, for the whole of the first half of the film, when you're on a wide shot with several characters in it, and you cut in to focus on a single character, you cut in from the same angle. If they're in profile in the wide shot, rather than showing them full-face, then you stay in the same viewpoint as you cut in, so they remain in profile. That's unusual and ungrammatical in filmmaking. But it added to the feeling that the whole thing had, that you can look at this, but you can't get inside it. You stay looking *at* the thing. That seemed to me a style of shooting that was absolutely in keeping with the subject. Later on, as you see slightly more homely scenes, like the fake Vanderhausen, the chap who turns up and wants his daughter painted, that's almost the first time you have conventional cross-cutting, a deep two-shot.

NEWTON: With regard to the voyeurism, the film appeared only a few years after Laura Mulvey's celebrated essay on "Visual Pleasure and Narrative Cinema." Were her ideas on your mind in making *Schalcken*?

MEGAHEY: Well, no, because I read Laura Mulvey much later. Someone wrote recently that because it's a 1970s film, it had to shoehorn in a few female nudes. The thing that I take enormous pleasure in (and don't take this the wrong way) is that there's a shot of the actor who plays Lesbia, Val Penny, and that I think is the most overtly...I don't know..."glamorous" shot. And I always thought that this is such a glowing image, and she seems to me to be glowing with life and health, and then she's going to be turned into one of these rather chilly, Schalcken-factory, classical nudes. So I thought that was absolutely the right image. But otherwise, with Laura Mulvey, which I read a few years ago, I'm actually very interested in that idea of "the male gaze," at least I think she invented it, because, yes, I'm a male, and I gaze, in order to make these films. I've certainly done a few films that have featured the body. She does a rather honest job on Godard, and on Godard's use of the female body, that showed an even-handedness in her approach.

NEWTON: When Lesbia is being washed and prepared to be painted, it reminded me somehow of the transformation scene in Hitchcock's *Vertigo*.

MEGAHEY: When Schalcken chooses the model from the group of women, one of those women is Cheryl Kennedy, who plays Rose. I put her in thinking this might be a clever idea if someone just happens to glimpse her and thinks "hang on a minute." But I don't think a single viewer has ever spotted her.

AUDIENCE QUESTION: Watching it, I was struck by how you don't slip us the heavy-handed cues that you find in a lot of contemporary horror films. What do you think about the pacing of *Schalcken*? Do we have a stricter short-hand structure now in Gothic films?

MEGAHEY: I think so. I have to confess that though I've just watched *Schalcken* again now, I don't normally sit in to watch the film. That's in part because having made it, I know what's going to happen. I think we pushed that idea of nothing apparently happening, but something brewing to its absolute limit. One of the people who has written about the film said that it begins with grueling real-time for about half an hour, and thereafter time speeds up, and it's almost vertiginous at certain moments. But that is an intention of the film. The aim was to show this pristine, neat Dutch interior, and to deal with it in a drama-documentary style, but just to worry people the whole time that something must be about to happen—you know, for God's sake, let something happen! And then when it does happen, apart from the low hum that comes in whenever Vanderhausen appears, but at no point is there ever a sudden stab of music to make you jump. It's all in that measured style, and even when the most terrible things happen—and in fact when the worst thing of all happens, at the end, when she gets onto the bed, the music plays as an ironical, little ditty, which I think makes it even worse, more frightening, and more terrible.

A classic thing now is that you tell the audience what is going to happen, you tell them what's happening while it's happening, and then you tell them what just happened. So you lead up, and the music builds, and then you get frenetic music when the horror comes, and then you have the downsweep afterward. I didn't want to use that at all. I wanted to use as little music as possible. A friend of mine said that the most frightening thing in *Schalcken* is when the heavy curtain swishes across the door, and you feel the heaviness of that curtain. It's those kind of details that I was after.

AUDIENCE QUESTION (FROM LAWRENCE JACKSON): Le Fanu's original story is so dense, so literary, what decisions did you make about visualizing such a tale?

MEGAHEY: Well, Lawrence, you've adapted quite a few works yourself, including "Schalcken" for radio, so you know how it is! I brought in the Le Fanu narrator, and I obviously added huge amounts of narration to it, but within that style. The narrator starts the story as though it were an art lecture, and I think he declares that some ancient relative actually owned the painting, and heard the story from the painter himself. So he turns it into an anecdote that kind of becomes a part of the art lecture. And in my version that becomes very much to do with the fact that it's television, and that you can see.

But there was something that I was most concerned about. I added all the brothel scenes—and those are based on me going to The Hague, to the Mauritshuis to look at paintings, and I'd already decided to have certain scenes in a brothel to be based on those Dutch paintings of men offering women money. And when I went to The Hague, to my surprise I found that Schalcken had actually made such paintings, the ones I'd described in the first draft of the script, and that he'd painted very much as I had set things out. And also in Dutch art of the time there are countless pictures that deal with a man, often a man in uniform, a military man, offering a young woman money. And you possibly know also that there was this extraordinary thing that happened to these works a hundred or so years after they were painted, which is that people started changing the titles to make them appear to be an innocent domestic scene. And you look at a painting by Gerard ter Borch, that's called "The Paternal Admonition," and it's a typical example of the genre, with a beautiful back-view of a young woman in fantastic robes, and the beautiful nape of her neck, and the hair up. And there's a man sitting while the woman is standing, and his finger is raised, and then there's an old woman sitting between them. And Goethe mentions this painting as a father telling his daughter how to behave. Well, it is now pretty much agreed by art historians, that originally it wasn't that at all, it was another of these pictures of a man presenting money for a young woman's honor, for her virginity. The old woman is the procuress. There are thousands of these paintings, and some are now presented as the return of a wandering son, or of a soldier back from the wars, and he's come back with his earnings. I don't know if when they were first painted it was coded, so that some people could feel they were in on it, or was it perfectly clear to everyone, and was it then some later puritanical reaction that made people seek to revise these works, changing them into domestic subjects. But it's interesting that they have that ambiguity, that you can read them both ways.

Later I did a platform event at the National Gallery in London with the keeper of Flemish art. Of all those paintings—and I've looked at hundreds of them—I only found one where the young woman not only doesn't acknowledge the presence of the man, but is actively ignoring him, sternly sewing and not registering his advances. And it's by a woman painter!

So the brothel scenes were all added to Le Fanu's tale. The thing I wanted to do most was to keep Le Fanu's rhythms, so that even when I was writing something which might sound like a much more modern part of the lecture, that somehow those rhythms remain. Apart from the absolutely new bits there, there's still a significant amount of Le Fanu in it. That's why I call it an adaptation, even though I added a lot to it. Because there are direct quotes from the story in it. So, throughout it, even though I've brought in material of my own, I believe he's informed the rhythms of the speech—as does Charles Gray's voice, which similarly has that wonderful urbane worldly quality.

AUDIENCE QUESTION: Also regarding the adaptation, I notice how in *Schalcken* you show us how Schalcken himself transforms reality in his paintings, producing something quite unlike what he sees before him. How much was your film consciously about the remolding of real life to produce art?

MEGAHEY: I think a lot of it is intending to say—and does say at some point—that a lot of these mythological and fantastic subjects that Schalcken paints, that they were done for money, and it's just a production line, really. But, as I read it, the more personal paintings, the theme of the woman with the candle in particular, that there's some quality to them that seems entirely different. I rationalized that for the drama, by saying, "well, it is different," because they come out of this terrible experience Schalcken had. Well, he didn't have it in real life, but there is something very particular about those paintings.

For the rest, I think I'm selling the idea that he sold out. Yet there was a part of him that was still capable of art, and possibly there was a part of him that was still capable of love, though you don't see much evidence of it there, as the social *mores* worked against that. Because he had no money, and therefore couldn't keep her, she was the property of Gerrit Dou. The film is meant to say that everything is for sale, and if you subscribe to that belief, then you actually lose everything. And for me, there are only two living creatures in the film really, one is Cheryl Kennedy who plays Rose, and the other is the model, Lesbia. Lesbia asks some questions that are not at all daft, but are perfectly sensible questions. She's meant to be Mary Magdalene, and then she wonders why she has one breast bare. And then she wonders who Ceres is, as she's in another erotic pose. It seems to me the two women are the living creatures. And the poor cat, of course!

By the way to set the viewer's mind at rest, that cat in the film was perfectly cool and happy! The scene where the cat is mishandled is based on another Dutch painting of students playing with—or rather perhaps torturing—a cat.

AUDIENCE QUESTION (FROM LENNEKE MAAN): During the film I was wondering if Vanderhausen was in some sense Schalcken's own ghost, a double for him? That's, in part, because I thought the actors rather resembled each other. Was this just my fancy, or was this something you intended?

MEGAHEY: I think that's a completely wonderful idea! It wasn't my intention at all, but it is a fantastic idea. Because Schalcken is indeed selling himself into death, a creative death. But those roles weren't cast because of any supposed physical resemblance. Jeremy Clyde as Schalcken was chosen in part because he does rather look like Schalcken, and John Justin, who plays Vanderhausen, was cast because he was a one-time matinée idol and had such a powerful face. I worked with John on radio long before that, and I really got on with him.

I've learnt much more about my film, and about the whole business of selling out, or selling your soul, or whatever, from what other people have said about it. You put things in unconsciously or subconsciously, but you don't ever when you're writing a script think, "well this has to demonstrate this metaphysical idea or this philosophical notion or this social intention, or whatever." You just don't do that. You write a story, and the rest of it is your instinct. And also it's informed by the research you've done, and the paintings you've seen.

NEWTON: As you say, John Justin was a very handsome young man, and a big British star, appearing most famously in *The Thief of Baghdad* (1940). I know this is a bit silly to remark upon, but it's central to *Schalcken* that he should appear to be repulsively ugly. What did Justin make of that?

MEGAHEY: Oh, he was great! That performance, well, he just turned up with it. If you think about it, it's not clear how Death should speak. I wrote a screenplay for an American version of *Faust*. We updated the story, and my instinct there was to make Mephistopheles fantastically articulate and suave, and smart and funny. Not the most original Mephistopheles in the world, it is true! But with Vanderhausen, I was really worried until the first day we shot with John about all these small things, such as how does Death—or the Devil—or your double—how does he speak? And when John turned up, and we were to begin rehearsing on set, he said, "I've got this voice!" And he did it, and it was immediately absolutely the voice. That voice sounds like John, but it sounds like John having gone through some dreadful trauma.

NEWTON: Was the voice done in post-production?

MEGAHEY: No, apart from Charles Gray's voiceover, there was no post-synching at all. So, John turned up with the voice, he turned up with that stance, that stiffness, and he just worked it out from the very beginning. The only problem I had with John was that he kept mistaking his own character's name, Vanderhausen, with Cheryl Kennedy's name, Rose Velderkaust.

AUDIENCE QUESTION: I was struck by the repetition of the phrase, "You will not pledge yourself unnecessarily," that Vanderhausen says to Dou. Was that in Le Fanu's story, or was it something that you added?

MEGAHEY: In Le Fanu, I think it's in once. In that moment, he seems to read Gerrit Dou's mind, that's all Le Fanu. The next times, I put it in—it's spoken in the brothel, and when the other visitor comes for a painter, and neither of those scenes are in the Le Fanu text. I wanted that line to be the tolling of three bells.

What strikes me in looking at some of the Dutch paintings that inspired my film is that sometimes when you look at them there's nothing there. There's a painting by Samuel van Hoogstraten in the Louvre, called "View of an Interior," or sometimes "The Slippers." And it looks as though it's a picture of a pair of slippers on the floor (we referenced them in *Schalcken*), and it's just an empty room, and then another empty room beyond. There is no one there, but there's a bunch of keys in the door. And you look at it, and you see there's a painting beyond, in the farther room. And that painting is of a beautiful woman, seen from behind, in a beautiful gown, her hair up so you can see the nape of her neck. And it's the painting I was talking about earlier, the Gerard ter Borch painting that ended up being renamed as "The Paternal Admonition." Hoogstraten, who presumably was a friend of ter Borch, and who certainly knew him, has painted this totally empty interior, but he's placed in it another man's painting on the wall. It's an interior, and it's beautifully painted, and yet there's nothing there. I tried to capture that feeling of nothing happening, and yet the eye is drawn by those details—by the keys, by the slippers, by the painting on the wall beyond. And something is going to happen, I'm not sure what. I wanted that wonderful freezing of action—and that emptiness.

11   A Tale of Two Carmillas

The Representation of Styria in Le Fanu's "Carmilla" and Its Web Series Adaptation

Rahel Sixta Schmitz

Joseph Sheridan Le Fanu's "Carmilla" (1872) is a key text in nineteenth-century gothic literature. In the story, the young girl Laura, living with her father in a remote Styrian castle, meets the mysterious and beautiful Carmilla Karnstein. Over the course of the tale, the two women develop an intimate romantic relationship. However, it is revealed that Carmilla is in truth a vampire and has been feeding on the girl. Laura's father can barely prevent the girl's death by dispatching the revenant in time.

Critics have widely discussed both the tale's treatment of English and Eastern European racial and national identities as well as its sexual politics. Le Fanu describes Carmilla's arrival at the castle in distinctly racial terms: while Carmilla is "absolutely beautiful" and is quickly taken in by Laura's father after a carriage accident, her traveling companions are "a hideous black woman, with a sort of coloured turban on her head" as well as "an ill-looking pack of men" with "strangely lean, and dark, and sullen" faces (219). Similarly, Laura's heritage is marked by her hybridity: even though she identifies as English throughout the novel, she has internalized this national identity exclusively due to her father's careful education—Laura has never been to England in her life. In fact, her mother was a Styrian and a direct descendant of the Karnstein family, making Laura and Carmilla blood relatives. The tale fames the relationship between the two girls in lesbian terms; in doing so it follows a path central to numerous gothic fictions, from Bram Stoker's *Dracula* (1897) to Anne Rice's *The Vampire Chronicles* (1976–2014), where the vampire is portrayed as a homoerotic and hence "abnormal" figure. It is through such transgressions of racial, national, and sexual categories that the West and the East are continuously contrasted and intermingled in "Carmilla."

There have been numerous adaptations across a wide range of media of Le Fanu's tale. One of the most recent examples is the Canadian web series *Carmilla*,[1] advertised as a loose adaptation of the original vampire story. Launched in 2014 on YouTube, the show consists of three seasons; one prequel season; one feature film, which concluded the series in 2017; and numerous transmedia elements, such as Twitter and Tumblr accounts by the franchise's fictional characters. The series recasts Laura and Carmilla as college students at Silas University[2] in Styria. Even though this is an Austrian university, the majority of enrolled students, including most of the show's characters, are non-natives, as Laura reveals on her Tumblr blog:

> through some fluke of the admissions office, most of the students are international—and even the Austrian students here aren't from the area. Come to mention it, none of the locals seem to attend here, or come within twenty miles of the campus...
>
> (laura2theletter, September 28, 2014)

While this "fluke" offers a simple explanation for why each character is a native English speaker and why life on campus strongly resembles that of a North American university, it also foregrounds that, while set in Styria, the campus appears to be a strange microcosm detached from the surrounding region.

The story is for the most part told in the form of a vlog—a video blog. Each episode comprises an entry in Laura's vlog—originally launched as an investigative journalism project for a university course after several female students have gone missing—in which she narrates the current developments at the university from her dorm room. After Laura's roommate disappears, she begins to investigate her new, unfriendly, languid roommate: Carmilla Karnstein. With the help of her friends, amongst them the floor don Lola Perry, as well as science student LaFontaine—both figures inspired by Laura's two governesses in the tale—Laura discovers that, while Carmilla is a vampire, she is not their true antagonist. Rather, she is herself a victim of an overbearing mother, the university's Dean, who forces her to abduct female students regularly for a human sacrifice. Carmilla herself is revealed to be a likeable, even loveable antihero who reluctantly aids Laura in repeatedly saving the world. While largely supplanting the tale's dark atmosphere for a light-hearted, even quirky tone, the web series is highly aware of its gothic heritage, oftentimes exploiting it for comic effect. The result is a grotesque fusion of the prose fiction's arcane atmosphere and the show's modern-day premise, where each character struggles to balance their life as conscientious college student with the fight against ancient demigods.

It is the comparison of both fictions that lies at the heart of this paper, examining in particular the narrative techniques of each text, and how both the prose story and the web series portray Styria and its inhabitants. After an examination of the tale's formal aspects and how they are transposed into the web series format in *Carmilla*, I discuss how and to what effect each narrative exploits its Eastern European setting. Significantly, both fictions describe Styria as an exotic, magical place. However, whereas "Carmilla" frames Styria as a poor and backward region in order to reflect critically on the supposed superiority of Western cultures, the online drama exposes this negative depiction of Eastern Europe through its reliance on pastiche. While doing so, *Carmilla* neglects the racial and national discourses of the original tale, instead focusing on its sexual politics exclusively. The web series specifically stands out due to its progressive take on queer representation. By rendering the topic a non-issue in light of the dangerous supernatural happenings within the region, it is foregrounded that it is fighting evil villains which comprises the center of the narrative, not a character's gender or sexuality.

Storytelling Techniques: Adapting Le Fanu's Tale to the Web Series Format

Embedded in the collection *In A Glass Darkly* (1872), which purports to be the casebook of occult detective Dr. Martin Hesselius, Le Fanu presents "Carmilla" as one of the doctor's cases. After a brief prologue by his secretary, the events are told by Laura, who takes on the roles of both the story's protagonist and its first-person narrator writing to Hesselius. Adding further levels of narration, at times Laura recounts tales and information relayed to her by other people. Due to this complex structure as well as the dream-like, even febrile experience of her time with Carmilla, large parts of the tale remain obscure and ambivalent. Through its use of multiple levels of narration, "Carmilla" establishes a "textual self-consciousness" (Sage 2004, 142) characteristic of the gothic mode. In his analysis of the text, W. J. McCormack (1980) identifies this as a discursive strategy typical for Le Fanu, where "pattern and metaphor overwhelm narrative and characterization" (191). The written tale foregrounds the process of narrative construction, thereby negotiating the power and limits of representation itself. Ultimately, it is storytelling that provides the solution to the mystery: "the narrator undergoes the ordeal and the victim of an interpolated story provides the sombre conclusion" (191). Carmilla's true nature is discovered through stories and events narrated by a wide range of characters. Furthermore, at no point can the reader forget that they are reading a tale that is narrated in hindsight by a person whose reliability is uncertain. For instance, Laura prepares her readers for the arrival of Carmilla at the *schloss* with the following words:

> I am now going to tell you something so strange that it will require all your faith in my veracity to believe my story. It is not only the truth, nevertheless, but truth of which I have been an eyewitness.
>
> (212)

Throughout the entire tale, Le Fanu signposts Laura's function as narrator through such inserts.

However, readers have to contend with a narration that has clearly been re-told and filtered multiple times, as Laura is often absent at key moments. The ritualistic disposal of Carmilla is undertaken by a group of men, with Laura being left behind at her family's castle. She gathers her "account of this last shocking scene" from the report of an "Imperial Commission" (269). At other times, central information regarding the mysterious "oupire" affliction is revealed through another character's narration. Le Fanu inserts General Spielsdorf's knowledge surrounding his ward's mysterious death into Laura's account. Similarly, her narration includes the tale of a woodsman at the former Karnstein village, who, in turn, retells the story of a Moravian nobleman fighting the last vampire at the town. The reader is repeatedly removed from the story's events through such complex narrative layers, as Laura herself can only re-narrate what other people have told her. At the same time, the reliability of each account is called into question, as it becomes obvious how each tale has been passed on multiple times by multiple people.

Le Fanu embeds Laura's narration within the editorial frame of Dr. Hesselius, a physician specializing in strange cases of the occult, carefully documenting and researching each case. While this frame adds a degree of scientific rationality to Laura's tale, it further extends the already remarkably extended time span. Through one of General Spielsdorf's narrations, it becomes clear that Carmilla must be very old:

> The house of Karnstein...has been long extinct: a hundred years at least. My dear wife was maternally descended from the Karnsteins. But the name and title have long ceased to exist. The castle is a ruin; the very village is deserted; it is fifty years since the smoke of a chimney was seen there.
>
> (251)

Earlier in her own narration, however, Laura mentions that she is writing her account of the events "after an interval of more than ten years" (225). The prologue provided by Hesselius's medical secretary finally reveals that the correspondence between Laura and the doctor occurred "so many years before," and that the girl has since died (207). Discussing this temporal complexity, Michael McAteer (2010) writes: "The deeper the narrative probes into a past through which its sense of tradition is conveyed, the more unstable it becomes" (213). Indeed, the intricate blood relations at the heart of the novella have been obscured by time; both Spielsdorf's ward and Laura are descendants of the Karnsteins. Together, these narrative techniques render "Carmilla" an obscure and ambivalent tale, in which small, yet important details are easily missed.

While losing the serious, dark tone of the original prose fiction and changing significant aspects of its plot, the web series *Carmilla* adapts the narrative strategies of Le Fanu's tale quite well.[3] By presenting the events in the form of vlogs created by Laura, the tale's first-person narration is transposed into the logic of the online drama: once again, Laura appears in the dual function of the story's protagonist and its narrator. The frame narrative of Dr. Hesselius, however, is discarded in favor of the immediacy implied by the narrative medium.

Since the vlog is supposedly created using the computer's webcam, the camera generally remains fixed within one room. While the setting of each season changes, and while Laura sometimes repositions her computer—thus offering a new perspective of a room—viewers remain restricted to this limited viewpoint. They therefore learn of many events only *after* they have happened, namely when Laura comes to the camera in order to narrate what has happened. This "tell, don't show" approach offers a twist on the passivity and repeated absence of Le Fanu's Laura. In both the prose story and the web series, readers/viewers get no direct access to the events, but only a re-narration; however, unlike in the tale, the show's Laura is highly active and even fearless when it comes to fighting villains. Here, it is the viewer who is absent and missing out on the action; they have to wait until Laura or one of her friends returns to the camera to narrate what has happened.

At the same time, these storytelling strategies significantly simplify the production of a web series in terms of time, effort, expense, and expertise. As Silke Jandl (2015) explains in her analysis of another highly successful web series adaptation, *The Lizzie Bennet Diaries* (2012–13), the vlog format emphasizes the intimate inner thoughts of the characters as well as their interpersonal dialogue; expensive film locations are superfluous in re-narrating a tale such as Jane Austen's 1813 novel *Pride and Prejudice* (170). Locating the story in a particular setting hence becomes a matter of verbal description. While *Carmilla* offers only little visualization of its Styrian context, the setting is repeatedly referred to, making it impossible for the viewer to forget where the narrative is taking place. Furthermore, few special effects and little make-up are needed since the most dramatic, supernatural events occur off-screen. In addition, when using a fixed, static camera as *Carmilla* does, no re-adjustments of camera angles, lighting, and similar technical issues are needed. Finally, the format does not rely on an extradiegetic soundtrack, which would diminish the supposed authenticity of the document.[4]

This appearance of authenticity, or what has been termed "inauthentic authenticity" (Burgess and Green 2009, 29), is a central element of YouTube web television. While it must be emphasized at this point that the web series is a narrative medium in its own right, it cannot be denied that it shares central characteristics with television. If television is characterized by its immediacy, intimacy, and hybridity, online drama takes these features a step further: first, in contrast to television's polished *mise-en-scène* and cinematography, the production quality of the

YouTube web series can make it appear more "real" and less of a performance (Creeber 2011, 597). Additionally, such shows are produced with particular delivery methods and consumption habits in mind—namely, as short videos running only a few minutes per episode, which are uploaded at regular, set times, and which are usually watched on smartphones or tablets; therefore, creating content for such viewing practices implies shorter and less complex takes, instead favoring "a strong emphasis on lower levels of detail and closer shots" (Treske 2008, 215). It is precisely this "rawness," foregrounding low production costs, which gives a web series such as *Carmilla* its "authentic" feel. At the same time, it once again mirrors the tale's storytelling and editorial frame: in both narratives, it is claimed that the tale is comprised of the unadulterated documents provided by Laura.

Second, if television is predominantly connected to the domestic viewing context of the living room, the webcam is associated with "the even more personal space of the bedroom and the lone viewer" (Creeber 2011, 597)—a sense of intimacy further increased by the continuous use of medium close-ups. *Carmilla* utilizes such intimacy to create a subtle sense of claustrophobia and to foreground the threat of invasion into Laura's private sphere, but also to focus on the developing relationship between Laura and Carmilla. The viewer can access the world of Silas University only through this restrictive frame. They have to accept that they often do not witness the goings-on themselves or that characters will not be placed optimally in the frame—if they fit into the frame at all (see Figure 11.1). However, since Laura's webcam is apparently running at all times, viewers will sometimes witness how villains tamper with Laura's private belongings or place dangerous traps in the room

Figure 11.1 Laura's friend Danny Lawrence is oftentimes out of frame, as she is too tall for the webcam set-up. *Carmilla.* Season 1, episode 7, "Town Hall." Uploaded 21 August 2014.

Figure 11.2 Carmilla tampers with the dorm room at night. *Carmilla*. Season 1, episode 13, "I, Spy." Uploaded 11 September 2014.

(see Figure 11.2). Especially Carmilla at first appears as such an invasive force into Laura's home. Yet, the show's restrictive frame eventually underlines the growing romantic intimacy of both women.

Finally, whereas television is a hybrid medium incorporating film, radio, newsprint, and other media, the web series can additionally tap the potential of the internet and online culture. It is in particular the possibility of interactivity, allowing the audience not only to watch but also to shape the content themselves, which makes such web series so appealing (Creeber 2011, 600). In *Carmilla*, every character as well as Silas University itself has at least one social media account, with which fans of the show can engage.[5] While the YouTube show comprises the centerpiece of the narrative, these transmedia extensions offer bonus content and are used to bridge the hiatus between seasons. For instance, Laura and her friends flee Silas University at the end of the first season, only to return unwillingly at the beginning of the second season. What they experience and how they eventually end up back on campus is revealed through a series of tweets by the members of the group. It is through the combination of the series and such transmedia content that *Carmilla* adapts the tale's narrative complexity. As a consequence of this transmedia environment, however, *Carmilla* partially loosens up Le Fanu's restricted focalization: Laura may still be the narrative's predominant narrator, but her friends are given an independent voice of their own. Furthermore, due to careful coordination, these contents sometimes are released almost simultaneously. Hence, while Le Fanu's tale was presented as one of Hesselius's carefully documented case files created over the course of several years, the show conflates this temporal dimension, creating a feeling of immediacy by suggesting that—at least at the time of the broadcast—everything is happening at this very moment. In the series, "Carmilla's" originally expansive time frame is conveyed exclusively on the story level through references to Carmilla's true age.

These narrative strategies are essential for the show's construction and fictionalization of Styria. In large part, viewers glean an impression of this magical region not through visualizations, but through verbal descriptions either within the show or through one of its transmedia extensions. The image they thereby gather of Eastern Europe and its inhabitants is not all that different from Le Fanu's Styria; the main difference between the two texts is how seriously they treat this setting and to what effect they utilize it.

"This Lonely and Primitive Place": The Representation of Styria and Its Inhabitants

Scholars have discussed whether the Styrian setting serves as a far-away, exoticized place through which Irish political problems could be explored, or whether Le Fanu was interested in Eastern Europe's specific political situation. For instance, McAteer (2010) claims that "Carmilla" casts Styria as a projection to investigate and negotiate questions related to the Irish political situation at the time (212). In contrast to this, Matthew Gibson (2006) has argued that Le Fanu's choice of setting might have been inspired by his genuine interest in the Austro-Hungarian *Ausgleich*, and by similarities between the political climates on the continent and in Ireland (44). While contrary, these views are by no means contradictory; both perspectives ascribe a central function to the fiction's setting.

Already the first sentence of "Carmilla" reveals its Styrian context:

> In Styria, we, though by no means magnificent people, inhabit a castle, or schloss. A small income, in that part of the world, goes a great way....Scantily enough would it answer among wealthy people at home. My father is English, and I bear an English name, although I never saw England. But here, in this lonely and primitive place, where everything is so marvellously cheap, I really don't see how ever so much more money would at all materially add to our comforts or even luxuries.
>
> (208)

The opening invokes "a general discourse of civilization versus barbarity" (McAteer 2010, 207). While Styria is described as "lonely and primitive," Laura and her father appear to be comparatively well-off due to their English heritage. At the same time, however, this wealth is pulled into question, as Laura emphasizes how their income would not grant them entry into wealthy society in England. Furthermore, the opening paragraph foregrounds Laura's own dubious heritage: her father may be English, but she herself has never been to the country. Therefore, while the opposition of barbarity and civilization is put center stage in the tale's opening lines, it is also already deconstructed within those sentences—a dynamic which persists throughout the entire narrative.

Laura goes on to describe the castle and its surroundings:

> Nothing can be more picturesque or solitary. It stands on a slight eminence in a forest. The road, very old and narrow, passes in front of its drawbridge, never raised in my time, and its moat, stocked with perch and sailed over by many swans [...]. Over all this the *schloss* shows its many-windowed front, its towers and its Gothic chapel.
>
> (208)

Close to the castle is the abandoned Karnstein village; the nearest inhabited township lies several miles away. Styria as it is depicted here is indeed a "lonely" place; Laura has spent much of her life isolated from people other than her father or the staff.

The villagers in the region are highly superstitious; it is through their depiction that the grotesque opposition of civilization and barbarity is further emphasized. When the peasants living near the castle begin to fall fatally ill, claiming that the epidemic is due to "oupire"—vampire— attacks (229), Laura's father dismisses their fears as mere irrationality: "These poor people infect one another with their superstitions, and so repeat in imagination the images of terror that have infested their neighbours" (230). The tale hence exoticizes Eastern Europe as a backward, poor, and superstitious region.

The most vivid portrayal of the Styrians comes in the form of a wandering salesman arriving at the castle:

> It was the figure of a hunchback, with the sharp lean features that generally accompany deformity. He wore a pointed black beard, and he was smiling from ear to ear, showing his white fangs. [...] He had a fiddle, a box of conjuring apparatus, a pair of foils and masks attached to his belt, several other mysterious cases dangling about him, and a black staff with copper ferrules in his hand.
>
> (228)

Having learned of the recent attack of the oupire in the region, the wanderer provides Laura and Carmilla with amulets and charms against the creature. Unlike Laura or her father, he is quick to notice Carmilla's pointed, sharp teeth, offering to file them down. Hence, while the hunchback appears to be a vivid image of the superstitious, primitive Styrians, he also seems to be best equipped to recognize and fight off a vampire.

Laura's own heritage and upbringing further problematize this opposition: while Laura's father is an Englishman working in the Austrian service, her mother was of an old-established Styrian family, the Karn-steins. Significantly, the vampire Carmilla is a Karnstein herself—in an incestuous twist to the already illicit sexual desire between the two women, Laura and Carmilla are blood-related. Laura's Englishness is due to her father's education: as we have seen, she admits that, even though her name may be English, she has never been to the country. Laura and her father speak English every day, "partly to prevents its becoming a lost language among us, and partly from patriotic mo-tives" (209); with similar regularity they drink tea, "for with his usual patriotic leanings, my father insisted that the national beverage should make its appearance regularly with our coffee and chocolate" (219); finally, Laura's father makes sure his daughter is familiar with the English classics, such as Shakespeare, "whom, by way of keeping up our English, he used to read aloud" (215). Laura's national identity is deceptive, willed, the result of her father's careful upbringing.

In line with the gothic tradition of turning the attention to the interplay of seemingly clear-cut, dichotomous categories and portraying the horrify-ing permeability of these boundaries, "Carmilla" illustrates its opposition of the West and the East—to be more precise, the British Isles and Eastern Europe—through the juxtaposition of categories such as civilization and barbarity, wealth and poverty, progress and backwardness, and rational-ity and superstitiousness. Through the editorial frame, Dr. Hesselius takes on the role of both an interstice between the rational and the supernatural and, himself being a German, an intermediary between the English and Styrian cultures. Yet, Hesselius never makes an appearance in the tale—even the prologue embedding the tale in his casebook is written by his secretary instead. The doctor as the figure of occult science and the bridge between opposing national identities is absent throughout the entire nar-rative. The knowledge concerning the vampire is provided instead by the local Styrians. The Western "experts" appearing throughout the tale are surprisingly incompetent and ignorant. As Nina Auerbach (1995) writes:

> Carmilla initially seems devoid of authorities; Dr. Hesselius, Le Fanu's guide to the supernatural in other tales, comes on only indirectly, in a brief prologue authenticating the 'conscientious par-ticularity' of Laura's narrative; he plays no rescuing role. Like many Victorian fathers, Laura's is a venerated fool, impervious to the plot that brings a vampire to his castle, laughing ever more affably as his daughter drifts closer to death....The General is as competent a father as Laura's is idiotic....More experts follow the General: a woodman expert in Karnstein revenants, a grotesque old baron who is a trove of vampire lore, a priest, and two medical men who au-thenticate Carmilla's decapitation.... Laura's point of view shrivels under this invasion of experts and official language.
>
> (45–46)

It is precisely through the information provided by people such as the hunchback or the "grotesque old baron" native to Styria that Carmilla is eventually found out. Scientific rationality and ancient superstitions are fused in the moment of her death: "Here, then, were all the *admitted signs and proofs* of vampirism. The body, therefore, *in accordance with the ancient practice*, was raised, and a sharp stake driven through the heart of the vampire" (269, emphases added). It is only through this fusion that Laura's life can be saved.

Laura is cast as a liminal figure, serving "to confuse the polarity between East and West, unreason and reason": "the young lady is mixed, in both a political and a rational sense: she is partly western and partly oriental; partly rational and partly governed by the same Dionysian urges that rage through the vampiric visitor" (Gibson 2006, 51). While the tale carefully establishes these dichotomous categories of West/East and rationality/superstitiousness, it also deconstructs them. Foregrounding the "ethos of progress central to British imperial advancement" through Laura's educated Englishness (McAteer 2010, 207), Le Fanu also questions that ideology: "Moving into an exoticised interior landscape, western European values of industry, progress and commercial power prove irrelevant and useless in the landscape of 'Carmilla'" (McAteer 2010, 211). In true gothic manner, the supposedly superior Western rationality ultimately proves powerless against the vampire. Instead, Laura's life depends on the archaic knowledge—dismissed as superstitious beliefs by her and her father—of the locals; only they know how to recognize and dispatch the creature.

As Barbara Korte (2010) claims in "Facing the East of Europe in Its Western Isles," "the European East has always been a construct of the imagination more than a geographical fact" (1). As such a construct, the East functions as the West's Other, illustrating the latter's supposed progressiveness through its own alleged primitiveness (2). This Othering of the East has been maintained since the Enlightenment up until today, rendering it a vital task to engage critically with the representations of both West and East. Significantly, as Korte goes on to explain, the East as Other can also deconstruct the West:

> [T]he East, for many writers in Britain today, is a space not only to be re-discovered, but also a mirror-space that helps the West to complement and destabilize its conceptions about itself, its stereotypes about the East, and its ideas about Europe and the European cultural heritage.
>
> (4)

In other words, the representation of Eastern Europe can not only serve as an Other that maintains the West's self-conception, but it can also function to deconstruct precisely that self-image.

Of course, Carmilla is killed at the end and the threat she poses—in terms of both transgressive sexuality and mixed identity—is thereby presumably contained. Yet, Laura's fate remains unclear: it is indicated that those people fed upon by the vampire "almost invariably" turn into a revenant themselves (271). By the time Dr. Hesselius's secretary finds her correspondence, Laura already has died prematurely, without her cause of death ever being detailed. Thus, while Carmilla is killed, the vampire Laura might still hunt for prey—and with her mixed heritage in addition to her lesbian desires, she represents an even greater transgressive danger than Carmilla did.

At several instances, the web series *Carmilla* picks up and expands on this subversive West/East disparity established in the tale. Already the beginning of the show's first episode alludes to the opening of Le Fanu's "Carmilla": "Silas University, in picturesque Styria, where nothing, not even the homecoming goat sacrifice, disturbs the pursuit of knowledge. But under the surface of this placid institute of higher education you'll find mystery after mystery" ("Disorientation" 2014). In both the tale and the web series, the story's Styrian setting is the first detail revealed to the reader/viewer. Le Fanu's Laura goes on to describe this part of the world as "lonely," "primitive," and "cheap," using this portrayal to foreground her own questionable wealth and superiority. In contrast, the web show makes both this disparity and Laura's obliviousness to it glaringly obvious through its use of irony. Silas University is both a place of higher education and homecoming goat sacrifices.

The show offers no visual portrayal of the university campus or Styria itself, except for old black-and-white photographs occasionally inserted into the vlog (see Figure 11.3).

Figure 11.3 An old photograph, supposedly portraying the Silas University Campus. *Carmilla*. Season 1, episode 1, "Disobedience." Uploaded 19 August 2014.

These images invoke Le Fanu's description of the *schloss*, but are ultimately of little relevance to the show, as the series is restricted to interior settings exclusively. The first season is entirely restricted to Laura's generic dorm room (see Figure 11.4). Not much can be gleaned from this room, at least nothing that would hint at its Eastern European context. During the following seasons, some additional insights are offered: the second season is set in the Dean's rustic quarters, sporting some antler decorations (see Figure 11.5). In the prequel season and the third season, the characters are stuck in different parts of the university library. The prequel season, in which Laura and Carmilla are stuck in the library's basement and watch old surveillance videos of Carmilla

Figure 11.4 Laura's dorm room. *Carmilla.* Season 1, episode 1, "Disobedience." Uploaded 19 August 2014.

Figure 11.5 The Dean's quarters. *Carmilla.* Season 2, episode 1, "Brave New World." Uploaded 2 June 2015.

interrogating some students on behalf of her mother, offers shots of both the girls' present dwelling and the interrogation room, which resembles a medieval torture chamber (see Figures 11.6 and 11.7). In contrast, the third season returns to the single viewpoint, static camera principle, with the exception of its last four episodes (see Figure 11.8). The feature film is the only entry in the franchise to offer outside shots, yet even here, the show restricts the majority of the action to relatively small rooms and sets.[6]

Viewers can therefore only gather any image of the outside world by studying these interiors—which offer little to no valuable information—and by means of the characters' narration, either through the vlogs or

Figure 11.6 The library basement. *Carmilla.* Season 0, episode 1, "Blast from the Past." Uploaded 22 October 2015.

Figure 11.7 The "interrogation room" in the library basement. *Carmilla.* Season 0, episode 1, "Blast from the Past." Uploaded 22 October 2015.

Figure 11.8 The university library. *Carmilla*. Season 3, episode 1, "I Know What You Didn't Do Last Summer." Uploaded 15 September 2016.

through their social media activities, again underlining the show's basic storytelling principles. As the story unfolds, viewers learn that supernatural creatures and horrifying occurrences are accepted as ordinary by students and staff alike. Occasionally, the official Twitter account of Silas University updates students on current developments, such as the solution to the university's literal troll problem: "The nefarious trolls who were charging a fee to cross over the bridge to Western Campus have been…removed" (@SilasUniversity, 31 July 2015). Over the course of the narrative, fans learn that the university library is a sentient being, that a gigantic anglerfish god lurks beneath the campus, and that vampires and zombies are simply part of everyday life.

Even though these goings-on on campus result in fatal casualties on a daily basis, they are seldom framed in uncanny terms. While the particular occurrences at Silas University are considered strange by the Styrian natives, it is suggested that magical beings are common to this part of Europe. For instance, hiking through the surrounding forested mountains in an attempt to flee the campus after the first season's finale, Laura and her friends encounter a cannibalistic gingerbread witch, are chased by a Styrian mob equipped with torches and pitchforks, and encounter a series of other gothic stereotypes. Of these events, only the confrontation with the gingerbread witch is visually portrayed, namely in the form of a Christmas special episode, taking place in a small diner. The remainder of the group's adventures is told exclusively in the form of social media posts and tweets. Fans following the show can learn through these channels that the group was chased out of the village after the Christmas special: "Terrific. The return of the torches and pitchforks. It's really hard to kill the people chasing you if they insist on being heavily armed" (@HeyCarmilla, 18 May 2015). The phrase "torches and pitchforks" develops into one of the show's running gags, thus alluding to the tale's portrayal of the Styrians as poor and backward.

In *Carmilla*, the existence of the supernatural is never a question, but rather always a given. Goat sacrifices and similar rituals are not a thing of mere superstitions, but often lead to tangible results. Modernizing the tale's clash of rationality and superstitiousness, the web series fuses both already at the very beginning. In the prose fiction, for instance, Laura's governess Mademoiselle LaFontaine is introduced as "something of a mystic" (214)—while she claims to understand diverse supernatural matters, her knowledge does not appear to be of any use when it comes to Laura's illness. The web series, in contrast, re-imagines her as the non-binary biology student LaFontaine, who not only researches the scientific basis for the strange events on campus, but can furthermore build complex devices and weapons for the fight against evil. LaFontaine is the first of the group to deduce that Carmilla must be a vampire.

While largely dismissing the gothic atmosphere of "Carmilla," the web show develops this Eastern European setting in ways that are strikingly similar to how Le Fanu frames the region in his tale, namely as an exotic, far-away, and magical place. By humorously foregrounding the absurdity of this fictionalization, *Carmilla* detaches the region from the dismal implications it carries in Le Fanu's tale. Both texts portray Eastern Europe as a dangerous place where supernatural beings roam freely; however, the web series specifically emphasizes that lesbian desire and queer identities are *not* among the dangers of the region. Setting a positive example for queer representation, the show treats such identities as a given rather than a driving force behind the plot. Only once is this queer representation turned into a central topic, namely when LaFontaine announces that they identify as non-binary; being best friends since childhood, Lola Perry at first struggles with LaFontaine's preferred pronouns, but comes around after a few episodes. In this fictionalized Styria, both deadly horrors and queer identities are part of everyday life.

Conclusion

The web series *Carmilla* does not merely transpose Le Fanu's original story into a new medium; rather, it re-invents and expands on the tale of the lesbian vampire. While doing so, the online drama adapts the narrative strategies employed in "Carmilla" to the logic of the web series format. Significantly, Styria is portrayed in similar terms in both texts: an exotic, remote region where supernatural beings exist. The main difference between each fiction is how this fictional Styria is constructed and the function it fulfills.

Le Fanu's "Carmilla" is pervaded by a serious atmosphere of darkness and foreboding; Styria hides "some of the profoundest arcana" (207).

Eastern Europe, functioning predominantly as a contrasting image of the British Isles, is a dangerous place, where the vampires act as a symbol of "incest anxiety," "homosexual anxieties," "male fears about the new woman," "Eastern Europe's unresolved racial mixture," and "the British public's fear of reverse colonisation" (Gibson 2006, 7). Significantly, the text puts the supposed stability of both sexual and national identities to the test not only by introducing Carmilla Karnstein as the Dionysiac lesbian vampire born in Styria but also by casting Laura herself as a hybrid figure, a symbol of the fragile distinction of East and West, rationality and superstitiousness.

The web series, in contrast, self-consciously foregrounds this fictionalization through its "tell, don't show" storytelling techniques, according to which viewers are offered only little visualization of the Eastern European setting and are instead provided with verbal descriptions. Exaggerating the exoticization of this region performed in the tale, *Carmilla* creates a comical tone. While it detaches the fiction from its racial and national discourses, the show furthermore singles out the tale's representation of lesbian desire and re-imagines it in more positive terms. Instead of portraying homosexuality as a dangerous transgression, the online drama grants the relationship between Laura and Carmilla a happy end. What is more, the show adds a plethora of queer characters to the narrative. While Le Fanu's tale must end with the ritualistic killing of the vampire as the symbol of numerous dangerous transgressions, *Carmilla* instead welcomes her and others like her. Thus, not only does the web series expose the artificiality of "Carmilla's" portrayal of Styria, but it goes on to deconstruct this conception completely. While the original tale features Eastern Europe as a region onto which "homosexual anxieties" and "male fears about the new woman" can be projected, *Carmilla* deliberately dismantles these concerns through its reinterpretation of Styria: here, it is deadly monsters that kill—not queer characters.

Notes

1 As the tale and the web share the same name, the title of Le Fanu's fiction, published in the collection *In a Glass Darkly*, is placed in quotation marks in this paper, whereas the online drama is referred to in italics.

2 The name of the university is an allusion to Le Fanu's gothic novel *Uncle Silas* (1864), told as a first-person narrative from the perspective of an adolescent woman.

3 When referring to *Carmilla*, this paper uses the terms "web series," "web show," and "online drama" synonymously as terms describing an episodic, fictional narrative produced to be broadcast and consumed via the Internet. As such, *Carmilla* is part of a larger emerging medium, "web television," which includes video platforms as diverse as Netflix or YouTube. "Vlogs" comprise a particular mode within web television: they can be either authentic video diaries or fictional constructs, and are usually marked by their conversational, oftentimes intimate mode of addressing a public audience.

For more information on the topic, consult Burgess and Green (2009), Creeber (2011), and Atkinson (2014).

4 For a discussion of the gothic potential of the web series as a narrative medium, consult Crawford (2015).

5 To this day, these accounts are still accessible; however, most of them have not been updated since October 2016, when the show's final season ended.

6 Along with a Christmas special airing between seasons 1 and 2, the film is also the only entry to utilize any editing techniques; all other videos are created by means of long takes.

References

Atkinson, Sarah. 2014. *Beyond the Screen: Emerging Cinema and Engaging Audiences*. New York and London: Bloomsbury Academic.

Auerbach, Nina. 1995. *Our Vampires, Ourselves*. Chicago: University of Chicago Press.

Burgess, Jean, and Joshua Green. 2009. *YouTube: Online Video and Participatory Culture*. Cambridge: Polity Press.

Carmilla. Season 1, episode 1, "Disorientation." Written by Jordan Hall. Posted by KindaTV. YouTube video, 2:37. Uploaded 19 August 2014. www.youtube.com/watch?v=h4QzRfvkJZ4&index=1&list=PLbvYWjKFvS5rX2yv-k5AJ8oxPoZ9zHcpe.

Crawford, Joseph. 2015. "Gothic Fiction and the Evolution of Media Technology." In *Technologies of the Gothic in Literature and Culture: Technogothics*, edited by Justin D. Edwards, 35–47. New York: Routledge.

Creeber, Glen. 2011. "It's Not TV, It's Online Drama: The Return of the Intimate Screen." *International Journal of Cultural Studies* 14, no. 6: 591–606.

Gibson, Matthew. 2006. *Dracula and the Eastern Question: British and French Vampire Narratives of the Nineteenth-Century near East*. New York: Palgrave Macmillan.

Jandl, Silke. 2015. "*The Lizzie Bennet Diaries*: Adapting Jane Austen in the Internet Age." *AAA – Arbeiten aus Anglistik und Amerikanistik* 40, no. 1/2: 167–96.

Karnstein, Carmilla (@HeyCarmilla). 2015. "Terrific. The Return of the Torches and Pitchforks. It's Really Hard to Kill the People Chasing You if They Insist on Being Heavily Armed." *Twitter*, 18 May 2015, 11:01 am, https://twitter.com/heycarmilla/status/600360589941157889.

Korte, Barbara. 2010. "Facing the East of Europe in Its Western Isles: Charting Backgrounds, Questions and Perspectives." In *Facing the East in the West: Images of Eastern Europe in British Literature, Film and Culture*, edited by Barbara Korte, Eva Ulrike Pirker, and Sissy Helff, 1–21. Amsterdam, New York: Rodopi.

laura2theletter. Tumblr. "What Country Is Silas in?" 28 September 2014. http://laura2theletter.tumblr.com/post/98648680796/what-country-is-silas-in-because-the-best-known.

Le Fanu, Joseph Sheridan. [1872] 2008. "Carmilla." In *In a Glass Darkly*, by Joseph Sheridan Le Fanu, 207–72. London: Wordsworth Editions.

McAteer, Michael. 2010. "A Troubled Union: Representations of Eastern Europe in Nineteenth-Century Irish Protestant Literature." In *Facing the East in the West: Images of Eastern Europe in British Literature, Film and*

Culture, edited by Barbara Korte, Eva Ulrike Pirker, and Sissy Helff, 205–18. Amsterdam and New York: Rodopi.

McCormack, William John. 1980. *Sheridan Le Fanu and Victorian Ireland*. Oxford: Clarendon Press.

Sage, Victor. 2012. "Irish Gothic: C. R. Maturin and J. S. LeFanu." In *A New Companion to the Gothic*, edited by David Punter, 135–47. Oxford: Blackwell.

Silas University (@SilasUniversity). 2015. "The Nefarious Trolls Who Were Charging a Fee to Cross Over the Bridge to Western Campus Have Been… Removed." *Twitter*, 31 July 2015, 11:00 am, https://twitter.com/SilasUniversity/status/627176926818373633.

Treske, Andreas. 2008. "Detailing and Pointing." In *Video Vortex Reader: Responses to YouTube*, edited by Geert Lovink and Sabine Niederer, 215–21. Amsterdam: Institute of Network Cultures.

12 Civilization versus "the Barbarian Turk"

Imperial Gothic and Western Self-Definition in Dracula Narratives from Fin-de-Siècle to the Post-9/11 World

Tuğçe Bıçakçı Syed

Bram Stoker's celebrated gothic tale *Dracula* (1897) has been widely discussed by scholars with regard to its approach to the political stresses of its time. Stephen D. Arata's concept of "reverse colonization" (Arata 1990) has proved useful in exploring the colonial incentives that shaped the Count's lust for British blood, while Matthew Gibson's in-depth research on Stoker's own views regarding the Eastern Question has provided further insight into the political allegories embedded in the novel. Moreover, *Dracula* is commonly read as a quintessential example of Patrick Brantlinger's concept of "imperial Gothic," a particular form of Gothic which expressed "anxieties about the ease with which civilization can revert to barbarism or savagery and thus about the weakening of Britain's imperial hegemony" during the late nineteenth and early twentieth centuries (Brantlinger 1988, 229). Accordingly, critics and readers have often regarded Stoker's iconic vampire as an Eastern savage or a barbarian through which Britain, or more broadly Christian Europe, defines its own civilized status. In this way Jonathan Harker's travels "among the traditions of Turkish rule" is depicted as the journey to the unknown, to the land of backwardness, superstition, and barbaric practices (Stoker 2013, 7).

Dracula was hardly the first Western gothic text to associate Turkish rule or the Ottoman Empire in particular, with barbarism. From the late eighteenth century onward the Ottoman Turks were used widely in Western texts alongside gothic motifs—such as female captivity or imprisonment, sexual and/or domestic violence—and were often reduced to Oriental despots like Hassan in Lord Byron's poem *The Giaour* (1813), or rapists like The Dey in the erotic epistolary novel *The Lustful Turk* (1828). This is because the construction of European identity, as Iver B. Neumann (1999) suggests, was strongly linked to the threat of the Ottoman Turk, known as "the dominant other" of the European states since the fourteenth century. Neumann argues that the conquest of Constantinople in 1453 triggered the unity of Christendom under the name of Europe against the Ottoman Turk. Moreover, this unity, which Neumann regards as central to the foundation of the European Union, implemented a political and religious rhetoric against the Turk by drawing on pejorative terms such as "infidel," "nonbeliever," "savage," and "barbarian."

Stoker's *Dracula* does not return to the events of 1453 and keeps Dracula's ancestor Vlad Tepeş's historical connection with the Ottoman Empire at bay. However, a number of Western Dracula narratives specifically center around the conquest of Constantinople and the feud between the Ottoman Sultan Mehmed II and Vlad Tepeş as leading motives in Dracula's journey to vampirism. Particularly, post-9/11 interpretations of the novel revive the civilization versus barbarism dichotomy in the political atmosphere of the period. In this essay, I shall explore the role of the Ottoman Empire as the leading Other of Europe by returning to the origins of the civilization versus barbarism dichotomy. Drawing on Johan Höglund's reconsideration of imperial Gothic in the context of post-9/11 American culture, I shall then discuss how the Ottoman Turk continues to be depicted as the forceful barbaric threat, the gothic adversary, who even surpasses Dracula's vampirism, in the post-9/11 Dracula narratives. By defining the Ottoman Turk in gothic terms, the texts and films discussed in this essay repeatedly evoke the dichotomy between civilization versus barbarism as a crucial tool of Western self-definition.

Gothic, the Barbarian Turks and *Dracula*

Hegel ([1807] 1977) once remarked that to define itself, the self, first, needs an "Other" to define: "Each is for the other the middle term through which each mediates itself" (112). This system of self-definition unsurprisingly dates back to ancient civilizations, specifically to Ancient Greece, when all people who did not speak Greek were considered to speak a language that the Greeks named "barbar." In other words, the origin of the word "barbar" springs from a linguistic difference, symbolizing a definitive lack in others while it emphasizes the normality of the Greeks (Boletsi 2013, 3). Maria Boletsi (2013) remarks that all words derived from "barbar" place the barbarian "outside the borders of civilisation" and make them seem "incomprehensible, unfamiliar, uncanny, improper," particularly from the perspective of the civilized (4). Hence, Gothic and the notion of the barbarian are strongly interconnected. Gothic writing is the quintessential form to speak for the improper, unfamiliar, and uncanny other of civilization—the barbarian.

In his ground-breaking work, *The Literature of Terror*, David Punter ([1980] 2013) names "the fear of the intrusion of the barbaric" as one of the three key "aspects of the terrifying to which Gothic constantly, and hauntedly, returns" (183–84). The civilized being attacked, invaded, or violated by the barbarian Other is a common theme in a wide range of gothic horror narratives from nineteenth-century vampire fiction to the contemporary post-apocalyptic horror sub-genre. The notion of the barbaric, Punter ([1980] 2013) argues, can manifest itself as the fear of "the past, "racial degeneracy," and of "the barbaric not only from the past but also in the present and even the future" (183–84). Overlapping with the emergence of the Gothic, Britain's eighteenth-century colonial expansion promoted the fear of racial degeneracy that Punter emphasizes. Therefore, with the help of the gothic mode, "the barbaric or colonized other" became another "way of constructing a civilized and progressive sense of selfhood" for British people (Edwards 2014, 60).

By this time, the Ottoman Turks were already disliked by Christian Europe and were considered Oriental despots—a stereotypical perception which formed the basis of Orientalist discourse—and as infidels, rapists, or barbarians (Pocock 2005, 12). Despite the fact that the Ottoman Empire is not widely included in the Orientalist discourse of today, the Empire played a significant part in the early development of the concept since the Sultans officially represented Islam. As mentioned earlier, the fall of Constantinople in 1453 was the defining moment for the perception of the Ottoman Turks by Christendom. Following this pivotal development, during the siege itself, the leader of the Catholic Church, Pope Nicholas V, "denounced" Mehmed II the Conqueror as "the cruelest persecutor of the Church of Christ, the son of Satan, the son of perdition, the son of death who thirsted for the blood of Christians" (Schwoebel 1967, 31). In Germany, Martin Luther's treatise named *On War Against the Turk* (1528) portrayed the Turks as "the devil incarnate: inhumanly violent, treacherous, demonically lascivious" and "grotesque slaughterers of children, beasts who even ripped unborn babies from their mother's wombs" (Miller 2000, 84). By the end of the sixteenth century the Turks were characterized by Cardinal Bessarion—who was born in Trebizond, Turkey and served in Constantinople for years—as "inhuman barbarians," "no better than savages," "ignorant and barbarous," and "wild beasts" together with many other negative attributes which degraded them to everything that the Western civilization was supposedly not (Migne 1857–58, 665–67; Marsh 1664, 65–66).

Although this propaganda continued until the Ottoman Empire lost its military power in the late seventeenth century, it was revived once again during the late nineteenth century. This repetitive pattern is, for Boletsi, a necessary occurrence because the civilized needs the barbarian to stay civilized:

> the concept of barbarism refers to an other who is rejected by, and excluded from, civilization. But since civilization constitutes itself by rejecting the barbarian other, the exclusion can never be complete. As a constitutive element of civilization, the excluded is also included, thus destabilizing the hierarchical opposition it is meant

to reinforce. In turn, the opposition's inherent instability and the other's subliminal presence provoke repeated and anxious efforts to restabilize the antithesis, ever new attempts to redraw the line between self and other and to expel the barbarian for good.

(Boletsi 2015, 17)

Boletsi identifies the line between the civilization and the barbarian other as consistently redrawn because these oppositions need each other to exist. In the past, "the Greeks, the Romans, Christianity, Europe, and the West," all made "repeated" efforts to keep their others outside their boundaries. "The Persians, the Scythians, the Gauls and Germans, the heathen Sarazens, the Mongols and Tartars, the Native Americans," on the other hand, played their role as the barbarians throughout history (Moser and Boletsi 2015, 15). Therefore, one should not be surprised to see Western statesmen, historians, and scholars reapply this discourse to the Ottoman Turks during the period leading up to World War I.

In *Evil, Barbarism and Empire: Britain and Abroad, c. 1830–2000*, Tom Crook, Rebecca Gill, and Bertrand Taithe (2011) point to the nineteenth century as the period when countries like Russia, China, British India, and the Ottoman Empire "fell awkwardly between two poles of the civilised and the barbarian" in the eyes of Western civilization (20). During the same period, Cardinal John Henry Newman defined Christianity as "the religion of civilisation" and claimed that Islam "subserves the reign of barbarism" (quoted in Crook, Gill, and Taithe 2011, 127). The English historian Edward Augustus Freeman similarly described the nations of Eastern Europe who were ruled by the Ottoman Empire at the time as being under the "barbarian yoke" (Freeman 1877, 121). Hence, the Eastern Question, or in other words, the fate of the Near East nations once they are disengaged from the barbarian yoke acquired a significant role in British imperial politics of the time (Gibson 2006, 2).

Many British writers in the nineteenth century, such as Lord Byron, John William Polidori, Joseph Sheridan Le Fanu, and Stoker, used this region in their gothic writings by combining the politics of the day specifically with the vampire myth. Gibson (2006) accounts for this by suggesting, "in the majority of cases, the vampire narrative set in the Near East is a deliberate and coded practice, which makes use of either careful dating, or else literary and contemporary allusion, to embed certain political ideas" (8). The use of these political ideas relating to the Balkan territories of the Ottoman Empire in gothic narratives of the time shows how significant this region was for the Western world because it occupied the Eastern Christian border and was a part of both Orientalist and Imperialist discourses of the West (Hughes 2003, 34).

Patrick Brantlinger's understanding of imperial Gothic is therefore intimately linked to these discourses. The three key themes of imperial gothic narratives for Brantlinger (1988) were "individual regression or going native;

an invasion of civilization by the forces of barbarism or demonism; and the diminution of opportunities for adventure and heroism in the modern world" (230). Indeed, Gothic and fantasy novels written by Stevenson, Haggard, Kipling, Doyle, and Stoker during the late-Victorian period accommodate at least one of these themes. They usually take place in imperial settings and the civilized characters are exposed to the barbaric practices of the natives or the barbaric Other travels to the heart of civilization by threatening the characters' civilized values.

In *Dracula*, the Count's journey to London as an Eastern barbarian is read as an attempt "to invert English imperialism, to colonize London, and to unleash an ontological and epistemological apocalypse by turning it into a kingdom of the undead" (Höglund 2018, 331). However, another motivation behind the Count's invasion of England can be seen to relate to the historical conflict between Vlad Tepeş and the Ottoman Sultan Mehmed II. Later in the novel, when the Count talks about his ancestor Voivode Dracul with pride, he tells Harker how shameful it was for his nation "when the flags of the Wallach and the Magyar went down beneath the Crescent" (Stoker 2013, 26). He also adds that the Voivode defeated the Turk to save Wallachia after his own brother "sold his people to the Turk and brought the shame of slavery on them" (26). In his speech, the Count evokes the age-long conflict between the Cross and the Crescent, representing Christianity and Islam respectively, and characterizes the Ottoman Turk as a tyrant enemy and a colonizer of his race. Therefore, Dracula's anger is directed both toward the British and the Ottoman Empires.

For Eleni Coundouriotis the Count also represents the centuries-long Ottoman history of the Balkan region for the Western readers. Coundouriotis (2000) argues that Dracula is a symbol for the oppressed European under the Ottoman rule and needs to be extinguished in order for the Ottoman rule to end definitely:

> Stoker's reinvention of the historical figure is driven by his desire to disclaim the Europe that the Count represents. The Count [...] symbolizes medieval, Christian Europe re-emerging into modernity, monstrously out of date. To hold this reality at bay, Eastern Europe can be left to linger behind the "iron curtain" of the Ottoman Empire. As this became politically untenable because of the spectacular violence against Christians, Eastern Europe had to be refigured without the traces of its Ottomanization. Brought under the cultural influence of Western Europe, these nations would have to be newly assimilated. Dracula, who fought against the Turks and then survived Ottoman rule, represents both Christianity and the history of Ottoman Europe. His hybridity — an Ottomanized European — results in a dissonant figure fitting uncomfortably, a blasphemous Christian hero.
> (Coundouriotis 2000, 153)

Although Coundouriotis's characterization of Dracula as a hybrid of both European and Ottoman heritage can be considered controversial, her overall argument relates to the political developments of the late nineteenth century in the Balkans as well as Britain's foreign policy at the time. After the brutal suppression of the Bulgarians by the Ottoman army in 1876, known as the April Uprising, the public outcry in Europe and the United States caused the Ottoman Empire to lose the very little support that it had from Christian Europe (Coundouriotis 2000, 149). The Eastern Question, in Britain, thus, gained more attention and significance as a sort of propaganda to be used against the Ottoman presence in Christian Europe. This is also why Brantlinger (1988) acknowledges *Dracula* as one of the epitomes of imperial gothic tradition of the period. As a vampire and an Ottomanized European, the Count represents the Balkan region as the zone where the West and the East, Christianity and Islam, civilization and barbarism, once again, come face to face. Therefore, for Coundouriotis, by destroying the vampire in *Dracula*, the British characters destroy the barbarian yoke of the Ottoman Empire.

The Return of the Barbarian after 9/11

As highlighted by Neumann (1999), Western representations of the Turks changed dramatically for the better after the foundation of the Republic of Turkey and "made the Turk less central as a constitutive other" to Europe (60). Nevertheless, the discourse of civilization versus barbarism was revived once again after the Cold War period under a different name. "Islamophobia" was first defined as "dread or hatred of Islam" and "unfounded hostility towards Islam" by the Commission on British Muslims and Islamophobia (1997), formed by the Runnymede Trust (1–4). The aim of this commission, according to Todd H. Green (2015), was "to analyze the discrimination experienced by many Muslims in Britain and to make policy recommendations to the government that would help combat this discrimination" (10–11). Indeed, as a result of the Israeli-Palestinian conflict and the Iranian Revolution of 1979, negative perceptions of Muslims and Islam increased in the West (Green 2015, 11). Furthermore, the fatwa issued by the Islamic leader of Iran against Salman Rushdie following the publication of *The Satanic Verses* (1988) created more controversy among Muslims and "gave rise to a backlash against Muslims in Britain" (11).

All these developments contributed to the atmosphere of cultural racism toward Muslims in the Western world; however, the attacks on the Twin Towers of the World Trade Center on 11 September 2001 became a culminating point for anti-Islam rhetoric in the United States. On the day of the attacks, in his "Address to the Nation," the US President George W. Bush (2001a) said "America was targeted for attack because we're the brightest beacon for freedom and opportunity in the world."

Four days later, on 15 September, he referred to Al-Qaeda, the Islamist extremist terrorist organization who performed the attacks, as "a group of barbarians" who did "barbaric acts" (2001b). In another meeting on 20 September, Prime Minister of the United Kingdom, Tony Blair (2001) showed his support for America's War on Terror by saying: "This is a struggle that concerns us all, the whole of the democratic and civilized and free world." In the same meeting, Bush (2001c) separated all Muslims from America's enemies: "The enemy of America is not our many Muslim friends. It is not our many Arab friends. Our enemy is a radical network of terrorists and every government that supports them." Nevertheless, both Bush and Blair evoked the civilization versus barbarism rhetoric, since Bush's words defined America as the symbol of civilization which sets an example for the uncivilized and undemocratic parts of the non-free world, and declared Islamist extremism and those who support them to be the barbarians of the twenty-first century.

The return of the discourse of barbarism after 9/11 had tremendous impact on the gothic mode's representation of cultural trauma, war, and the "Other" through gothic monsters, such as vampires, zombies, werewolves, demons, shapeshifters, and many more. Linnie Blake (2012) considers the Gothic of this period as reflecting "the national zeitgeist" of America through these monsters that signified "the dark forces against which the [American] nation must struggle" (39). These dark forces were, in other words, the new barbarians of American society in the post-9/11 world, mostly conveyed through invasion narratives, which called forth the re-emergence of the previously discussed nineteenth-century sensation, imperial Gothic.

Adapting Brantlinger's idea of imperial Gothic in *The American Imperial Gothic: Popular Culture, Empire, Violence*, Johan Höglund (2014) investigates American gothic narratives which "accompanied and mapped the development of the American imperial state" from the late eighteenth century to the present with a specific focus on the post-9/11 era (167). He argues that the imperial Gothic of this period reinforces the use of civilization versus barbarism discourse in the disguise of an existentialist good versus evil conflict that America—as the empire of archetypal modernity, democracy, and freedom—holds against its barbaric enemies with the help of the gothic mode:

> The Imperial Gothic in both its extroverted and its introverted forms is a mode of writing capable of supporting the building of empire and the fortification of imperial borders with the help of gothic metaphor. It imagines global conflict as a Manichean struggle between good and evil and in its American guise, it typically suggests that the gothic Other must be contained through perpetual military violence.
>
> (Höglund 2014, 90)

For Höglund (2014), American imperial Gothic repeats the tropes and motifs of British imperial Gothic, as Brantlinger has described them: it "depicts the Other that inhabits the frontier space as not only a primitive barbarian but also a gothic and monstrous creature" (85).

British imperial gothic narratives frequently demarcate the primitive Eastern threat as the Other. Hence, as discussed earlier, the Ottoman Empire left a mark on the most influential vampire narrative of the nineteenth century. American imperial Gothic, on the other hand, has a more contemporary yet complex relationship with the image of the Turk as the Other. After the fall of the Ottoman Empire, the Republic of Turkey has developed strong relationships with the West and, indeed, became military allies with the United States after World War II. Moreover, although it has a predominantly Muslim population, Turkey took a foreign-policy stand against Islamic extremism and has worked side by side with the West in line with this purpose. Therefore, it is not surprising to find that Turkey is absent in the analyses of American imperial gothic narratives that Höglund offers in his study while Afghanistan and Iraq take the stage frequently. However, *Dracula*'s reincarnations in the post-9/11 American literature and film fill this gap.

The American author Elizabeth Kostova's international bestseller *The Historian* (2005) draws inspiration from *Dracula* and centers around the medieval conflict between Vlad III and the Ottoman Sultan Mehmed II particularly. The novel provides a long story of three generations of historians who, upon receiving an empty book with a dragon print in the middle, set out on a quest to find the owner of the book, Vlad III, not only in the archives of several libraries in Turkey, Bulgaria, and Hungary but also in real life. Spreading over a time period from the 1930s to the early 2000s, the novel is narrated by several characters in a manner that revives the epistolary form of Stoker's gothic tale. Nevertheless, Kostova's novel is not another adaptation of Stoker's text, but rather uses it as inspiration to tell a completely different story about family history, academic research, and Dracula. Mentioned as "Turk-killer," "Turk-slayer," and "one who kills Turks" several times in the novel, Dracula is, of course, the real source of evil in the story; however, the Ottoman Sultan Mehmed II is shown to be as evil as Vlad III in the eyes of the most Western characters. Deriving from the momentous conquest of Constantinople in 1453 and its aftermath, this perception of good versus evil is reutilized in the novel to introduce the West versus the East conflict in post-9/11 America.

Kostova's novel opens with a foreword written by the young woman that the sixteen-year-old, unnamed narrator of the main story will grow up to be. Having found, at the age of sixteen, a letter addressed to herself in her father's library, this young girl narrates the story of a History Professor Bartolomeo Rossi, (her grandfather), his master's degree student Paul (her father), his daughter Helen Rossi (her mother) and their search for the tomb of Dracula. In "A Note to the Reader," she explains her story as "a search for history" that continues generation after generation (Kostova 2006, vii). She admits that as a historian she not only used the diaries, letters, archives, and documents that she already has relating to his family's search but she also carried out her own research on the near history and adds: "The glimpses of religious and territorial conflict between an Islamic East and a Judeo-Christian West will be painfully familiar to a modern reader" (Kostova 2006, viii). This early revelation sets the main focus of this novel that is hidden behind the Dracula myth. From this very first moment, the novel aims to follow the conflict between the West and the East or the Cross and the Crescent, and trace its beginnings which, for Kostova, is the conquest of Constantinople that all her characters keep coming back to rediscover.

The main story starts when postgraduate student Paul shows the book he has received to his supervisor Professor Rossi. Having revealed that he was given a copy of the same book years ago, the Professor mysteriously disappears that night and Paul, together with Rossi's daughter Helen, an anthropology student, sets out on a journey to find him. At their first stop, in Istanbul, Paul gazes at the city. While reading that "*Istanbul* is a Byzantine word that meant *the city*" from his guidebook, he remarks: "You see, even the Ottomans couldn't demolish Constantinople [...] [the] Byzantine Empire lasted from 333 to 1453. Imagine — what a long, long afternoon of power" (Kostova 2006, 203). Paul's words seem to reopen old wounds for Helen whose country, Romania, stayed under Ottoman rule for centuries. She comments:

> The conquest of Constantinople in 1453 by Mehmed II was one of the greatest tragedies in history. He broke down these walls with his cannonballs and then he sent his armies in to pillage and murder for three days. The soldiers raped young girls and boys on the altars of the churches, even in Saint Sophia. They stole the icons and all the other holy treasures to melt down the gold, and they threw the relics of the saints in the streets for the dogs to chew.
>
> (Kostova 2006, 203–4)

Unlike Paul, who is an American and supposedly does not have much knowledge or ancestral experience of the Ottoman Empire, Helen knows what it means to have a national history influenced immensely by the Ottoman hegemony. The Ottoman "sediment" that she believes her nation still carries is not only the reminder of their sorrowful past but also of the fallen Eastern Roman Empire that once threatened Christendom. The way she narrates the events after the conquest shows what an evil tyrant she believes Sultan Mehmed II to have been.

In other respects, the Turkish Professor Turgut Bora, whom Paul and Helen meet unexpectedly in a café in Istanbul, mentions a story which asserts that it was the Byzantines who were evil: "there is a story that the most bloodthirsty of the emperors of Byzantium were vampires, that some of them understood the Christian communion as an invitation to quaff the blood of mortals" (Kostova 2006, 214). While the Western characters Paul and Helen believe in the atrocities of the Ottoman Sultan and cherish the history of the Byzantine Empire, Turgut Bora reminds them of the stories that Turkish people were told about the evil acts of the Christian Byzantines. To put it differently, the two opposite perspectives are referenced here, yet both at heart concern themselves with the same West versus East debate. Later when Helen reminds Turgut that the Sultan "enslaved more than fifty thousand" Byzantines after the conquest, he accepts the conquest "was not so delightfully done" but defends the Ottoman tolerance for other religions and races and affirms "our Sultans were not monsters" (Kostova 2006, 295–96). This dialogue reconstitutes the image of the Ottoman Sultan as a slave master, an evil despot in Helen's eyes and as a tolerant but successful leader in Turgut's eyes. In a way, both sides define the other as evil to assure themselves that they are "the good one."

The novel revisits the image of the Sultan as an evil despot when Paul wanders inside the Topkapı Palace. He explains his feelings in the corridors of the Ottoman Empire in the following way:

> everywhere I sensed something sinister or perilous, which could simply have been the overwhelming evidence of the sultan's supreme power, a power not so much concealed as revealed by the narrow corridors, twisting passages, barred windows, cloistered gardens. At last, seeking a little relief from the mingled sensuality and imprisonment, the elegance and the oppression, I wandered back outside to the sunlit trees of the outer court. Out there, however, I met the most alarming ghosts of all, for my guidebook located there the executioner's block and explained in generous detail the sultan's custom of beheading officials and anyone else with whom he disagreed. Their heads were displayed on the spikes of the sultan's gates, a stern example to the populace. The sultan and the renegade from Wallachia were a pleasant match, I thought, turning away in disgust.
>
> (Kostova 2006, 311–12)

Paul's words gothicize the Topkapı Palace, the home of the Ottoman Empire for almost four hundred years. It is likened to a mediaeval castle with its "narrow corridors, twisting passages, barred windows, cloistered gardens" and Paul feels himself standing in the dungeon of that gothic castle as if he is the prisoner. Surrounded by the ghosts of the people beheaded and spiked, Paul believes that the Sultan was as evil as his enemy Vlad III. He even seems to understand why Vlad III, who spent his childhood in that very palace as a sort of prisoner, turned out to be as evil as he was.

Moreover, this is not the first or last comparison between Vlad and the Sultan Mehmed II. Later in the novel, upon hearing a story about Ottoman cruelty by Helen's aunt Eva in Budapest, Paul makes a remark which, again, compares the Sultan's cruelty to Vlad's; however, this time, he seems more certain who is the superior evil:

> The Ottomans again, I thought—how clever they were, and cruel, such a strange mixture of aesthetic refinement and barbaric tactics....Vlad Dracula's fight against them, like that of many of his Christian compatriots, had been the struggle of a David against a Goliath, with far less success than David achieved.
>
> (Kostova 2006, 333)

Paul's "perverse admiration for Dracula," as he puts it, derives from his perception of the Sultan as the giant oppressor and of Dracula as the ultimate underdog. According to Edward A. Gosselin (1980), however, in the late medieval period, this celebrated fight between Goliath, a giant Philistine warrior, and David, an Israeli shepherd, was interpreted by Christian scholars as the fight between Christ and Satan (57). Paul's words, therefore, define the Sultan as a superior evil to Dracula and reconstitute their fight as between Christianity and Islam rather than Christ and Satan. This is also why, while traveling from Istanbul to Budapest, Paul observes the region as a place where the good encountered the evil for centuries:

> There is something vastly mysterious for me about the shift one sees, along that route, from the Islamic world to the Christian, from the Ottoman to the Austro-Hungarian, from the Muslim to the Catholic and Protestant....I would also see it alternately as benign and bathed in blood — this is the other trick of historical sight, to be unrelentingly torn between good and evil, peace and war.
>
> (Kostova 2006, 316)

Clearly, by representing Sultan Mehmed II as an evil despot, his palace as a gothic castle, his conquest as barbaric, and his religion as Satanic, Kostova echoes previous examples of the civilization versus barbarism dichotomy used against the Ottoman Empire. However, interestingly, until the end of the novel America is kept separate from all these, from "the West" to which Paul keeps referring. Alan S. Ambrisco (2015) considers this situation as promoting "America's myth of itself as a pacifist nation and safe haven" while registering Europe as a "terror-ridden" region (29). He argues that Kostova's novel "presents Dracula as a terrorist and tyrant" who reappears "in history's most violent moments" (28).

Although Dracula's evil deeds are surely emphasized throughout the novel, the Ottoman Sultan Mehmed II is considered guiltier than Dracula in perpetuating evil in the world. If Dracula is a terrorist as

Ambrisco suggests, then Kostova's novel demonstrates him to be the apprentice of Sultan Mehmed II. Earlier in the novel, for example, while the sixteen-year-old unnamed narrator reads about Vlad III in a library, she learns that he learned his torture technique, "impaling," from the Ottomans, as he was brought up in the Ottoman palace (Kostova 2006, 40). Höglund (2012) maintains that *The Historian* does not depict the vampire figure as the embodiment of the East as Stoker's *Dracula* does and therefore is less an example of imperial gothic. However, I argue that Dracula in *The Historian* does not merely represent the West or the East. He is indeed an embodiment of the centuries-old West versus East, good versus bad, civilization versus barbarism debate which turn up at the door of the United States in the post-9/11 world as shown in the Epilogue of the novel.

The end of the novel presents the unnamed narrator, now an elderly history professor, looking over "the federal building that had been bombed" (Kostova 2006, 700). This end, as Ambrisco (2015) argues, transforms America from a safe haven, "from a peace-loving and peace-keeping" country to a place doomed to be haunted by the "ghostly violence from Europe's past" (30). This is, indeed, the same violence that developed out of the West versus the East conflict which has been around since Ancient Greece. Kostova gothicizes this conflict in the novel. By imagining Dracula as the defender of Christian Europe and the Ottoman Sultan Mehmed II as the evil Eastern despot, Kostova returns to the beginning of terrorism that supposedly spread the evil in the first place. Once again, the conquest of Constantinople in 1453, which "is the worst date in history" for Dracula himself, serves as the starting point of the civilization versus barbarism rhetoric (Kostova 2006, 632). Therefore, as "a modern Gothic travel narrative," Kostova's *The Historian*, I argue, is far more an example of American imperial Gothic than Höglund (2012) initially claimed. The fall of the safe and peaceful American empire; the adventures of the main characters in Turkey, Bulgaria, and Hungary; the constant fear of Dracula's existence; and the possibility of his invasion through terrorism all demonstrate the features of imperial gothic narratives that Brantlinger described. *The Historian* does not refer to the present-day Islamic threat as much as the other American imperial gothic narratives discussed in Höglund's study, but demonizes its origin in the West, the Ottoman Empire.

Similarly, inspired by Stoker's *Dracula*, Gary Shore's film *Dracula Untold* (2014) similarly demonizes the Ottoman Empire. It is as if all evil in the world, including vampirism, has a reason to justify itself except for the evil despot from the East who can best be embodied in the Ottoman Sultan and his conquest of Constantinople. As a post-9/11 American narrative, *Dracula Untold* is fully inspired by the conflict between the Prince of Transylvania Vlad III and the Ottoman Sultan Mehmed II and embeds the myth of becoming a vampire as a necessary price to pay in order to defeat the evil Turk. In the opening story of *Dracula Untold*, Vlad's son tells the audience how the paths of two sides of the conflict crossed way before 1453:

> In the year of our Lord, 1442 the Turkish sultan enslaved one thousand Transylvanian boys to fill the ranks of his army. These child slaves were beaten without mercy, trained to kill without conscience, to crave the blood of all who defied the Turks. From among these boys, one grew into a warrior so fierce that entire armies would retreat in terror at the mention of his name. The Impaling Voivode. Son of the Dragon. Sickened by his monstrous acts, Vlad came to bury his past with the dead and returned to Transylvania to rule in peace. His subjects called him Prince. I called him Father. But the world would come to know him as Dracula.
>
> (*Dracula Untold*)

In predicting the troublesome years to come under the hegemony of the Ottoman Sultan, the opening serves as an explanation for the primary reason of Vlad's anger toward the Turks. As a former slave who killed relentlessly for the Turk, the novel represents Vlad as a homesick repentant and a peaceful Prince whose only wish was to protect his subjects who "live in enough fear of the Turks' return" (*Dracula Untold*). He later emphasizes his wish for peace when Hamza Bey, a soldier of the Sultan, unexpectedly arrives at the Easter celebration in Vlad's court. Hamza Bey asks for a thousand boys to be taken for the Sultan's army including Vlad's one and only son. In order to convince Sultan Mehmed II, with whom he grew up as brothers in the Ottoman court, to spare his son, Vlad goes to the Ottoman camp nearby.

In this scene, the movie depicts the military power, the wealth, and the magnificence of the Ottoman Empire of the time in detail to show the audience that Dracula cannot compete with the Sultan. The camera first shows the vast land that the Ottoman camp occupies and its all too numerous military tents. Seeing the camp, Dumitru, Vlad's comrade in arms, comments: "Soon the entire world will be Turk" (*Dracula Untold*)—a comment that emphasizes the extent of Ottoman expansion. Inside the Sultan Mehmed II's tent, almost everywhere is plated with gold, from the table on which the war territory is engraved to the Turkish coffee cups. When the Sultan Mehmed II asks for Vlad's son also to be taken to the court alongside the one thousand boys, the film highlights Vlad's helplessness before the Sultan in his beseeching tone: "Mehmet, my brother, I will grant you anything else…Please don't do this to me" (*Dracula Untold*) In this scene, the Sultan signs his request as an agreement between him and Vlad. Elest Ali characterizes this scene as Islamophobic because he argues that by showing the Sultan's "bloody thumb-print" right next to an Arabic stamp saying Allah, the film aims to depict the Sultan's villainy to be the order of Allah (Ali 2014). However, I would argue that this scene and the film as a whole establish more than just the vilification of Islam. In order to protect his people and save his own son from the fate he endured for years, Vlad has no other choice but to seek a supernatural solution to defeat his enemy. Following the recent trend of softening and humanizing the undead in gothic horror, the film justifies Vlad's violent comeback as a vampire, while demonizing the Ottoman Sultan. In doing so, the audience feels more sympathy toward the undead and considers him as a hero compared to the Sultan who is depicted as the source of evil.

According to Christian Moser and Maria Boletsi (2015), the rhetorical antithesis between civilization and barbarism "unleashes a dynamics of increasing violence against the barbarians" (17). The civilization versus barbarism dichotomy allows the civilized to take violent action in order to protect itself from the barbarian threat. For Höglund (2014) as well, the violence against the barbarian is a necessary outcome in imperial gothic narratives because "the gothic Other can only be exorcised through violence" (64). The War on Terror that the United States commenced and many NATO countries, particularly Britain, supported is another example of this sort of violence. *Dracula Untold* makes use of this rhetoric by making Prince Vlad and his army turn into a vampire for protection from the barbarian that is the Ottoman Turk. They crush the Ottoman army using their vampire bites and demonstrating supernatural strength. In the climax of the film, Vlad, now as Dracula, faces the Sultan who tries to use Dracula's weakness for silver against him. Yet, Dracula vows to "strike" the Sultan's name "from the history books" (*Dracula Untold*). After a fight sequence, Dracula puts a stake through the Sultan's chest and kills him with his vampire bite. Years later, his son remembers Dracula in this way:

> The Turks never conquered the capital of Europe. Prince Vlad Dracula was a hero but there are no pictures, no statues of him. I am his legacy. His sacrifice taught me that even after the darkest night, the sun will rise again.
>
> (*Dracula Untold*)

Hence, Dracula's vampirism becomes a heroic sacrifice, a necessary price to pay for the future of his country just as the War on Terror was considered necessary for America's safety. However, the last scene where Dracula unexpectedly encounters Mina's reincarnation who talks in an American accent in between skyscrapers evokes the end of *The Historian* where American safety is compromised. This open end of the film leaves an unanswered question: has Dracula come to America to fight against the threat of evil known as Islamic terrorism in the post-9/11 world or, once again, to repent and leave the evil past behind?

Conclusion

Having provided a theoretical ground which elucidates the relationship between the word "barbarian," Gothic, and Turkish identity, this essay has examined the image of the Ottoman Turk as the barbarian Other in Dracula narratives. I have argued that, considered within the civilization versus barbarism dichotomy, Stoker's *Dracula* represents the Ottoman Turk that Christian Europe needs to shake off through the Count's Eastern characterization because by pushing the barbarian out of its borders, Europe can redefine itself as safe, civilized, and fully *Christian*. Drawing on Johan Höglund's analyses of American imperial gothic narratives of the post-9/11 era, I have argued that Elizabeth Kostova's novel *The Historian* and Gary Shore's film *Dracula Untold* similarly utilize the civilization versus barbarism dichotomy. In fact, these narratives legitimize the deeds of the vampire and demonize the Ottoman past of Turkey and the Sultan Mehmed II by persistently going back to the conquest of Constantinople, the most destructive moment in history for the West. In the post-9/11 world, the good is—as always—versus the evil; the East is still the antithesis of the West; civilization is once more threatened by barbarism; and the Ottoman Turk is again "the Other." This gothic otherness attached to the identity of the Ottoman Turk is what has interlinked Gothic and Turkish identity for centuries. By reading the identity of the Ottoman Turk in gothic terms as despots, barbarians, and evil, Western Gothic not only contributes to the Western process of self-definition but perhaps also lays the foundations of Turkish Gothic.

References

Ali, Elest. 2014. "What the Historical Inaccuracies in *Dracula Untold* Tell Us About the Rise of Islamophobia." *The New Statesman*. https://www.newstatesman.com/culture/2014/10/what-historical-inaccuracies-dracula-untold-tell-us-about-rise-islamophobia. Accessed on 8 January 2019.

Ambrisco, Alan S. 2015. "Suicide, Spectral Politics and the Ghosts of History in Elizabeth Kostova's *The Historian*." *Horror Studies* 6, no.1: 19–37.

Arata, Stephen D. 1990. "The Occidental Tourist: 'Dracula' and the Anxiety of Reverse Colonization." *Victorian Studies* 33, no. 4: 621–45.

Blair, Tony. 2001. "Remarks with Prime Minister Tony Blair of the United Kingdom and an Exchange with Reporters September 20, 2001." In *Public Papers of the Presidents of the United States: George W. Bush (2001, Book II)*. Washington, DC: United States Government Printing Office. https://www.govinfo.gov/content/pkg/PPP-2001-book2/pdf/PPP-2001-book2-doc-pg1138-2.pdf. Accessed on 8 January 2019.

Blake, Linnie. 2012. "Vampires, Mad Scientists and the Unquiet Dead: Gothic Ubiquity in Post-9/11 US Television." In *The Gothic in Contemporary Literature and Popular Culture: Pop Goth*, edited by Justin D. Edwards and Agnieszka Soltysik Monnet, 37–56. New York: Routledge.

Boletsi, Maria. 2015. "Waiting for the Barbarians after 9/11: Functions of a Topos in Liminal Times." In *Barbarism Revisited: New Perspectives on an Old Concept*, edited by Christian Moser and Maria Boletsi, 355–76. Leiden: Brill.

Boletsi, Maria. 2013. *Barbarism and Its Discontents*. Stanford: Stanford University Press.

Brantlinger, Patrick. 1988. *The Rule of Darkness: British Literature and Imperialism, 1830–1914*. New York: Cornell University Press.

Bush, George W. 2001a. "Address to the Nation on the Terrorist Attacks September 11, 2001." In *Public Papers of the Presidents of the United States: George W. Bush (2001, Book II)*. Washington, DC: United States Government Printing Office. https://www.govinfo.gov/content/pkg/PPP-2001-book2/pdf/PPP-2001-book2-doc-pg1099.pdf. Accessed on 8 January 2019.

Bush, George W. 2001b. "Remarks in a Meeting with the National Security Team and an Exchange with Reporters at Camp David, Maryland September 15, 2001." In *Public Papers of the Presidents of the United States: George W. Bush (2001, Book II)*. Washington, DC: United States Government Printing Office. https://www.govinfo.gov/content/pkg/PPP-2001-book2/pdf/PPP-2001-book2-doc-pg1111.pdf. Accessed on 9 January 2018.

Bush, George W. 2001c. "Address Before a Joint Session of the Congress on the United States Response to the Terrorist Attacks of September 11 September 20, 2001." In *Public Papers of the Presidents of the United States: George W. Bush (2001, Book II)*. Washington, DC: United States Government Printing Office. https://www.govinfo.gov/content/pkg/PPP-2001-book2/pdf/PPP-2001-book2-doc-pg1140.pdf. Accessed on 8 January 2019.

Commission on British Muslims and Islamophobia. 1997. *Islamophobia: A Challenge for Us All*. London: Runnymede Trust.

Coundouriotis, Eleni. 2000. "*Dracula* and the Idea of Europe." *Connotations* 9, no. 2: 143–59.

Crook, Tom, Rebecca Gill, and Bertrand Taithe. 2011. *Evil, Barbarism and Empire: Britain and Abroad, c. 1830–2000*. London: Palgrave.

Dracula Untold. 2014. Directed by Gary Shore. Universal City, CA: Universal and Legendary Pictures. 2015. DVD.

Edwards, Justin D. 2014. "British Gothic Nationhood, 1760–1830." In *The Gothic World*, edited by Glennis Byron and Dale Townshend, 51–61. Oxford: Routledge.

Freeman, E. A. 1877. *The Ottoman Power in Europe: Its Nature, Its Growth and Its Decline*. London: Macmillan.

Gibson, Matthew. 2006. *Dracula and the Eastern Question: British and French Vampire Narratives of the Nineteenth Century near East*. Basingstoke: Palgrave Macmillan.

Gosselin, Edward A. 1980. "Two Views of the Evangelical David: Lefevre d'Etaples and Theodore Beza." In *The David Myth in Western Literature*, edited by Raymond-Jean Frontain and Jan Wojcik, 56–69. Indiana: Purdue University Press.

Green, Todd H. 2015. *The Fear of Islam: An Introduction to Islamophobia in the West*. Minneapolis: Augsburg Fortress.

Hegel, Georg Wilhelm Friedrich. (1807) 1977. *Phenomenology of Spirit*. Translated by A. V. Miller. Oxford: Oxford University Press.

Höglund, Johan. 2018. "Imperial Horror and Terrorism." In *The Palgrave Handbook to Horror Literature*, edited by Kevin Costerphine and Laura R. Kremmel, 327–38. Switzerland: Palgrave Macmillan.

Höglund, Johan. 2014. *The American Imperial Gothic: Popular Culture, Empire, Violence*. Surrey: Ashgate.

Höglund, Johan. 2012. "Catastrophic Transculturation and Gothic Modernity in *Dracula* and *The Historian*." *Transnational Literature* 5, no. 1. https://dspace.flinders.edu.au/xmlui/bitstream/handle/2328/26432/Catastrophic_Transculturation.pdf;jsessionid=9E138C21D59FF98A4F51F0DA9D244115?sequence=1. Accessed on 8 January 2019.

Hughes, William. 2003. "'To build together a new nation': Colonising Europe in Bram Stoker's *The Lady of the Shroud*." *Gothic Studies* 5, no. 2: 33–46.

Kostova, Elizabeth. 2006. *The Historian*. London: Sphere.

Marsh, Henry. 1664. *A New Survey of the Turkish Empire*. London: Henry Marsh.

Migne, Paul Jacques. 1857–1858. *Patrologia Greaca*. Vol. 161, 665–67.

Miller, Gregory J. 2000. "Luther on the Turks and Islam." *Lutheran Quarterly* 14: 79–97.

Moser, Christian, and Maria Boletsi. 2015. *Barbarism Revisited: New Perspectives on an Old Concept*. Leiden: Brill.

Neumann, Iver B. 1999. *Uses of the Other: "The East" in European Identity Formation*. Minneapolis: University of Minnesota Press, 1999.

Pocock, J. G. A. 2005. *Barbarism and Religion: Barbarians, Savages and Empires*. Vol. 4. Cambridge: Cambridge University Press.

Punter, David. [1980] 2013. *The Literature of Terror: A History of Gothic Fictions from 1765 to the Present Day, Volume 2: Modern Gothic*. Oxon: Routledge. Reprint.

Schwoebel, Robert. 1967. *The Shadow of the Crescent: The Renaissance Image of the Turk 1453–1517*. Nieuwkoop: B. de Graaf.

Stoker, Bram. 2013. *Dracula, and Other Horror Classics*. New York: Barnes & Noble.

13 Acephalous Times
The Severed Head in Contemporary Fiction and Film

Roger Luckhurst

One of the most startling moments in Joseph Conrad's *Heart of Darkness* (1899) is when Marlow, in a classic instance of the technique of "delayed decoding," reveals, after a long and tortuous digression, what he first sees when he views Kurtz's compound from the Congo River through his field glasses:

> I made a brusque movement, and one of the remaining posts of that vanished fence leaped up in the field of my glass...These round knobs were not ornamental but symbolic; they were expressive and puzzling, striking and disturbing—food for thought and also for the vultures if there had been any looking down from the sky... They would have been even more impressive, those heads on the stakes, if their faces had not been turned to the house. Only one, the first I had made out, was facing my way. I was not so shocked as you may think.
>
> (Conrad 1983, 86)

Conrad's orchestrated delay, holding off this first encounter for several thousand words and then revealing the severed heads only in a subordinate clause, comes after Marlow's long eulogy of praise for Kurtz. "All Europe contributed to the making of Kurtz" (Conrad 1983, 86), says Marlow. The severed head is meant to serve, in colonial discourse, as the utmost sign of savagery. The trophy head is a sentinel on the edge of European civilization, marking the descent into the violent, primitive world beyond. Yet in Conrad's tale, Europe's representative inverts the binaries of light and dark, civility and savagery, Europe and Africa. The heads face both ways, leaving us with an unsettling ambiguity.

European modernity is sometimes said to have been inaugurated by the elegant machine designed by the French revolutionary deputy, Joseph-Ignace Guillotin, and first put into use in 1792. The guillotine was meant to end the spectacle of torturous tyranny—the horrific public display of prolonged and violent execution of enemies of the Crown, bodies hanged, drawn and quartered, heads boiled and placed on spikes to be displayed for weeks, months, or even years. Instead, the guillotine was a democratic device of the new republican law: fast, efficient, rational, and humane. It promised the rapid descent of an unfailing blade, heads disappearing into the waiting basket. There was to be no more class hierarchy of execution: the axe, the firing squad, the rope. From the king to the highwayman, all would be inserted into the same unerring machine ensemble. The guillotine expressed the European ideals of the new democratic republic in practice.

Although the guillotine remained in use in France until 1977 (the last such execution was of the Tunisian Hamida Djandoubi for murder), these executions were progressively moved out of public display and became highly restricted acts of the state's management of bodies inside closed institutions. This happened through the course of the nineteenth century, and the classic account of this movement from public spectacle to institutional biopolitics remains that of Michel Foucault (1975) in *Surveiller et punir* (*Discipline and Punish*). By Conrad's time, the spectacle of the severed head was meant to have been returned to the non-modern, non-European ethos of the Other. What has most haunted European civilization in the twenty-first century is the YouTube terrorism of the beheading of Western hostages: a calculated gesture of "savagery," designed to offend European or "Western" values.

Conrad's provocative inversion—"All Europe contributed to the making of Kurtz"—stands as a sentinel on the brink of the twentieth century, in part facing back to the racial hierarchies of the imperial past. Yet the severed head has remained an intrusive presence in popular culture of both Europe and America, and even intensified in the contemporary moment. In what follows, I want to trace the range of these representations, and to propose a series of capsule explanations for the possible meanings for the persistence of the cultural sign of the severed head. After this set of explorations, I will circle back to the question of Europe, ending with a reading of Arnaud Desplechin's film *The Sentinel* (1992). The film is a self-conscious reflection on the condition of Europe after the end of the Cold War that turns on the discovery of a severed head in the luggage of a trainee surgeon at a Customs check on the border of France and Germany. Since we are spared no details in his excavation of this severed head for clues, I want to do the same: to ask why Europe remains so haunted by this decapitated figure.

Cultural representations of heads rolling, of elegant decollation, messy decapitation, or vicious head wounds remain ubiquitous. Horror fiction and film have always punished the eyes for the very act of watching these transgressions, from E. T. A. Hoffmann's "The Sandman" (1816) or the razor through the eye in Luis Buñuel's *L'Âge d'or* (1930) to Lucio Fulci's obsession with putting out eyes in his Italian *giallo* films such as *The Beyond* (1981). Horror has also been gleefully lopping off heads from Washington Irving's "The Legend of Sleepy Hollow" (1820), a story rooted in ancient legends of vengeful headless horsemen. The first wave of the gothic romance bled into the French *genre noir,* which reached a peak of horrific realism, full of guillotined heads, in the 1820s.

The primitive sensations in these early "terror novels" so often condemned by arbiters of taste have been far from superseded. They have, if anything, been amplified in the late twentieth century. The zombie, that ubiquitous monster, is put down not with a stake through the heart but by a bullet or a vicious blow to the head. The director George Romero established this rule in one of the inaugural films of the genre, *Night of the Living Dead* (1968). By the third film of his series, *Day of the Dead* (1985), the mad doctor among the survivors' toys with a severed head for much of the movie's running time, seeking the mysterious neurological spark that keeps the zombie *un*-dead, suspended in this odd shuffling limbo between life and death. The camera surveys his charnel-house of body parts with unflinching gaze.

George Romero's first three zombie films contained such uncompromising images of opened torsos and heads that they were unrated by the classification board of the Motion Picture Association of America, effectively declaring them to be outside the boundaries of acceptable taste. Yet thirty years later, the same special effects team around Greg Nicotero that worked on *Day of the Dead* provide a weekly gamut of gruesome images for *The Walking Dead* (AMC, 2010–), one of the most successful syndicated cable TV shows ever made. *The Walking Dead* is a veritable smorgasbord of heads bashed, smashed, and severed in both glorious CGI and analogue detail. A central character, Mischonne, specializes in samurai-sword decapitation of zombies, while a key figure among the human survivors in the early series, the patriarch Hershel Greene, is formally beheaded in an exercise of frontier justice by the fascistic Governor. Hershel's severed head, of course, is still subject to zombification, remaining sentient because it has merely been decollated, severed at the neck. Even the beloved Hershel needs an extra knife through the skull to destroy the brain to finish him off decisively. We discover, in one of the more hallucinatory sequences of this early series, that the Governor, who wears an eye-patch over his lost eye, communes with severed heads that he keeps in an aquarium in his private office as an expression of his absolute power over his private fiefdom.

These exorbitant wounds, this violence toward the head, are everywhere in mainstream visual culture. Ari Aster's *Hereditary* (2018) involved a spectacularly staged decapitation of a child in its opening act. Luca Guadagnino's remake of *Suspiria* (2018) ends drenched in blood showering from the exploding heads of the witches' coven as the new Mother decapitates her opposition. In the TV series *The Strain* (2014–17), it is a shock to discover that the vampires—if that is what these creatures invading the New York subways are—can be dispatched by simply smashing their heads to bits by jumping up and down on them, as our sophisticated, cutting-edge, scientific hero Dr. Ephraim Goodweather

210   *Roger Luckhurst*

from the Center for Disease Control does with much finesse in an early episode. In the survival horror video-game world, the *Resident Evil* zombie shoot-'em-up franchise established the delighted gamer riposte "Boom, Headshot!" in common parlance.

This trope has leapt the species barrier and moved beyond horror. In the crime series, *Breaking Bad* (2008–13), a Mexican informant is sent back by the drug cartel to officers of the Drug Enforcement Agency as a severed head mounted on a tortoise. At least since Martin Scorsese's *Goodfellas* (1990), a mafioso's charming psychosis is illustrated by stamping a rival's head to destruction, as Joe Pesci's character Tommy DeVito does, instantly annoyed that he has ruined a pair of perfectly good shoes. This strange lurch between comedy and desensitized horror appears again in Quentin Tarantino's accidental gunshot to the head in *Pulp Fiction* (1994). "Ah man, I just shot Marvin in the face," John Travolta sighs, drenched in blood. It is also a scene of sudden violence echoed in several sequences in *The Sopranos* (1999–2007), for instance in the murder and decapitation of Ralph Cifaretto. The audience glimpses a severed head in Patrick Bateman's fridge in *American Psycho* (2000), both book and film emblematic of a blank, post-ironic attitude to this extreme, misogynistic violence.

Meanwhile, in fantasy, *Game of Thrones* (2011–19) suggests the absolute power of feudal tyranny is best represented through decapitation, the symbol of the lord's sovereign right over the life and death of subjects and rivals. *Game of Thrones* made its mark by declaring early on the absolute right of the show-runners to take the head off one of its leading stars, the first season concluding with the beheading of Ned Stark (played by Sean Bean). Stark's head, placed on a pike and raised above the gates of the city, as is the traditional fate of the traitor, continues to brutalize his captured daughters, setting up a long narrative chain of revenge across several seasons. As this story unfolds, heads roll in the hundreds—possibly the thousands.

The severed head features in science fiction, too. There is a long cultural tradition in Western culture of tales of uncanny "brazen heads" constructed by men of arcane, possibly devilish knowledge. These talking oracular heads, somewhere between biology and mechanism, life and death, utter unpalatable truths and prophecies when animated (see Kang 2011). Directly updated from tales of dangerous knowledge involving Albertus Magnus or Roger Bacon, we have instead the robot Ash in *Alien* (1979), the crew member who sabotages every chance of survival and who only speaks the truth of the doom of the crew of the spaceship Nostromo once his head has been knocked off and briefly sparked back to life. In Michael Crichton's film *Westworld* (1973) the technicians might open up the head of Yul Brynner's Gunslinger to fix his malfunctioning circuits, but he will still become an implacable murdering machine, the embodiment of the death drive. David Cronenberg's

Scanners (1981) featured another notorious threshold of graphic horror when a rogue telepath explodes a rival's head by thought alone. In the same year, John Carpenter's remake of *The Thing* featured a head glooping to the floor from an autopsy table and sprouting spider legs to scuttle away. "You've gotta be fucking kidding" says one character, in a meta-textual comment on the special effect itself (see Neale 1990).

In Dennis Potter's last TV drama, *Cold Lazarus* (1996), the cryogenically preserved head of the writer Daniel Feeld is reanimated three hundred years after his death as a team of scientists try to commodify his flickering memories. The TV series *Fringe* (2008–13) focused obsessively on violent intrusions to the head, whether by surgery, drugs, or neurological re-wiring, as much as by blunt-force trauma. *Fringe* worked to return the metaphor of psychic trauma back to its original meaning of the *physical* wound, the lesion. All the central protagonists are bound together by a traumatized, partial amnesia as a result of pharmacological and surgical experiments on the neurology of their brains conducted by a shadowy agency in the 1970s. Each has their head messed with, and the series jumped from one rogue surgeon to another, all hidden away in basement laboratories cluttered with brains floating in formaldehyde. The characters offered the spectrum of what the philosopher Catherine Malabou has called *les nouveaux blessés*, the new wounded (Malabou 2012).

Down a notch from the explicit body horror of these images, there was a cluster of head wounds and severed heads that featured in fine art in the early 1990s. Was this one starting point for the wider cultural circulation of such images? The generation of Young British Artists (YBAs) was launched by Damien Hirst at the 1988 exhibition in London called *Freeze*. The show was named after the freeze-frame photograph called *Bullet Hole* by the artist Matt Collishaw, which featured an intense close-up of a violent head wound. The image (of a wound inflicted by an ice-pick, in fact) had been appropriated from a pathology manual, but placed in the neutralizing grid of conceptual art. That this image named the show "Freeze" suggested it was emblematic of the new generation's confrontational mode, its jarring mix of registers: horror in fine art. When the YBAs appeared in the "Sensation" exhibition at the Royal Academy of Art in 1997, the show included Marc Quinn's *Self*, the bust of Quinn's own head, but sculpted out of several pints of his own frozen blood. This is a project Quinn has updated every five years since, a series of heads bobbing in refrigerated vitrines, tracking mortality rather as Rembrandt did in his self-portraits.

These images recall several of the paintings of severed heads by the French artist Théodore Géricault, completed in 1819, and intended as a political protest about the repressive use of the guillotine by the Restoration government (Athanassoglou-Kallymer 1992). But the seriousness of the engagement of the YBAs with art history has long been thrown into doubt by the photograph of Damien Hirst called *With Dead Head*. This was an image snapped illicitly in a morgue at Leeds University when Hirst was still a teenager, grinning alongside a surgically removed head. It is an image that continues to cause outrage for its puerility and insensitivity, and was denounced again as exploitative by a group of academics at Leicester University when displayed in a gallery in Walsall in 2013 (Jones 2013). These days, Hirst surpasses the flesh and prefers the bling of diamond-encrusted skulls. *For the Love of God*, a skull decorated with over eight thousand diamonds, sold for $100m in 2007.

In contrast to these gleeful displays, at the same time there were two heads in boxes that audiences significantly never got to see. One was in *Barton Fink* (1991), the film by the Coen brothers that continually puns around keeping your head or losing it, and ends with the protagonist carrying a box that may or may not contain the head of the woman who died in his hotel room. Perhaps it is another mark of our shifting sensibilities that the TV series of *Fargo* (2014–), which elaborates on the universe of the Coen brothers' films in various ways, recalls the head in the box in its third series and allows the viewer a glimpse inside of the head it most definitely holds.

The other celebrated cinematic moment was in the culminating scene of David Fincher's serial killer film *Se7en* (1995). *Se7en* involved groundbreaking graphic detail for mainstream Hollywood, and the director had to fight hard to keep the head in the box in the script. Notoriously, Fincher was initially sent the wrong draft of the script, in which Gwyneth Paltrow's severed head had been written out and replaced by a redemptive rescue, more in keeping with Hollywood convention. Fincher asked to revert to the earlier ending, but the producer told him, "There's no way that there will be a head in the box at the end of this movie, there is absolutely no way that will ever happen" (Salisbury 2014, 27). Even if it did make it into the final cut, *Se7en* refused to reveal the contents of the box to the viewer, relying instead on the imagination to complete the arc of the crime.

To decapitate is to bring the high low, dethrone reason and prioritize guts and gore. But if the representation of the severed head wrecks taste and beauty (as the painter Jean-Auguste-Dominique Ingres complained of Géricault's *Guillotined Heads*), this transgressive act fascinates the avant-garde. Georges Bataille set up the secret society and journal *L'Acéphale* (1936–39)—The Headless—marked by the drawn image of a man without a head in mockery of Leonardo da Vinci's perfectly proportioned Vitruvian Man. Bataille celebrated pulling the sacred down to the profane, the reasoning head undone by bodily desires, and in ritualistic prose *L'Acéphale* praised the decapitation of Louis XVI, the new republic born from his sacrificial blood. Acephaly means not just losing your head, but losing your head of state (Bataille 2018). Samuel Beckett's work after the war was populated by detached heads babbling streams of words to ward off the emptiness (in *The Unnamable, Happy Days,*

Play, and further reduced to an isolated mouth that appears in the darkness somewhere above the stage in *Not I*. In *That Time* the floating head of the Listener says nothing, however). The trope continues across the European continent in experimental fiction: the allegory of totalitarian power focused on the display of severed heads in Ismail Kadare's *The Traitor's Niche* (first published in Albania in 1978, but only translated into English in 2017) or in Antonio Tabucchi's *The Missing Head of Damasceno Monteiro* (1997), a metaphysical detective fiction without solution based on the true story of a man murdered, decapitated, and dumped by the Portuguese police under the fascist regime.

This accumulation of examples is intended to move across different media, cultures, and high and low forms. It is enough of a sample to pose the question: where are all these heads coming from? "Beheadings appear in the midst of schisms and discord," Julia Kristeva (2012) observes in her study, *The Severed Head* (104). "Where there is a head, there is a crisis," Regina Janes (2005) adds in her account of the cultural meanings of beheading (95). For Janes it is perhaps the inaugural human act of symbolization stretching back far into prehistory, since severing a head turns it into a sign (significantly, these prehistoric heads bob back up at the end of Sarah Moss's novella about an archaeological dig, *Ghost Wall* [2018]). So what is the contemporary crisis? What is being signaled in the current profusion of severed heads, and our apparent willingness to contemplate them?

The following sections offer several explanations, each time adjusting the historical framework further back to ground our contemporary obsession in wider and wider frameworks.

Pakistan, 1 February 2002

The most immediate explanation for the contemporary contemplation of the severed head has to evoke terrorism and the propaganda spectacle of the beheading of captives. In the twenty-first century, the execution video, recorded and uploaded to the internet, became the defining new terrorist act of the times. In Pakistan, on the 1st of February 2002, from the crucible of the emergent "War on Terror," a recording of the *Wall Street Journal* journalist Daniel Pearl reading a statement denouncing America was released by his captors. As the tape ran on, his throat was cut and his head was severed with a knife. This was an avowedly anti-Western and anti-Semitic act (Pearl was explicitly targeted as a Jew). The pitiless staging inaugurated a new threshold in obscene visibility of terrorism. Video execution was simple and quick to stage, and the internet disseminated the recording across the globe in an instant.

The tactic was then used by fundamentalist groups after the invasion of Iraq in 2003 against American contractors, and then in the Sunni-Shi'ite civil war that followed. There were 64 video beheadings of captives in

Iraq in 2004, and their dissemination was usually associated with the al-Qaeda group led by Abu Musab al-Zarqawi, although internal debates among the ideologues of terrorist groups in Iraq debated the efficacy of the tactic. Martyrdom through suicide bombing was considered more acceptable, and this is commonly an act of *self*-beheading, since the force of a suicide bomb typically decollates the head and leaves it intact, while the rest of the body is destroyed. In Sinan Antoon's remarkable novel, *The Corpse Washer* (2013), one scene of the ritual washing of a body before Islamic burial features only the surviving head. The analyst Martin Harrow observes that the terrorist tactic of video-recorded decapitations peaked in 2004, but then tailed off, since it consolidated support among extremists but rarely persuaded others of the legitimacy of the cause (Harrow 2011). Al-Zarqawi was executed by drone strike in 2006.

Nevertheless, the triple execution in 2014 of the journalists James Foley and Steven Sotloff and aid worker David Haines in Syria shows that the act of video beheading retains its potency. The executioner of Western abductees in the Syrian cases, Mohammed Emwazi, who grew up in Britain, was nicknamed "Jihadi John" by the British tabloid press. He was himself killed by drone strike in November 2015, a tactic of targeting for extrajudicial killing that is technically termed "decapitation." This parallelism tends to reinforce the symbiotic relation of terrorist and state violence. Drone strikes are surrounded by the language of the "surgical" strike and "clinical" precision, but they are also intended as symbolic acts of terror in their ubiquitous, extra-territorial reach (see Cronin 2009; Combs 2017).

Media-literate groups like al-Qaeda and Islamic State have used 24-hour news cycles and horizontal internet networks to get the global media system to circulate images and amplify terror by using highly mediated symbols. Beheading is the emblematic mark of the barbarians at the gate who target and accuse so-called "civilization." The act of beheading *defines* the barbaric, and this form of terrorism defiantly embraces the accusation. The Italian philosopher Adriana Cavarero has proposed that the contemporary situation has so upped the stakes in terms of cruelty, visibility, and the reduction of the other to "bare life" stamped out, that this stage of terrorism deserves a new name: horrorism. Horrorism is a further extension of the repugnance we feel at violence directed toward the defenseless: it is "a particular form of violence that exceeds death itself" (Cavarero 2009, 32). In Cavarero's book, the political philosophy is continually interrupted by descriptive reportage of particular acts of violence so that the suicide bomb and ritualized beheading are a continual point of reference for her, testing the limits of thought. The French philosopher Bernard-Henri Levy (2004) regarded the beheading and mutilation of Daniel Pearl as a starting point for a philosophical investigation of the challenges to the premise of European, Jewish, and "Western" identity represented by the execution.

Don DeLillo's novel *Mao II* (1990) argued for a new epoch of mediatized modes of terrorism, a new level of spectacle amplified by global networks. But the act of beheading, as the threshold between barbarism and civilization, has always operated as a cultural marker, at least since ancient Greece. Greek writers (such as Diodorus Siculus) abused the Celts as senseless savages from beyond the *polis,* who cut off the heads of their enemies, preserved and displayed these trophies as a mark of their savagery. At least the Greeks and the Romans, if they admitted that they also cut heads off (which they did), did so *for a reason* and within a strict hierarchy of meaning. This was the punishment of the law, not the arbitrary cruelty of heathens. The spectacle of terrorist beheading therefore runs on ancient ritualistic lines, but repurposed.

Contemporary cultural expressions of horrorism in fiction and film can be read by placing this limit act of terrorism inside the wider context of the intensification of biopolitical control of populations in global networks. This political control of *bios,* of life itself, is a return of an absolutist control over the right to determine who lives and dies, and so often is also a *thanatopolitics* (Agamben 1998) or a necropolitics (Mbembe 2003). At the borders of the First World, along the US-Mexico border or in the waters of the Mediterranean on the edges of Europe, there is now the operation of *gore capitalism,* a commodification of death that is "the price the Third World pays for adhering to the increasingly demanding logic of capitalism." "Contemporary history is no longer based on the experience of survivors," Mexican theorist Sayak Valencia (2018) argues, "but rather on the vast numbers of the dead" (19 and 28).

Boston, 5 August 1968

The second explanation pushes the frame back to 1968. As I have already suggested, George Romero transformed the ancient cemetery ghoul into the modern zombie in *Night of the Living Dead* in 1968. This epochal film happened to coincide with a significant redefinition of the medical conception of death. In 1968, the parameters of death were changed by a small group of doctors headed by Henry Beecher that came together in a group called the Ad Hoc Committee of the Harvard Medical School. This group's reflections were prompted by medical advances that had invented new beings, inside a new technological assemblage: the Intensive Care Unit (ICU). The ICU had improved survival rates for the critically ill but created a novel problem. The success of new artificial respirators meant that the cardio-pulmonary system could be sustained separately from brain function. There were now patients with a complete absence of cortical activity—who were "brain dead"—but who continued to live on within the biotechnical apparatus of the ICU. These paradoxical "beating heart cadavers" or "neomorts," as they were first called, were new beings that also happened to emerge just as transplant surgery was making significant new strides (the first heart transplant was attempted in 1967, for instance). The brain dead became a potential source for the exploration of transplant surgery, but whilst death continued to be legally defined as the cessation of the heart, such a surgical intervention constituted medical malpractice at best and wrongful death at worst (Lock 2002; Teresi 2012).

As a solution to this crisis, the Ad Hoc Committee set out to relocate death from the heart to the brain, and established the criteria for determining what they called "irreversible coma" in a paper published in the *Journal of the American Medical Association* on 5 August 1968. The new construct of death marked it as a complete absence of responsiveness in both autonomic systems and the higher neo-cortex. If the patient met the criteria for unresponsiveness, brain death could be declared, the respirators turned off, and biological death be allowed to follow ("A Definition" 1968). Or not, as sometimes happened in those rare, uncanny cases of liminal beings who lived on in twilight states without the support of the ICU assemblage.

The creation of this interval between brain death and full biological death shifted death from a decisive moment to an ongoing process. No wonder that after 1968 you have to shoot Romero's ghouls in the head. As the TV announcer in *Night of the Living Dead* explains in the film:

> The Survival Center at the Pentagon has disclosed that a ghoul can be killed by a shot in the head or a heavy blow to the skull. Officials are quoted as explaining that since the brain of a ghoul has been activated by radiation, *kill the brain and you kill the ghoul.*

The rules for killing the modern zombie, strangely enough, might have been written by the Ad Hoc Medical Committee.

The liminal territory of the space between life and death has been further charted since 1968, in part to try to resolve continuing anomalies with the category of brain death (see Truog 2018). Doctors coined the term Persistent Vegetative State in 1972 and debated when this slips into Permanent Vegetative State. A presidential commission called "Defining Death" in 1981 tried to develop a federal standard, but a further flurry of diagnostic and definitional work was undertaken in the 1990s. A task force specializing in neurology produced an entirely new category in 1997, the "minimally conscious state," broadly defined as a severely altered consciousness in which the person demonstrates a minimal but definitely behavioral evidence of self or environmental awareness. This encompassed not just severe physical trauma, but many forms of late-stage dementia. The medical anthropologist Margaret Lock has termed these new medical definitions a process of "making up the good-as-dead," and polemically contends that it could be read as the cultural work of demarcating ever more categories of *social* rather than *biological* death. "In late modernity," Lock (2001) argues, "the numbers of people recognized as candidates for social death have increased exponentially" (189).

This medical context spills beyond not just zombies and body horror, but into a whole array of cultural representations of brain neurology, from coma to dementia to memory and identity loss and the disorders of memory associated that exist in the contested vanishing point between neurological and psychical trauma (see Luckhurst 2015). The mysteries of brain damage and brain neurology now become the basis for best-selling accounts, such as Henry Marsh's *Do No Harm: Stories of Life, Death and Brain Surgery* (2014), or Clark Elliott's *Ghost in My Brain* (2015), a memoir about stroke recovery and the neuroplasticity of the brain. The Wellcome Collection's 2012 exhibition, *Brains: The Mind as Matter*, had a whole section, "Cutting/Treating," that explored through surgical records, etchings and photographs, trephination and brain surgery (see Kwint and Wingate 2012). In popular culture, the head wound or losing your head expresses this relocation of selfhood from heart to brain.

Vienna, 1922

In cultural reflections on decapitation, neurology has not been much of a focus until the recent turn toward medicine in the humanities. This is because interpretation of the severed head has been dominated for a century by the paradigm inherited from psychoanalysis. After Freud, only a naïve fool would treat decapitation as a *literal* signifier. Using the decoding of symbols most fully developed in his *Interpretation of Dreams*, the triple law of displacement, condensation, and considerations of representability, Freud asserts that decapitation really signals the fear of castration. In his short note "Medusa's Head," written in 1922, but only published posthumously in 1940, Freud wrote:

> To decapitate = to castrate. The terror of Medusa is thus a terror of castration that is linked to the sight of something.... It occurs when a boy, who has hitherto been unwilling to believe the threat of castration, catches sight of the female genitals.
>
> (Freud 1955, 273)

In compensation for the traumatic *absence* of the penis, the writhing hair of serpents multiplies the reassuring *presence* of the male organ, and the horror at the sight of the Medusa "makes the spectator stiff with terror, turns him to stone," the horror becoming oddly reassuring for the male gaze (Freud 1955, 273). Medusa castrates castration by transferring castration to the woman. In this reading of symbolic displacement, the high is switched with the low, the cerebral with the instinctual, the sacred with the profane, and the male with the female.

Janes (2005) suggests that "Freud's hermeneutic swept all before it" for over a century, to not always useful effect (126). Hélène Cixous (1976) mocked this castration anxiety over forty years ago (just after her expulsion from the Lacanian psychoanalytic school): "You only have to look at the Medusa straight on to see her. And she's not deadly. She's beautiful and she's laughing" (885). Nevertheless, this reading survives, at least in cultural interpretation. Julia Kristeva's *The Severed Head: Capital Visions* sits inside this paradigm, in which the solemn myths of Medusa, Salome, and Judith underpin Western gender models, and perhaps even signification itself, in the logic of the murder of the thing resurrected in the sign. "Cut off the monster's head," Kristeva reads through an array of classical cultural symptoms: "that is the only way to protect yourself from death and from the female genitals that could swallow you." Woman here acts "as supreme castrator, beheader, devourer" (Kristeva 2012, 33). Although one could never imagine Julia Kristeva at a midnight monster movie, she makes sure to disdain the trivialization of decapitation in modern mass culture. "We are far from the sacred taboos of the distant past," Kristeva (2012) says: "How interesting it is to cut, how obvious, how amusing…let us wed historical or contemporary subjects with this way of seeing the established horror, increasingly conformist, affected, theatrical, museumized" (84).

Freud wrote from within a fin-de-siècle European culture that certainly managed a crisis of gender through the language of classical and biblical myth. It has been estimated that nearly three thousand versions of the story of Salomé, Herodias and John the Baptist were produced in various art forms between 1860 and 1910. Salomé appeared in the early poetry of Stephane Mallarmé ("Herodiade," started in 1864). Oscar Wilde's banned play *Salomé* (1891) was published with illustrations by Aubrey Beardsley, and the play was turned into an opera by Richard Strauss (1905). The painter Gustave Moreau was repeatedly drawn to the figure of Salomé, as was Gustav Klimt, Lovis Corinth, and Pierre Bonnard. Ella Ferris Pell's painting *Salomé* (1890) takes the castrating figure out of the male gaze and "makes a revolutionary statement simply by being nothing but the portrait of a young, strong, and radiantly self-possessed woman who looks upon the world around her with confidence" (Dijkstra 1986, 392). Filtering the sexual anarchy of the European fin de siècle, Freud harped on the vengeance of the daughters, idols of perversity that slashed at patriarchy with such menace. But is this paradigm still relevant for our contemporary glut of severed heads? Can sexual anarchy in the late Victorian be transposed to contemporary gender trouble?

It is worth tarrying with the Freudian formula where it is evidently folded into the resonances of texts. In Fincher's *Se7en,* the female head in a box signifies only displaced transactions between men inside the brutal and misogynistic semiotics of John Doe's exorbitant crimes. In contrast, the Coen brothers seem more slyly in control in *Barton Fink*. Audrey's head in the box (if that is what it is) is avowedly sacrificed to male narcissism, and Fink's impotence and writer's block are freed as soon as she is sacrificed. Someone even says, "there's been a balls up at head office," neatly literalizing Freud's logic of substitution. This is the Coens' satirical decapitation of the life of the mind in overtly gendered terms, in a plot coiled around the Biblical motifs less of Salomé and John the Baptist than a displaced and inverted Judith and Holofernes. Freud's castration complex seems integral to the study of masculinity in *Barton Fink*, yet incorporates it with such a knowing self-referentiality that it becomes part of the icy formalism of the film.

Regina Janes (2005) objects that after a hundred years of applying the formula *to decapitate* = *to castrate*, "in this magician's trick, once the interpretation is easy it is no longer interesting" (xiii). More substantively, she also points out that the dominance of this psychoanalytic account eclipses the longer history of the embedded symbolic meanings of cutting off a head. Let's turn away from the symbolic, then, to turn back to reconsider the more embedded historical significance of the severed head.

London, 30 January 1661

For centuries, the symbolic function of decapitation has been to assert absolute political power. The most persistent role of the severed head across many cultures, from prehistory to the present, is to play the *trophy* head, the mark of military or political triumph, or the *presentation* head, a gift offered in deference to sovereign power (see Larson 2014). Heads roll in war, in occupation, in transitions of political sovereignty. The parliamentary rebellion in the English Civil War was secured by the beheading of Charles the First in 1649. In a purposive echo, after the Restoration of the monarchy, Cromwell's corpse was dug up on the twelfth anniversary of the King's execution, on 30 January 1661, dragged through the streets, the corpse hanged at Tyburn and then decapitated, with the head impaled on a spike on the roof of Westminster Hall (a traditional spot for traitors), where it stayed for forty years until blown down in a storm. Executed heads were typically parboiled to preserve their power to signify longer (those mounted on London Bridge at the entrance to the city were managed by a dedicated civil servant, the Keeper of Heads), but this uncanny preservation gave the heads unexpected potency. Cromwell's head became a curio in the eighteenth century, even as public tortures and executions were toned down. The Lord Protector's head was only finally laid to rest in the ante-chapel of Sidney Sussex College in Cambridge in 1960, three hundred years after it had been transformed into a symbol of revolutionary disorder (Larson 2014, xiii–xviii). Even so, Cromwell's dishonored corpse, this time complete with head, is still said to haunt Red Lion Square in London, one of the sites where the disinterred body was put on display (Clark 2007, 56–58).

The Hobbesian theory of the commonwealth as a "leviathan," an artificial body organized under the command of a sovereign head, dominated seventeenth-century political philosophy. Hobbes published *Leviathan* in 1651, two years after the beheading of the King, an event that much disturbed the political philosopher for its assault on authority, and which had been described to him in graphic detail by an eyewitness. It is unsurprising that a key image of the disordered polity at the time, as David Cressy has explored, was of the "Headless Monster." At the time of Civil War the acephalic body was a monstrous portent that signaled chaos on the cosmic level. In 1642, one pamphlet recorded that Mary Wilmore of Northamptonshire "was delivered of a childe without a head." In 1646, a "Strange and Wonderfull Monster" was born in Lancashire to a "Popish gentleman," "the face of it upon the breast, and without a head" (Cressy 2004, 40–42). As Cressy (2004) observes, "If the head signifies reason, guiding the members and governing the state," then "a headless monster could point to a commonwealth that had lost its way and lost its mind" (63).

Paris, 25 April 1792

The truly modern European model of the democratic state, however, is still premised on the taking off of the head of France's absolutist monarch. After the revolutionary overthrow of Louis XVI in 1789, the new penal code of the new Republic did not abolish capital punishment, but democratized it, making the punishment the same for all social classes. Machines for decapitation had been used in different parts of Europe before (the *Mannaia* in Italy, the "Halifax gibbet" in England), while the guillotine was first used in Paris on 25 April 1792. Its first victim was Nicolas Pelletier, a highwayman, but it became synonymous not with criminal justice but the spirit of the Revolution.

The device was first proposed by the physician and revolutionary deputy Joseph-Ignace Guillotin, but designed and tested on corpses by another radical, Dr. Antoine Louis. It was intended to de-dramatize the scene of execution through its speed and efficiency. In the instant decollation by the falling blade and the disappearance of the severed head into a basket, the device did away with the spectacle of the dying man. The first crowds expressed loud complaint at the lack of spectacle, but the guillotine was meant to *end* disordered emotions and terror, not invoke them.

Following the execution of the king, however, and the intensification of threats to the leaders of the Revolution, the guillotine became the political machine for The Terror of 1793–94, where tens of thousands of the perceived political enemies of the Committee of Public Safety were sent for execution for "moral" as well as "material" deviations from revolutionary commitment. They were dispatched at vast speed by the new device (Gough 1998, 55). The guillotine stood precisely "at the junction of body and body politic. From the field of medicine its blade passes through the political to attain the metaphysical" (Arasse 1989, 34). The device became what the materialist medic and reluctant deputy Pierre Cabanis termed "the ensign of tyranny," rather than of liberty (Arasse 1989, 33).

A controversy emerged over whether the guillotine was in fact *too* instantaneous, allowing the consciousness of severed heads to survive seconds or even minutes after the blade had fallen. In this interval, "What could be more horrible than the perception of one's own execution, followed by the afterthought of one's having been executed?" asked the surgeon and anti-guillotine campaigner, Jean-Joseph Sue (cited in Arasse 1989, 38). This debate fed directly into the horrors of the *genre noir* of the 1820s: Jules Janin's notorious *The Dead Donkey and the Guillotined Woman* (1829) starts with the flaying of a piteous donkey and ends with the beheading of the anti-heroine, her corpse stolen from the unconsecrated grave, and taken, in final ignomimy, for medical school dissection (this extra final chapter was added by Balzac). European conservative political philosophy has pointed to the horrors of the guillotine as the symbol of the dangers of revolutionary thought ever since.

Haunted Europe, 1992

Around the bicentenary of the French Revolution in 1989, there were numerous philosophical reflections on the implicit and explicit violence of the exclusions inherent in eighteenth-century claims to represent "we, the people" in the new revolutionary democracies (Lyotard 1988; Balibar 2004). Another text that reflected on this, and that circled around reflections on the head, was Jacques Derrida's *L'Autre Cap* (translated as *The Other Heading*). This was an address first delivered to a colloquium on European cultural identity in May 1990, just as the Soviet bloc was collapsing, German unification was only months away, and just before the Maastricht treaty transformed the European Community into a Union in November 1993. Derrida puns around the "cap"—*la capitale* (the city) and *le capital* (money), *le cap* (the headland)—to explore where Europe is heading, and so on (see Weber 2014). Derrida (1992) refers to beheading when he speaks of "a relation of identity with the other that no longer obeys the form, the sign, or the logic of the heading, nor even of the *anti-heading*—of beheading, decapitation" (15). Derrida, as always, aims to deconstruct a binary articulation of European power, of self and other, of heading or beheading, exploring instead ways to let the other occupy this head-space. "All the propositions and injunctions are divided, the heading splits, the capital is de-identified...[Europe] has begun to open itself onto the shore of the other heading" (Derrida 1992, 75–76).

Two years later, in April 1993, Derrida (1994) delivered his lectures on the ghosts haunting Europe in *Spectres of Marx,* amplifying the gothic resonances of this displacement of the binary of capitation and decapitation into a full-scale "hauntology." The gothic mode became only more relevant for the European condition, as the meaning of borders and the place of the non-European in Europe has been increasingly contested in the twenty-first century, from Brexit Britain to Viktor Orbàn's Hungary. After the surge of refugees coming from Libya and Syria across the Mediterranean in the summer of 2014, Europe was forced to confront the question "why do so many people continue to die at the edges of modern, civilized and democratic states?" (Jones 2016, 4).

This turn to Europe, to the issue of legacy, and where the continent is heading, brings this essay back to Arnaud Desplechin's film, *The Sentinel* (1992). *The Sentinel* could almost be titled *The Other Head* and be read as exploring the challenge to Europe at a time of crisis that, as Derrida (1992) puts it, is "well guarded by the vigilant sentinels of being" (26). The severed head that turns up in the luggage of a German medical student when stopped at the French border undoes certainty, constituting a spectral yet brutally physical return of a European history that might be erased just as the Cold War ends and a new political Union begins. This severed head is a very material *revenant*: like the zombie, it is abjectly corporeal.

Desplechin's film begins with a prefatory scene, which involves an anecdote told between diplomats at an embassy in Bonn about how Stalin and Churchill divided up Europe at the Yalta conference in 1945. That is the deep context for a film set in the present as the Soviet Union collapses and the borders of Europe are hurriedly re-drawn. The central character, Mathias, is a German medical student training in pathology in Paris, but he comes from a diplomatic family long enmeshed in murky Cold War conspiracies. The mummified head bobs up out of that past and sets up an obligation to bear witness. The head seems obscurely implicated in an atrocious history, of the Soviet gulag and dark passages of genocide, displaced persons, refugees, and cynical *Realpolitik* from the end of World War II. It is a history rapidly sinking out of sight in the era of *perestroika* and reunification.

Excavating something of this history takes the form of a slow autopsy on this displaced head, but this only succeeds in unravelling the privilege and security of the protagonist. Mathias ends up losing his head, and, confined to a mental institution, his own identity undone, his breach of diplomatic protocols is brushed under the carpet as an embarrassment. The obligation asked of him is too much: an act of what Derrida terms *impossible mourning*. The history Mathias thinks he has uncovered is destabilized by his mental state, and Europe is intent on taking another heading, suppressing the past he has uncovered. The head is the emblem of what is cut off for the new Europe to unify, and yet which continues to haunt. This is a different kind of European political cinema, one full of roving ghosts and shifting generic markers that destabilize rational certainties (Bingham 2008; Grandena, 2008). The protagonist who loses his mind has "the anguish...of a mind haunted by a familiar and unknown guest," as the philosopher Jean-Francois Lyotard (1991) puts it in his contemporaneous reflections on what was being left out of Europe's grand narratives (2).

As with Desplechin's first short film, *The Life of the Dead* (1991), there is an interest in investigating this suspensive state between life and death, this odd interval between two deaths, the literal and the symbolic. Decapitation addresses here the identity of Europe, center and border, capital and periphery, the body politic and its headless state. "Where there is a head there is a crisis," Regina Janes argues, and the number of heads rolling in contemporary culture suggests that the Gothic remains a privileged register for addressing the overdetermined wounds of contemporary European identity.

References

"A Definition of Irreversible Coma: A Report of the Ad Hoc Committee of the Harvard Medical School to Examine the Definition of Brain Death." 1968. *Journal of the American Medical Association* 205, no. 6 (5 August): 337–40.

Agamben, Giorgio. 1998. *Homo Sacer: Sovereign Power and Bare Life*. Translated by Daniel Heller-Roazen. Stanford: Stanford University Press.

Arasse, Daniel. 1989. *The Guillotine and the Terror*. Translated by C. Miller. London: Penguin.

Athanassoglou-Kallmyer, Nina. 1992. "Géricault's Severed Heads and Limbs: The Politics and Aesthetics of the Scaffold." *Art Bulletin* 74, no. 4: 599–618.

Balibar, Étienne. 2004. *We, the People of Europe: Reflections on Transnational Citizenship*. Princeton: Princeton University Press.

Bataille, Georges. 2018. *The Sacred Conspiracy: The Internal Papers of the Secret Society of Acephale and Lectures to the College of Sociology*. London: Atlas.

Bingham, Adam. 2008. "Paris Doesn't Belong to Us Anymore: Arnaud Desplechin's Absurd Theatre of Life in *La Sentinelle*." *Senses of Cinema* 48. http://sensesofcinema.com/2008/cteq/sentinelle. Accessed on 1 June 2016.

Cavarero, Adriana. 2009. *Horrorism: Naming Contemporary Violence*. Translated by W. McCuaig. New York: Columbia University Press.

Cixous, Hélène. 1976. "The Laugh of the Medusa." Translated by K. Cohen and P. Cohen. *Signs* 1, no. 4: 875–93.

Clark, James. 2007. *Haunted London*. Stroud: Tempus.

Combs, Cynthia. 2017. *Terrorism in the Twenty-First Century*. 8th ed. London: Routledge.

Conrad, Joseph. 1983. *Heart of Darkness*. Harmondsworth: Penguin.

Cressy, David. 2004. "Lamentable, Strange, and Wonderful: Headless Monsters in the English Revolution." In *Monstrous Bodies/Political Monstrosities*, edited by L. L. Knoppers and J. B. Landes, 40–63. Ithaca: Cornell University Press.

Cronin, Audrey. 2009. *How Terrorism Ends*. Princeton: Princeton University Press.

Derrida, Jacques. 1994. *Specters of Marx: The State of the Debt, the Work of Mourning, and the New International*. Translated by P. Kamuf. London: Routledge.

Derrida, Jacques. 1992. *The Other Heading: Reflections on Today's Europe*. Translated by P. A. Brault and M. Naas. Bloomington: Indiana University Press.

Dijkstra, Bram. 1986. *Idols of Perversity: Fantasies of Feminine Evil in Fin-de-Siècle*. Oxford: Oxford University Press.

Foucault, Michel. 1975. *Surveiller et punir*. Paris: Gallimard.

Freud, Sigmund. 1955. "Medusa's Head." In *Standard Edition of the Complete Psychological Works of Sigmund Freud*, Vol. 18, edited and translated by J. Strachey, 273–74. London: Hogarth.

Gough, Hugh. 1998. *The Terror in the French Revolution*. New York: St. Martin's.

Grandena, Florian. 2008. *Showing the World to the World: Political Fictions in French Cinema of the 1990s and Early 2000s*. Newcastle: Cambridge Scholars.

Harrow, Martin. 2011. "Video-Recorded Decapitations: A Seemingly Perfect Terrorist Tactic That Did Not Spread." *Working Paper for Danish Institute for International Studies*. Copenhagen: DIIS. Online.

Janes, Regina. 2005. *Losing Our Heads: Beheading in Literature and Culture*. New York: New York University Press.

Jones, Jonathan. 2013. "Don't Lose Your Head Over Hirst." *Guardian* (17 July). www.guardian.co.uk. Accessed on 20 October 2018.

Jones, Reece. 2016. *Violent Borders: Refugees and the Right to Move*. London: Verso.

Kang, Minsoo. 2011. *Sublime Dreams of Living Machines: The Automaton in the European Imagination*. Cambridge: Harvard University Press.

Kristeva, Julia. 2012. *The Severed Head: Capital Visions*. Translated by J. Gladding. New York: Columbia.

Kwint, Marius and Richard Wingate. 2012. *Brains: The Mind as Matter*. London: Wellcome.

Larson, Frances. 2014. *Severed: A History of Heads Lost and Heads Found*. London: Granta.

Levy, Bernard-Henri. 2004. *Who Killed Daniel Pearl?* Translated by J. Mitchell. London: Duckworth.

Lock, Margaret. 2002. *Twice Dead: Organ Transplants and the Reinvention of Death*. Berkeley: University of California Press.

Lock, Margaret. 2001. "On Making up the Good-as-Dead in a Utilitarian World." In *Remaking Life and Death: Toward an Anthropology of Biosciences*, edited by T. Franklin and M. Lock, 165–92. Santa Fe: School of America Research Press.

Luckhurst, Roger. 2015. "Biomedical Horror: The New Death and the New Dead." In *Technologies of the Gothic in Literature and Culture*, edited by Justin D. Edwards, 84–98. London: Routledge.

Lyotard, Jean-Francois. 1991. *The Inhuman: Reflections on Time.* Translated by R. Bowlby. Cambridge: Polity.

Lyotard, Jean-Francois. 1988. *The Differend: Phrases in Dispute.* Translated by G. Van den Abeele. Minneapolis: University of Minnesota Press.

Malabou, Catherine. 2012. *The New Wounded: From Neurosis to Brain Damage.* Translated by S. Miller. New York: Fordham University Press.

Mbembe, Achille. 2003. "Necropolitics." *Public Culture* 15, no. 1: 11–40.

Neale, Steve. 1990. "'You've Gotta Be Fucking Kidding': Knowledge, Belief and Judgment in Science Fiction." In *Alien Zone: Cultural Theory and Contemporary Science Fiction*, edited by A. Kuhn, 160–68. London: Verso.

Salisbury, Mark. 2014 "Seventh Hell." In *David Fincher Interviews*, edited by Laurence F. Knapp, 24–32. Jackson: University of Mississippi Press.

Teresi, Dick. 2012. *The Undead: How Medicine Is Blurring the Line between Life and Death.* New York: Pantheon.

Truog, Robert D. 2018. "The 50-Year Legacy of the Harvard Report on Brain Death." *JAMA* (7 June): E1–2. www.jama.com. Accessed on 20 October 2018.

Valencia, Sayak. 2018. *Gore Capitalism.* Translated by J. Pluecker. New York: Semiotext(e).

Weber, Samuel. 2014. "Mind the 'Cap'." In *Europe after Derrida: Crisis and Potentiality*, edited by A. Gajka and B. Isyar, 9–29. Edinburgh: Edinburgh University Press.

Index

For Product Safety Concerns and Information please contact our EU
representative GPSR@taylorandfrancis.com
Taylor & Francis Verlag GmbH, Kaufingerstraße 24, 80331 München, Germany